BUSINESS MATH
DEMYSTIFIED

Demystified Series

Accounting Demystified
Advanced Statistics Demystified
Algebra Demystified
Anatomy Demystified
asp.net 2.0 Demystified
Astronomy Demystified
Biology Demystified
Biotechnology Demystified
Business Calculus Demystified
Business Math Demystified
Business Statistics Demystified
C++ Demystified
Calculus Demystified
Chemistry Demystified
College Algebra Demystified
Corporate Finance Demystified
Data Structures Demystified
Databases Demystified
Differential Equations Demystified
Digital Electronics Demystified
Earth Science Demystified
Electricity Demystified
Electronics Demystified
Environmental Science Demystified
Everyday Math Demystified
Forensics Demystified
Genetics Demystified
Geometry Demystified
Home Networking Demystified
Investing Demystified
Java Demystified
JavaScript Demystified
Linear Algebra Demystified
Macroeconomics Demystified

Management Accounting Demystified
Math Proofs Demystified
Math Word Problems Demystified
Medical Terminology Demystified
Meteorology Demystified
Microbiology Demystified
Microeconomics Demystified
Nanotechnology Demystified
OOP Demystified
Options Demystified
Organic Chemistry Demystified
Personal Computing Demystified
Pharmacology Demystified
Physics Demystified
Physiology Demystified
Pre-Algebra Demystified
Precalculus Demystified
Probability Demystified
Project Management Demystified
Psychology Demystified
Quality Management Demystified
Quantum Mechanics Demystified
Relativity Demystified
Robotics Demystified
Six Sigma Demystified
sql Demystified
Statistics Demystified
Technical Math Demystified
Trigonometry Demystified
uml Demystified
Visual Basic 2005 Demystified
Visual C# 2005 Demystified
xml Demystified

BUSINESS MATH
DEMYSTIFIED

ALLAN G. BLUMAN

McGRAW-HILL
New York   Chicago   San Francisco   Lisbon   London
Madrid   Mexico City   Milan   New Delhi   San Juan
Seoul   Singapore   Sydney   Toronto

The McGraw-Hill Companies

Library of Congress Cataloging-in-Publication Data

Bluman, Allan G.
    Business math demystified / Allan G. Bluman.
        p.   cm.—(Demystified series)
    Includes index.
    ISBN 0-07-146470-0
    1. Business mathematics.   I. Title.   II. McGraw-Hill "Demystified" series.
HF5691.B666   2006
650.01′513—dc22

2006042034

5 6 7 8 9 0   DOC/DOC   1 7 6 5 4 3 2

ISBN 0-07-146470-0

The sponsoring editor for this book was Judy Bass and the production supervisor was Pamela A. Pelton. It was set in Times Roman by TechBooks. The art director for the cover was Margaret Webster-Shapiro; the cover designer was Handel Low.

This book is printed on acid-free paper.

McGraw-Hill books are available at special quantity discounts to use as premiums and sales promotions, or for use in corporate training programs. For more information, please write to the Director of Special Sales, McGraw-Hill Professional, Two Penn Plaza, New York, NY 10121-2298. Or contact your local bookstore.

CONTENTS

CONTENTS

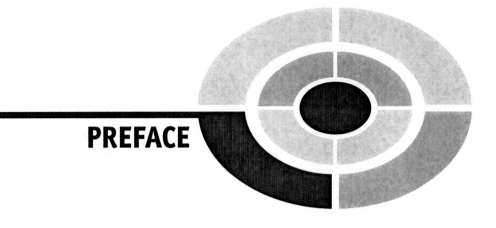

PREFACE

The purpose of this book is to provide the mathematical skills and knowledge to students who are either entering or are already in the business profession.

This book presents the mathematical concepts in a straightforward, easy-to-understand way. It does require, however, a knowledge of arithmetic (fractions, decimals, and percents) and a knowledge of algebra (formulas, exponents, and order of operations). Chapters 1 through 4 provide a brief review of these concepts. If you need a more in-depth presentation of these topics, you can consult another one of my books in the series entitled *Pre-Algebra Demystified*.

This book can be used as a self-study guide or as a supplementary textbook for those taking a business mathematics course at a junior college, a community college, a business or technical school, or a 4-year college. It should be pointed out that this book is **not** for students taking a high-level course in mathematics for business with topics such as linear programming, quantitative analysis, elementary functions, or matrices.

It is recommended that you use a scientific calculator for some of the more complex formulas found in Chapters 10 through 13. Also, some calculators are not able to handle several nested parentheses; that is, parentheses inside of parentheses. If you get an error message while trying to do this, it is recommended that you do some of the operations inside the parentheses first and use these numbers omitting the parentheses.

I hope you will find this book helpful in improving your mathematical skills in business and enabling you to succeed in your endeavors.

Good luck!

Allan G. Bluman

Acknowledgments

I would like to thank my editor Judy Bass for her assistance in the publication of this book and Carrie Green for her helpful suggestions and error checking. Finally I would like to thank my wife Betty Claire for her proofreading, typing, and encouragement. Without her, this book would not be possible.

Note: All names of people and businesses in this book are fictitious and are used to make the concepts presented more business-world oriented. Any resemblance to actual persons or businesses is purely coincidental.

BUSINESS MATH
DEMYSTIFIED

CHAPTER

Fractions—Review

Basic Concepts

In a fraction, the top number is called the **numerator** and the bottom number is called the **denominator**.

To reduce a fraction to lowest terms, divide the numerator and denominator by the largest number that divides evenly into both.

EXAMPLE: Reduce $\dfrac{28}{36}$.

SOLUTION:

$$\frac{28}{36} = \frac{28 \div 4}{36 \div 4} = \frac{7}{9}$$

To change a fraction to higher terms, divide the smaller denominator into the larger denominator, and then multiply the smaller numerator by that answer.

EXAMPLE: Change $\dfrac{3}{5}$ to 30ths.

SOLUTION:

Divide $30 \div 5$ and multiply $3 \times 6 = 18$. Hence, $\dfrac{3}{5} = \dfrac{18}{30}$. This can be written

as $\dfrac{3}{5} = \dfrac{3 \times 6}{5 \times 6} = \dfrac{18}{30}$.

An **improper fraction** is a fraction whose numerator is greater than or equal to its denominator; for example, $\frac{18}{5}$, $\frac{8}{3}$, and $\frac{7}{7}$ are improper fractions. A **mixed number** is a whole number and a fraction; $6\frac{3}{4}$, $3\frac{1}{9}$, and $2\frac{7}{8}$ are mixed numbers.

To change an improper fraction to a mixed number, divide the numerator by the denominator and write the remainder as the numerator of a fraction whose denominator is the divisor. Reduce the fraction if possible.

EXAMPLE: Change $\dfrac{28}{6}$ to a mixed number.

SOLUTION:

$$6\overline{)28} \quad \dfrac{28}{6} = 4\dfrac{4}{6} = 4\dfrac{2}{3}$$
$$\underline{24}$$
$$4$$

To change a mixed number to an improper fraction, multiply the denominator of the fraction by the whole number and add the numerator; this will be the numerator of the improper fraction. Use the same number for the denominator of the improper fraction as the number in the denominator of the fraction in the mixed number.

EXAMPLE: Change $7\dfrac{3}{4}$ to an improper fraction.

SOLUTION:

$$7\dfrac{3}{4} = \dfrac{4 \times 7 + 3}{4} = \dfrac{31}{4}$$

PRACTICE:

1. Reduce to lowest terms: $\frac{10}{30}$.

2. Reduce to lowest terms: $\frac{45}{48}$.

3. Reduce to lowest terms: $\frac{27}{33}$.

4. Change $\frac{3}{4}$ to 28ths.

5. Change $\frac{5}{8}$ to 72nds.

6. Change $\frac{9}{10}$ to 40ths.

7. Change $\frac{21}{15}$ to a mixed number.

8. Change $\frac{13}{6}$ to a mixed number.

9. Change $5\frac{3}{7}$ to an improper fraction.

10. Change $9\frac{1}{8}$ to an improper fraction.

SOLUTIONS:

1. $\dfrac{10}{30} = \dfrac{10 \div 10}{30 \div 10} = \dfrac{1}{3}$

2. $\dfrac{45}{48} = \dfrac{45 \div 3}{48 \div 3} = \dfrac{15}{16}$

3. $\dfrac{27}{33} = \dfrac{27 \div 3}{33 \div 3} = \dfrac{9}{11}$

4. $\dfrac{3}{4} = \dfrac{3 \times 7}{4 \times 7} = \dfrac{21}{28}$

5. $\dfrac{5}{8} = \dfrac{5 \times 9}{8 \times 9} = \dfrac{45}{72}$

6. $\dfrac{9}{10} = \dfrac{9 \times 4}{10 \times 4} = \dfrac{36}{40}$

7. $15\overline{\smash{)}21}$ gives 1 remainder 6 ; $\quad \dfrac{21}{15} = 1\dfrac{6}{15} = 1\dfrac{2}{5}$
$$\begin{array}{r} 1 \\ 15\overline{)21} \\ \underline{15} \\ 6 \end{array}$$

8. $6\overline{\smash{)}13}$ gives 2 remainder 1 ; $\quad \dfrac{13}{6} = 2\dfrac{1}{6}$
$$\begin{array}{r} 2 \\ 6\overline{)13} \\ \underline{12} \\ 1 \end{array}$$

9. $5\dfrac{3}{7} = \dfrac{7 \times 5 + 3}{7} = \dfrac{38}{7}$

10. $9\dfrac{1}{8} = \dfrac{8 \times 9 + 1}{8} = \dfrac{73}{8}$

Operations with Fractions

In order to add or subtract fractions, you need to find the **lowest common denominator** (LCD) of the fractions. The LCD of the fractions is the smallest number that can be divided evenly by all the denominator numbers. For example, the LCD of $\frac{1}{6}$, $\frac{2}{3}$, and $\frac{7}{9}$ is 18 since 18 can be divided evenly by 3, 6, and 9. There are several mathematical methods for finding the LCD; however, we will use the guess method. That is, just look at the denominators and figure out the LCD. If needed, you can look at an arithmetic or prealgebra book for a mathematical method to find the LCD.

To add or subtract fractions

1. Find the LCD.
2. Change the fractions to higher terms.
3. Add or subtract the numerators. Use the LCD.
4. Reduce or simplify the answer if necessary.

EXAMPLE: Add $\dfrac{1}{3} + \dfrac{3}{8} + \dfrac{5}{6}$.

SOLUTION:
Use 24 as the LCD.

$$\frac{1}{3} = \frac{8}{24}$$

$$\frac{3}{8} = \frac{9}{24}$$

$$+\frac{5}{6} = \frac{20}{24}$$

$$\overline{\qquad\qquad}$$

$$\frac{37}{24} = 1\frac{13}{24}$$

EXAMPLE: Subtract $\dfrac{11}{12} - \dfrac{7}{9}$.

SOLUTION:
Use 36 as the LCD.

$$\frac{11}{12} = \frac{33}{36}$$

$$-\frac{7}{9} = \frac{28}{36}$$

$$\overline{\qquad\qquad}$$

$$\frac{5}{36}$$

To multiply two or more fractions, cancel if possible, multiply numerators, and then multiply denominators.

EXAMPLE: Multiply $\dfrac{9}{10} \times \dfrac{2}{3}$.

SOLUTION:
Cancel then multiply.

$$\frac{9}{10} \times \frac{2}{3} = \frac{\cancel{9}^3}{\cancel{10}^5} \times \frac{\cancel{2}^1}{\cancel{3}^1} = \frac{3 \times 1}{5 \times 1} = \frac{3}{5}$$

To divide two fractions, invert (turn upside down) the fraction after the $\div$ sign and multiply.

EXAMPLE: Divide $\dfrac{2}{3} \div \dfrac{8}{9}$.

SOLUTION:

$$\frac{2}{3} \div \frac{8}{9} = \frac{\cancel{2}^1}{\cancel{3}^1} \times \frac{\cancel{9}^3}{\cancel{8}^4} = \frac{1 \times 3}{1 \times 4} = \frac{3}{4}$$

PRACTICE:
Perform the indicated operation. Reduce all answers to lowest terms.

1. $\dfrac{5}{8} + \dfrac{3}{4}$

2. $\dfrac{2}{5} + \dfrac{3}{8}$

3. $\dfrac{1}{2} + \dfrac{5}{8} + \dfrac{5}{6}$

4. $\dfrac{9}{10} - \dfrac{2}{5}$

5. $\dfrac{7}{12} - \dfrac{1}{8}$

6. $\dfrac{5}{7} \times \dfrac{2}{5}$

7. $\dfrac{1}{8} \times \dfrac{4}{5}$

8. $\dfrac{7}{8} \times \dfrac{3}{5} \times \dfrac{4}{7}$

9. $\dfrac{2}{3} \div \dfrac{5}{9}$

10. $\dfrac{8}{9} \div \dfrac{2}{3}$

SOLUTIONS:

1. $\dfrac{5}{8} + \dfrac{3}{4} = \dfrac{5}{8} + \dfrac{6}{8} = \dfrac{11}{8} = 1\dfrac{3}{8}$

2. $\dfrac{2}{5} + \dfrac{3}{8} = \dfrac{16}{40} + \dfrac{15}{40} = \dfrac{31}{40}$

3. $\dfrac{1}{2} + \dfrac{5}{8} + \dfrac{5}{6} = \dfrac{12}{24} + \dfrac{15}{24} + \dfrac{20}{24} = \dfrac{47}{24} = 1\dfrac{23}{24}$

4. $\dfrac{9}{10} - \dfrac{2}{5} = \dfrac{9}{10} - \dfrac{4}{10} = \dfrac{5}{10} = \dfrac{1}{2}$

5. $\dfrac{7}{12} - \dfrac{1}{8} = \dfrac{14}{24} - \dfrac{3}{24} = \dfrac{11}{24}$

6. $\dfrac{5}{7} \times \dfrac{2}{5} = \dfrac{\cancel{5}^{1}}{7} \times \dfrac{2}{\cancel{5}^{1}} = \dfrac{1 \times 2}{7 \times 1} = \dfrac{2}{7}$

7. $\dfrac{1}{8} \times \dfrac{4}{5} = \dfrac{1}{\cancel{8}^{2}} \times \dfrac{\cancel{4}^{1}}{5} = \dfrac{1 \times 1}{2 \times 5} = \dfrac{1}{10}$

8. $\dfrac{7}{8} \times \dfrac{3}{5} \times \dfrac{4}{7} = \dfrac{\cancel{7}^{1}}{\cancel{8}^{2}} \times \dfrac{3}{5} \times \dfrac{\cancel{4}^{1}}{\cancel{7}^{1}} = \dfrac{1 \times 3 \times 1}{2 \times 5 \times 1} = \dfrac{3}{10}$

9. $\dfrac{2}{3} \div \dfrac{5}{9} = \dfrac{2}{\cancel{3}^{1}} \times \dfrac{\cancel{9}^{3}}{5} = \dfrac{2 \times 3}{1 \times 5} = \dfrac{6}{5} = 1\dfrac{1}{5}$

10. $\dfrac{8}{9} \div \dfrac{2}{3} = \dfrac{\cancel{8}^{4}}{\cancel{9}^{3}} \times \dfrac{\cancel{3}^{1}}{\cancel{2}^{1}} = \dfrac{4 \times 1}{3 \times 1} = \dfrac{4}{3} = 1\dfrac{1}{3}$

Operations with Mixed Numbers

To add mixed numbers, add the fractions, and then add the whole numbers. Simplify the answer when necessary.

EXAMPLE: Add $8\dfrac{3}{4} + 6\dfrac{2}{5}$.

SOLUTION:

$$
\begin{aligned}
8\frac{3}{4} &= 8\frac{15}{20} \\
+\,6\frac{2}{5} &= 6\frac{8}{20} \\
\hline
14\frac{23}{20} &= 15\frac{3}{20}
\end{aligned}
$$

To subtract mixed numbers, borrow if necessary, subtract the fractions, and then subtract the whole numbers. Simplify the answer when necessary.

EXAMPLE: $15\dfrac{11}{12} - 7\dfrac{3}{8}$.

SOLUTION:

$$
\begin{aligned}
15\frac{11}{12} &= 15\frac{22}{24} \\
-\,7\frac{3}{8} &= 7\frac{9}{24} \\
\hline
8\frac{13}{24}
\end{aligned}
$$

No borrowing is necessary here.

When borrowing is necessary, take one away from the whole number and add it to the fraction. For example,

$$9\frac{5}{6} = 9 + \frac{5}{6} = 8 + 1 + \frac{5}{6} = 8 + \frac{6}{6} + \frac{5}{6} = 8\frac{11}{6}$$

Another example:

$$15\frac{5}{7} = 15 + \frac{5}{7} = 14 + 1 + \frac{5}{7} = 14 + \frac{7}{7} + \frac{5}{7} = 14\frac{12}{7}$$

EXAMPLE: Subtract $9\dfrac{1}{3} - 6\dfrac{3}{4}$.

SOLUTION:

$$9\dfrac{1}{3} = 9\dfrac{4}{12} = 8\dfrac{16}{12}$$
$$-6\dfrac{3}{4} = 6\dfrac{9}{12} = 6\dfrac{9}{12}$$
$$\overline{\phantom{-6\dfrac{3}{4} = 6\dfrac{9}{12} = {}}2\dfrac{7}{12}}$$

To multiply or divide mixed numbers, change the mixed numbers to improper fractions and then multiply or divide as shown before.

EXAMPLE: Multiply $5\dfrac{1}{2} \times 3\dfrac{5}{11}$.

SOLUTION:

$$5\dfrac{1}{2} \times 3\dfrac{5}{11} = \dfrac{\cancel{11}^{1}}{\cancel{2}^{1}} \times \dfrac{\cancel{38}^{19}}{\cancel{11}^{1}} = \dfrac{19}{1} = 19$$

EXAMPLE: Divide $9\dfrac{1}{3} \div 2\dfrac{2}{3}$.

SOLUTION:

$$9\dfrac{1}{3} \div 2\dfrac{2}{3} = \dfrac{28}{3} \div \dfrac{8}{3} = \dfrac{\cancel{28}^{7}}{\cancel{3}^{1}} \times \dfrac{\cancel{3}^{1}}{\cancel{8}^{2}} = \dfrac{7}{2} = 3\dfrac{1}{2}$$

PRACTICE:
Perform the indicated operations.

1. $1\dfrac{5}{6} + 2\dfrac{3}{8}$

2. $12\dfrac{1}{9} + 3\dfrac{2}{3}$

3. $4\dfrac{1}{5} + 5\dfrac{2}{3} + 3\dfrac{9}{10}$

4. $15\dfrac{11}{12} - 8\dfrac{1}{8}$

5. $23\dfrac{1}{6} - 7\dfrac{2}{3}$

6. $1\dfrac{1}{2} \times 6\dfrac{2}{3}$

7. $6\dfrac{1}{4} \times 2\dfrac{2}{5}$

8. $2\dfrac{1}{8} \times 3\dfrac{1}{2} \times \dfrac{5}{7}$

9. $8\dfrac{1}{8} \div 2\dfrac{1}{2}$

10. $7\dfrac{1}{2} \div 4\dfrac{3}{4}$

SOLUTIONS:

1. $1\dfrac{5}{6} + 2\dfrac{3}{8} = 1\dfrac{20}{24} + 2\dfrac{9}{24} = 3\dfrac{29}{24} = 4\dfrac{5}{24}$

2. $12\dfrac{1}{9} + 3\dfrac{2}{3} = 12\dfrac{1}{9} + 3\dfrac{6}{9} = 15\dfrac{7}{9}$

3. $4\dfrac{1}{5} + 5\dfrac{2}{3} + 3\dfrac{9}{10} = 4\dfrac{6}{30} + 5\dfrac{20}{30} + 3\dfrac{27}{30} = 12\dfrac{53}{30} = 13\dfrac{23}{30}$

4. $15\dfrac{11}{12} - 8\dfrac{1}{8} = 15\dfrac{22}{24} - 8\dfrac{3}{24} = 7\dfrac{19}{24}$

5. $23\dfrac{1}{6} - 7\dfrac{2}{3} = 23\dfrac{1}{6} - 7\dfrac{4}{6} = 22\dfrac{7}{6} - 7\dfrac{4}{6} = 15\dfrac{3}{6} = 15\dfrac{1}{2}$

6. $1\dfrac{1}{2} \times 6\dfrac{2}{3} = \dfrac{\cancel{3}^{1}}{\cancel{2}^{1}} \times \dfrac{\cancel{20}^{10}}{\cancel{3}^{1}} = \dfrac{10}{1} = 10$

7. $6\dfrac{1}{4} \times 2\dfrac{2}{5} = \dfrac{\cancel{25}^{5}}{\cancel{4}^{1}} \times \dfrac{\cancel{12}^{3}}{\cancel{5}^{1}} = \dfrac{15}{1} = 15$

8. $2\dfrac{1}{8} \times 3\dfrac{1}{2} \times \dfrac{5}{7} = \dfrac{17}{8} \times \dfrac{\cancel{7}^{1}}{2} \times \dfrac{5}{\cancel{7}^{1}} = \dfrac{85}{16} = 5\dfrac{5}{16}$

9. $8\dfrac{1}{8} \div 2\dfrac{1}{2} = \dfrac{65}{8} \div \dfrac{5}{2} = \dfrac{\cancel{65}^{13}}{\cancel{8}^{4}} \times \dfrac{\cancel{2}^{1}}{\cancel{5}^{1}} = \dfrac{13}{4} = 3\dfrac{1}{4}$

10. $7\dfrac{1}{2} \div 4\dfrac{3}{4} = \dfrac{15}{2} \div \dfrac{19}{4} = \dfrac{15}{\cancel{2}^{1}} \times \dfrac{\cancel{4}^{2}}{19} = \dfrac{30}{19} = 1\dfrac{11}{19}$

Calculator Tip

Almost all of the new scientific calculators have a fraction key. With this key, all of the operations with fractions can be performed on the calculator. Since various brands of calculators perform operations with fractions differently, it is necessary that you read the instruction manual in order to learn how to use the fraction key. Although it is not absolutely necessary that you know how to use a calculator to do fractions for this book, it will save you time if you are able to use the calculator.

Quiz

1. Reduce $\dfrac{36}{45}$.

   (a) $\dfrac{2}{3}$

   (b) $\dfrac{3}{4}$

   (c) $\dfrac{4}{5}$

   (d) $\dfrac{7}{8}$

2. Reduce $\dfrac{15}{60}$.

   (a) $\dfrac{1}{5}$

   (b) $\dfrac{2}{3}$

   (c) $\dfrac{3}{4}$

   (d) $\dfrac{1}{4}$

3. Change $\dfrac{5}{9}$ to 36ths.

    (a) $\dfrac{20}{36}$

    (b) $\dfrac{5}{36}$

    (c) $\dfrac{8}{36}$

    (d) $\dfrac{15}{36}$

4. Change $\dfrac{3}{10}$ to 40ths.

    (a) $\dfrac{8}{40}$

    (b) $\dfrac{9}{40}$

    (c) $\dfrac{12}{40}$

    (d) $\dfrac{10}{40}$

5. Write $5\dfrac{4}{7}$ as an improper fraction.

    (a) $\dfrac{27}{4}$

    (b) $\dfrac{39}{7}$

    (c) $\dfrac{16}{7}$

    (d) $\dfrac{27}{5}$

6. Write $7\frac{3}{4}$ as an improper fraction.

   (a) $\frac{31}{4}$

   (b) $\frac{25}{4}$

   (c) $\frac{14}{14}$

   (d) $\frac{31}{3}$

7. Change $\frac{15}{6}$ to a mixed number.

   (a) $1\frac{5}{6}$

   (b) $2\frac{1}{3}$

   (c) $1\frac{1}{6}$

   (d) $2\frac{1}{2}$

8. Change $\frac{12}{7}$ to a mixed number.

   (a) $1\frac{5}{7}$

   (b) $2\frac{2}{7}$

   (c) $1\frac{5}{12}$

   (d) $1\frac{1}{4}$

9. $\frac{7}{10} + \frac{2}{3} = ?$

   (a) $\frac{9}{13}$

(b) $\dfrac{1}{30}$

(c) $\dfrac{7}{15}$

(d) $1\dfrac{11}{30}$

10. $\dfrac{3}{4} + \dfrac{1}{2} + \dfrac{5}{6} = ?$

(a) $2\dfrac{1}{12}$

(b) $\dfrac{1}{30}$

(c) $\dfrac{7}{15}$

(d) $1\dfrac{1}{20}$

11. $\dfrac{11}{12} - \dfrac{3}{8} = ?$

(a) $1\dfrac{7}{24}$

(b) $\dfrac{13}{24}$

(c) $\dfrac{11}{32}$

(d) $2\dfrac{4}{9}$

12. $\dfrac{7}{10} - \dfrac{3}{5} = ?$

(a) $\dfrac{21}{50}$

(b) $\dfrac{1}{10}$

(c) $1\frac{1}{6}$

(d) $1\frac{3}{10}$

13. $\frac{3}{4} \times \frac{5}{6} \times \frac{2}{15} = ?$

(a) $1\frac{43}{60}$

(b) $6\frac{3}{4}$

(c) $1\frac{7}{10}$

(d) $\frac{1}{12}$

14. $3\frac{1}{4} + 5\frac{2}{3} = ?$

(a) $8\frac{11}{12}$

(b) $2\frac{5}{12}$

(c) $8\frac{5}{12}$

(d) $\frac{39}{68}$

15. $1\frac{9}{10} + 5\frac{2}{3} + 3\frac{1}{5} = ?$

(a) $4\frac{11}{30}$

(b) $10\frac{23}{30}$

(c) $6\dfrac{29}{30}$

(d) $9\dfrac{2}{3}$

16. $9\dfrac{1}{8} - 5\dfrac{2}{3} = ?$

   (a) $14\dfrac{19}{24}$

   (b) $51\dfrac{17}{24}$

   (c) $3\dfrac{11}{24}$

   (d) $1\dfrac{83}{136}$

17. $3\dfrac{3}{4} \times 1\dfrac{2}{5} = ?$

   (a) $2\dfrac{19}{24}$

   (b) $2\dfrac{7}{20}$

   (c) $\dfrac{28}{75}$

   (d) $5\dfrac{1}{4}$

18. $2\dfrac{5}{8} \times 4\dfrac{1}{3} = ?$

   (a) $1\dfrac{17}{24}$

   (b) $11\dfrac{3}{8}$

(c) $\dfrac{63}{104}$

(d) $6\dfrac{23}{24}$

19. $6\dfrac{1}{5} \div 2\dfrac{1}{2} = ?$

(a) $2\dfrac{12}{25}$

(b) $15\dfrac{1}{2}$

(c) $3\dfrac{7}{10}$

(d) $8\dfrac{7}{10}$

20. $4\dfrac{2}{3} \div 2\dfrac{1}{3} = ?$

(a) $10\dfrac{8}{9}$

(b) 7

(c) $2\dfrac{1}{3}$

(d) 2

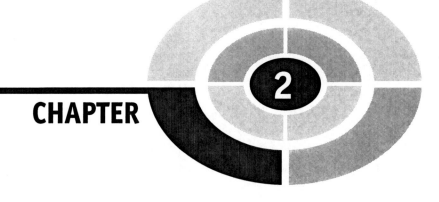

CHAPTER 2

Decimals—Review

Rounding Decimals

Each digit of a decimal has a place value. The place-value names are shown in Figure 2-1.

For example, in the number 0.8731, the 3 is in the thousandths place. The 1 is in the ten-thousandths place.

Decimals are rounded to a specific place value as follows: First locate that place-value digit in the number. If the digit to the right is 0, 1, 2, 3, or 4, the place-value digit remains the same. If the digit to the right of the place-value digit is 5, 6, 7, 8, or 9, add one to the place-value digit. In either case, all digits to the right of the place-value digit are dropped.

EXAMPLE: Round 0.16832 to the nearest hundredth.

SOLUTION:
We are rounding to the hundredths place, which is the digit 6. Since the digit to the right of the 6 is 8, raise the 6 to a 7 and drop all digits to the right of the 6. Hence, the answer is 0.17.

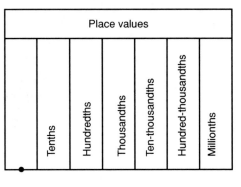

Fig. 2-1.

EXAMPLE: Round 62.5412 to the nearest thousandth.

SOLUTION:
The digit in the thousandths place is 1 and since the digit to the right of 1 is 2, the 1 remains the same. Drop all digits to the right of 1. Hence, the answer is 62.541.

Zeros can be affixed to the end of a decimal on the right side of the decimal point. For example, 0.62 can be written as 0.620 or 0.6200. Likewise, the zeros can be dropped if they are at the end of a decimal on the right side of the decimal point. For example, 0.3750 can be written as 0.375.

PRACTICE:
1. Round 0.67 to the nearest tenth.
2. Round 0.5431 to the nearest hundredth.
3. Round 83.2173 to the nearest thousandth.
4. Round 3.99999 to the nearest ten-thousandth.
5. Round 4.7261 to the nearest one (whole number).

SOLUTIONS:

1. 0.7
2. 0.54
3. 83.217
4. 4
5. 5

Notes on rounding: If an item sells at a cost of 3/$1.00, and you purchase one item, the exact cost is $1.00 ÷ 3 or 0.33\frac{1}{3}$. Now in the real world, you would pay $0.34 for the item. In other words, you "pay the extra penny." However, most business math books, including this one, follow the rounding rules used in mathematics; therefore, the cost of an item, if rounded to the nearest cent, would be $0.33. That is just the way business math books are written.

Also, round all answers involving money to the nearest cent following the rounding rules given in this chapter. Percents generally are rounded to one or two decimal places.

Addition of Decimals

In order to add two or more decimals, write the numbers in a column, placing the decimal points of the numbers in a vertical line. Add the numbers and place the decimal point in the sum directly under the other decimal points above.

EXAMPLE: Add $5.6 + 32.31 + 472.815$.

SOLUTION:

$$
\begin{array}{r}
5.600 \text{ (Zeros are annexed to keep the columns straight.)} \\
32.310 \\
+ \ 472.815 \\
\hline
510.725
\end{array}
$$

EXAMPLE: Add $58.129 + 321.6 + 0.05$.

SOLUTION:

$$
\begin{array}{r}
58.129 \\
321.600 \\
+ \ 0.050 \\
\hline
379.779
\end{array}
$$

PRACTICE:
Add

1. $0.15 + 6.7 + 3.211$
2. $86.5 + 327.6 + 0.153$
3. $4.711 + 0.003 + 12.18$
4. $19.2 + 7.1 + 3.6 + 18.273$
5. $156.03 + 432.7 + 1372.1$

SOLUTION:

1. 10.061
2. 414.253
3. 16.894
4. 48.173
5. 1960.83

Subtraction of Decimals

Subtracting decimals is similar to adding decimals. To subtract two decimals, write the decimals in a column, placing the decimal points in a vertical line. Subtract the numbers and place the decimal point in the difference directly under the other decimal points.

EXAMPLE: Subtract 156.31 − 18.623.

SOLUTION:

```
  156.310 (Annex a zero to keep the columns straight.)
 − 18.623
  137.687
```

EXAMPLE: Subtract 28.6 − 14.7132.

SOLUTION:

```
  28.6000 (Annex zeros to keep the columns straight.)
 − 14.7132
  13.8868
```

PRACTICE:
Subtract
1. 18.321 − 13.5
2. 643.8 − 261.732
3. 9.62 − 3.31
4. 8.631 − 0.0006
5. 473 − 0.02

SOLUTIONS:

1. 4.821
2. 382.068
3. 6.31
4. 8.6304
5. 472.98

Multiplication of Decimals

To multiply two decimals, multiply the two numbers, disregarding the decimal points, and then count the total number of digits to the right of the decimal points in the two numbers. Count the same number of places from the right in the product and place the decimal point there. If there are fewer digits in the product than are places, prefix as many zeros as needed.

EXAMPLE: 47.6 × 0.58.

SOLUTION:

$$
\begin{array}{r}
47.6 \text{ (Three decimal places are needed in the answer.)} \\
\times\ 0.58 \\
\hline
3808 \\
2380 \\
\hline
27.608
\end{array}
$$

EXAMPLE: Multiply 18.3 × 0.003.

SOLUTION:

$$
\begin{array}{r}
18.3 \\
\times\ 0.003 \\
\hline
0.0549
\end{array}
$$

Since five places are needed in the answer, it is necessary to use one zero in front of the product.

PRACTICE:
Multiply
1. 156.3 × 0.22
2. 54.6 × 7.7
3. 0.005 × 0.02
4. 6.03 × 0.4
5. 16.21 × 143.7

SOLUTIONS:
1. 34.386
2. 420.42
3. 0.0001
4. 2.412
5. 2329.377

Division of Decimals

When dividing two decimals, it is important to find the correct location of the decimal point in the quotient. There are two cases:

Case 1: To divide a decimal by a whole number, divide as though both numbers were whole numbers and place the decimal point in the quotient directly above the decimal point in the dividend.

EXAMPLE: Divide $318.2 \div 37$.

SOLUTION:

$$
\begin{array}{r}
8.6 \\
37\overline{)318.2} \\
\underline{296} \\
222 \\
\underline{222} \\
0
\end{array}
$$

EXAMPLE: Divide 0.00036 by 9.

SOLUTION:

$$
\begin{array}{r}
0.00004 \\
9\overline{)0.00036} \\
\underline{36} \\
0
\end{array}
$$

Case 2: When the divisor contains a decimal point, move the point to the right of the last digit in the divisor. Then move the point to the right to the same number of places in the dividend. Divide and place the point in the quotient directly above the point in the dividend.

EXAMPLE: Divide 2.4075 by 0.75.

SOLUTION:

$$
0.75\overline{)2.4075}
$$

Move the point two places to the right as shown:

$$
\begin{array}{r}
3.21 \\
75\overline{)240.75} \\
\underline{225} \\
157 \\
\underline{150} \\
75 \\
\underline{75} \\
0
\end{array}
$$

Sometimes it is necessary to place zeros in the dividend.

EXAMPLE: Divide $6 \div 0.375$.

SOLUTION:

$$0.375 \overline{)6}$$

Move the point three places to the right after annexing three zeros:

$$
\begin{array}{r}
16 \\
375 \overline{)6000.} \\
\underline{375} \\
2250 \\
\underline{2250} \\
0
\end{array}
$$

Sometimes it is necessary to round an answer.

EXAMPLE: Divide 42 by 7.2 and round the answer to the nearest hundredth.

SOLUTION:

$$7.2 \overline{)42}$$

Carry the answer to three decimal places (i.e., thousandths), as shown:

$$
\begin{array}{r}
5.833 \\
72 \overline{)420.000} \\
\underline{360} \\
600 \\
\underline{576} \\
240 \\
\underline{216} \\
240 \\
\underline{216} \\
24
\end{array}
$$

Now round 5.833 to the nearest hundredth. The answer is 5.83.

PRACTICE:

1. $124 \div 8$
2. $14.454 \div 22$
3. $17.856 \div 3.72$
4. $14.84 \div 2.12$
5. $0.012 \div 24$

SOLUTIONS:

1. 15.5
2. 0.657
3. 4.8
4. 7
5. 0.0005

Comparing Decimals

To compare two or more decimals, place the numbers in a vertical column with the decimal points in a straight line with each other. Add zeros to the ends of the decimals so that they all have the same number of decimal places. Then compare the numbers, ignoring decimal points.

EXAMPLE: Which is larger, 0.27 or 0.635?

SOLUTION:
$0.27 \rightarrow 0.270 \rightarrow 270$
$0.635 \rightarrow 0.635 \rightarrow 635$
Since 635 is larger than 270, 0.635 is larger than 0.27.

EXAMPLE: Arrange the decimals 0.84, 0.341, 5.2, and 0.6 in order of size, smallest to largest.

SOLUTION:
$0.84 \rightarrow 840$
$0.341 \rightarrow 341$
$5.2 \rightarrow 5200$
$0.6 \rightarrow 600$
In order: 0.341, 0.6, 0.84, and 5.2.

PRACTICE:

1. Which is larger, 0.13 or 0.263?
2. Which is smaller, 0.003 or 0.0256?
3. Arrange in order (smallest first): 0.837, 0.6, 0.53.
4. Arrange in order (largest first): 0.9, 0.009, 9.0.
5. Arrange in order (largest first): 0.02, 0.2, 2.0, 0.002.

SOLUTION:

1. 0.263
2. 0.003
3. 0.53, 0.6, 0.837
4. 9.0, 0.9, 0.009
5. 2.0, 0.2, 0.02, 0.002

Changing Fractions to Decimals

A fraction can be converted to an equivalent decimal. For example, $\frac{1}{4} = 0.25$. When a fraction is converted to a decimal, it will be in one of two forms: a **terminating decimal** or a **repeating decimal.**
  To change a fraction to a decimal, divide the numerator by the denominator.

EXAMPLE: Change $\frac{3}{8}$ to a decimal.

SOLUTION:

$$
\begin{array}{r}
0.375 \\
8\,)\overline{3.000} \\
\underline{24} \\
60 \\
\underline{56} \\
40 \\
\underline{40} \\
0
\end{array}
$$

Hence, $\frac{3}{8} = 0.375$.

EXAMPLE: Change $\frac{1}{4}$ to a decimal.

SOLUTION:

$$
\begin{array}{r}
0.25 \\
4\overline{)1.00} \\
8 \\
\overline{20} \\
20 \\
\overline{0}
\end{array}
$$

Hence, $\frac{1}{4} = 0.25$.

EXAMPLE: Change $\frac{7}{11}$ to a decimal.

SOLUTION:

$$
\begin{array}{r}
0.6363 \\
11\overline{)7.0000} \\
66 \\
\overline{40} \\
33 \\
\overline{70} \\
66 \\
\overline{40} \\
33 \\
\overline{7}
\end{array}
$$

Hence, $\frac{7}{11} = 0.6363\ldots$

The repeating decimal can be written as $0.\overline{63}$

EXAMPLE: Change $\frac{1}{6}$ to a decimal.

SOLUTION:

$$
\begin{array}{r}
0.166 \\
6\overline{)1.000} \\
6 \\
\overline{40} \\
36 \\
\overline{40} \\
36 \\
\overline{4}
\end{array}
$$

Hence, $\frac{1}{6} = 0.166\ldots$ or $0.1\overline{6}$.

A mixed number can be changed to a decimal by first changing it to an improper fraction and then dividing the numerator by the denominator.

EXAMPLE: Change $4\frac{3}{5}$ to a decimal.

SOLUTION:

$$4\frac{3}{5} = \frac{23}{5}$$

$$5\overline{)23.0}$$
$$\begin{array}{r} 4.6 \\ \underline{20} \\ 30 \\ \underline{30} \\ 0 \end{array}$$

Hence, $4\frac{3}{5} = 4.6$.

PRACTICE:
Change each of the following fractions to a decimal:

1. $\frac{7}{8}$
2. $\frac{5}{6}$
3. $\frac{13}{20}$
4. $\frac{7}{12}$
5. $5\frac{2}{3}$

SOLUTIONS:

1. 0.875
2. $0.8\overline{3}$
3. 0.65
4. $0.58\overline{3}$
5. $5.\overline{6}$

Changing Decimals to Fractions

To change a terminating decimal to a fraction, drop the decimal point and place the digits to the right of the decimal in the numerator of a fraction whose denominator corresponds to the place value of the last digit in the decimal. Reduce the answer if possible.

EXAMPLE: Change 0.6 to a fraction.

SOLUTION:

$$0.6 = \frac{6}{10} = \frac{3}{5}$$

Hence, $0.6 = \frac{3}{5}$.

EXAMPLE: Change 0.54 to a fraction.

SOLUTION:

$$0.54 = \frac{54}{100} = \frac{27}{50}$$

Hence, $0.54 = \frac{27}{50}$.

EXAMPLE: Change 0.0085 to a fraction.

SOLUTION:

$$0.0085 = \frac{85}{10,000} = \frac{17}{2000}$$

Hence, $0.0085 = \frac{17}{2000}$.

PRACTICE:
Change each of the following decimals to a reduced fraction:

1. 0.45
2. 0.08
3. 0.7
4. 0.375
5. 0.0025

SOLUTIONS:

1. $\frac{9}{20}$
2. $\frac{2}{25}$
3. $\frac{7}{10}$
4. $\frac{3}{8}$
5. $\frac{1}{400}$

Calculator Tip

Operations with decimals are performed on the calculator by just imputing the decimal numbers and using the operations signs $(+, -, \times, \div)$. Some calculators will change fractions to decimals or decimals to fractions. One such key looks like this: F $\leftrightarrow$ D. Don't be alarmed if your calculator does not have this type of key; you can still do these problems using the techniques shown in this chapter.

Changing a repeating decimal to a fraction requires a more complex procedure, and this procedure is beyond the scope of this book. However, Table 2-1 can be used for some common repeating decimals.

Table 2-1

$\frac{1}{12} = 0.08\overline{3}$	$\frac{1}{6} = 0.1\overline{6}$	$\frac{1}{3} = 0.\overline{3}$	$\frac{5}{12} = 0.41\overline{6}$
$\frac{7}{12} = 0.58\overline{3}$	$\frac{2}{3} = 0.\overline{6}$	$\frac{5}{6} = 0.8\overline{3}$	$\frac{11}{12} = 0.91\overline{6}$

Quiz

1. In the number 0.039724, the place value of the 9 is
    (a) hundredths
    (b) thousandths
    (c) ten-thousandths
    (d) hundred-thousandths

2. Round 0.62154 to the nearest thousandth.
    (a) 0.62
    (b) 0.6
    (c) 0.621
    (d) 0.622

3. Round 5.998 to the nearest hundredth.
    (a) 5.99
    (b) 5.9
    (c) 6
    (d) 5.98

4. Add $4.13 + 5.2 + 16.213$.
   (a) 26.3214
   (b) 25.543
   (c) 25.453
   (d) 24.371

5. Subtract $38.7 - 16.152$.
   (a) 21.312
   (b) 22.548
   (c) 24.17
   (d) 22.46

6. Multiply 0.27×13.3.
   (a) 35.91
   (b) 0.3591
   (c) 359.1
   (d) 3.591

7. Multiply 0.005×0.0007.
   (a) 0.0000035
   (b) 0.035
   (c) 0.00035
   (d) 0.035

8. Divide $29.376 \div 8.64$.
   (a) 0.34
   (b) 3.4
   (c) 34
   (d) 0.034

9. Divide $20.52 \div 57$.
   (a) 36
   (b) 0.036
   (c) 0.36
   (d) 3.6

10. Arrange in order of smallest to largest: 22, 0.22, 0.022, 2.2.
    (a) 22, 0.22, 0.022, 2.2
    (b) 2.2, 0.022, 0.22, 22
    (c) 0.22, 22, 0.022, 2.2
    (d) 0.022, 0.22, 2.2, 22

11. Change $\frac{7}{16}$ to a decimal.
    (a) 0.128
    (b) 0.4375

(c) 0.3125

(d) 2.28

12. Change $\frac{5}{12}$ to a decimal.

(a) $0.\overline{416}$

(b) $0.4\overline{16}$

(c) $0.41\overline{6}$

(d) $0.\overline{41}$

13. Change 0.35 to a reduced fraction.

(a) $\frac{7}{20}$

(b) $\frac{35}{10}$

(c) $3\frac{1}{2}$

(d) $\frac{35}{100}$

14. Change 0.165 to a reduced fraction.

(a) $\frac{3}{20}$

(b) $\frac{1}{8}$

(c) $\frac{33}{200}$

(d) $\frac{4}{25}$

15. Change $0.\overline{3}$ to a reduced fraction.

(a) $\frac{33}{100}$

(b) $\frac{333}{1000}$

(c) $\frac{3}{10}$

(d) $\frac{1}{3}$

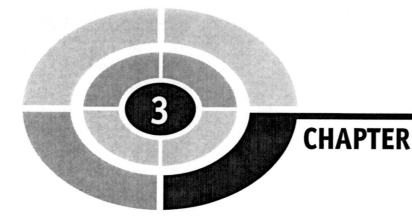

CHAPTER

Percent—Review

Basic Concepts

Percents are most often used in business. For example, sales tax rates are given in percents. Interest rates for borrowing and investing are given in percents. Commissions are usually computed as a percent of sales, and so on.

Percent means hundredths. For example, 24% means $\frac{24}{100}$ or 0.24. Another way to think of 24% is to think of 24 equal parts out of 100 equal parts (see Figure 3-1).

Remember that 100% means $\frac{100}{100}$ or 1.

Changing Percents to Decimals

To change a percent to a decimal, drop the percent sign and move the decimal point two places to the left. (If there is no decimal point in the percent, it is at the end of the number; i.e., 4% = 4.0%.)

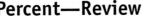

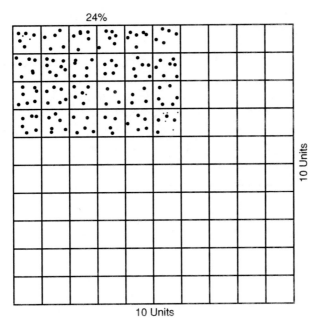

Fig. 3-1.

EXAMPLE: Write 4% as a decimal.

SOLUTION:
    4% = 0.04

EXAMPLE: Write 85% as a decimal.

SOLUTION:
    85% = 0.85

EXAMPLE: Write 156% as a decimal.

SOLUTION:
    156% = 1.56

EXAMPLE: Write 27.8% as a decimal.

SOLUTION:
    27.8% = 0.278

EXAMPLE: Write 0.7% as a decimal.

SOLUTION:
    0.7% = 0.007

Calculator Tip

If you are using a scientific calculator, all you have to do to change a percent to a decimal is to divide the percent by 100; for example, 27% = 27 ÷ 100 = 0.27. Also, many scientific calculators have a % key. These keys have different uses on different calculators. On some calculators, the key will change a percent to a decimal; for example, if you enter 27 and press the % key, you get 0.27. If your calculator does not do this, you will have to read the instructions to see how to use the % key.

PRACTICE:
Write each of the following percent values as a decimal:

1. 77%
2. 6%
3. 144%
4. 0.6%
5. 42.3%

SOLUTIONS:
For each problem, drop the percent sign and move the decimal point two places to the left.

1. 0.77
2. 0.06
3. 1.44
4. 0.006
5. 0.423

Changing Decimals to Percents

To change a decimal to a percent, move the decimal point two places to the right and affix the percent sign. If the decimal is located at the end of the number, do not write it.

EXAMPLE: Write 0.35 as a percent.

SOLUTION:
0.35 = 35%

Calculator Tip

If you are using a calculator, you can change a decimal to a percent by multiplying it by 100. For example, $0.538 = 0.538 \times 100 = 53.8\%$.

EXAMPLE: Write 0.09 as a percent.

SOLUTION:
  $0.09 = 9\%$

EXAMPLE: Write 3.41 as a percent.

SOLUTION:
  $3.41 = 341\%$

EXAMPLE: Write 0.172 as a percent.

SOLUTION:
  $0.172 = 17.2\%$

EXAMPLE: Write 6 as a percent.

SOLUTION:
  $6 = 6.00 = 600\%$

EXAMPLE: Write 0.0352 as a percent.

SOLUTION:
  $0.0352 = 3.52\%$

PRACTICE:
Write each of the following decimals as percents:
  1. 0.08
  2. 0.89
  3. 0.612
  4. 2
  5. 0.0035

SOLUTIONS:
Move the decimal point two places to the right and affix a percent sign.

  1. $0.08 = 8\%$
  2. $0.89 = 89\%$

3. $0.612 = 61.2\%$
4. $2 = 2.00 = 200\%$
5. $0.0035 = 0.35\%$

Changing Fractions to Percents

To change a fraction to a percent, change the fraction to a decimal (i.e., divide the numerator by the denominator) and then move the decimal two places to the right and affix the percent sign.

EXAMPLE: Write $\frac{3}{5}$ as a percent.

SOLUTION:
Divide 3 by 5 as shown:

$$
\begin{array}{r}
0.6 \\
5\overline{)3.0} \\
\underline{30} \\
0
\end{array}
$$

$$\frac{3}{5} = 0.6 = 60\%$$

EXAMPLE: Write $\frac{1}{4}$ as a percent.

SOLUTION:
Divide 1 by 4 as shown:

$$
\begin{array}{r}
0.25 \\
4\overline{)1.00} \\
\underline{8} \\
20 \\
\underline{20} \\
0
\end{array}
$$

$$\frac{1}{4} = 0.25 = 25\%$$

EXAMPLE: Write $\frac{5}{8}$ as a percent.

SOLUTION:

Divide 5 by 8 as shown:

$$
\begin{array}{r}
0.625 \\
8\overline{\smash{)}5.000} \\
\underline{48} \\
20 \\
\underline{16} \\
40 \\
\underline{40} \\
0
\end{array}
$$

$$\frac{5}{8} = 0.625 = 62.5\%$$

EXAMPLE: Write $2\frac{3}{4}$ as a percent.

SOLUTION:

$$2\frac{3}{4} = \frac{11}{4}$$

$$
\begin{array}{r}
2.75 \\
4\overline{\smash{)}11.00} \\
\underline{8} \\
30 \\
\underline{28} \\
20 \\
\underline{20} \\
0
\end{array}
$$

$$2\frac{3}{4} = 2.75 = 275\%$$

EXAMPLE: Write $\frac{5}{6}$ as a percent.

SOLUTION:

$$
\begin{array}{r}
0.833 \\
6\overline{\smash{)}5.000} \\
\underline{48} \\
20 \\
\underline{18} \\
20 \\
\underline{18} \\
2
\end{array}
$$

$$\frac{5}{6} = 0.83\overline{3} = 83.\overline{3}\%$$

PRACTICE:
Write each of the following fractions as percents:

1. $\dfrac{3}{8}$

2. $\dfrac{1}{2}$

3. $\dfrac{17}{50}$

4. $5\dfrac{1}{2}$

5. $\dfrac{7}{12}$

SOLUTIONS:
Change each fraction to a decimal and then change the decimal to a percent.

1. 37.5%
2. 50%
3. 34%
4. 550%
5. $58.\overline{3}\%$

Changing Percents to Fractions

To change a percent to a fraction, write the numeral in front of the percent sign as the numerator of a fraction whose denominator is 100. Reduce the fraction if possible.

EXAMPLE: Write 65% as a fraction.

SOLUTION:

$$65\% = \frac{65}{100} = \frac{13}{20}$$

EXAMPLE: Write 9% as a fraction.

SOLUTION:

$$9\% = \frac{9}{100}$$

EXAMPLE: Write 40% as a fraction.

SOLUTION:

$$40\% = \frac{40}{100} = \frac{2}{5}$$

EXAMPLE: Write 225% as a fraction.

SOLUTION:

$$225\% = \frac{225}{100} = 2\frac{25}{100} = 2\frac{1}{4}$$

PRACTICE:
Write each of the following percents as fractions:

1. 75%
2. 160%
3. 5%
4. 60%
5. 87%

SOLUTIONS:

1. $75\% = \frac{75}{100} = \frac{3}{4}$

2. $160\% = \frac{160}{100} = 1\frac{60}{100} = 1\frac{3}{5}$

3. $5\% = \frac{5}{100} = \frac{1}{20}$

4. $60\% = \frac{60}{100} = \frac{3}{5}$

5. $87\% = \frac{87}{100}$

Three Types of Percent Problems

A percent word problem has three values: the base (B) or whole, the rate (R) or percent, and the part (P). For example, if you got 40 correct answers on a 50-point exam, the base is 50, the part is 40, and your grade (rate) would be $\frac{40}{50} = 0.80 = 80\%$.

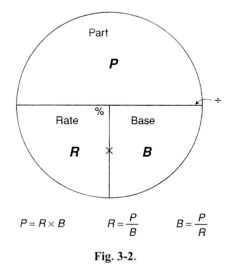

$$P = R \times B \qquad R = \frac{P}{B} \qquad B = \frac{P}{R}$$

Fig. 3-2.

Every percent problem contains three variables. They are the base (B), the rate (R) or percent, and the part (P). When you solve a percent problem, you are given the values of two of the three variables and you are asked to find the value of the third variable. The relationship of the three variables can be pictured in the circle shown in Figure 3-2.

$$P = R \times B$$
$$R = \frac{P}{B}$$
$$B = \frac{P}{R}$$

There are three types of percent problems.

TYPE 1: FINDING THE PART

Type 1 problems can be stated as follows:

Find 20% of 60.
What is 20% of 60?
20% of 60 is what number?

In Type 1 problems, you are given the base and the rate and are asked to find the part. Use the formula $P = R \times B$ and multiply the rate by the base. Be sure to change the percent to a decimal or fraction before multiplying.

EXAMPLE: Find 60% of 90.

SOLUTION:
Change the percent to a decimal and multiply: $0.60 \times 90 = 54$.

EXAMPLE: Find 45% of 80.

SOLUTION:
Use the formula $P = R \times B$. Change 45% to a decimal and multiply: $0.45 \times 80 = 36$.

PRACTICE:
1. Find 70% of 45.
2. Find 84% of 15.
3. What is 33% of 66?
4. 62.5% of 64 is what number?
5. Find 18% of 630.

SOLUTIONS:
1. $0.70 \times 45 = 31.5$
2. $0.84 \times 15 = 12.6$
3. $0.33 \times 66 = 21.78$
4. $0.625 \times 64 = 40$
5. $0.18 \times 630 = 113.4$

TYPE 2: FINDING THE RATE

Type 2 problems can be stated as follows:

> What percent of 16 is 10?
> 10 is what percent of 16?

In Type 2 problems, you are given the base and the part and are asked to find the rate or percent. The formula is $R = \frac{P}{B}$. In this case, divide the part by the base and then change the answer to a percent.

EXAMPLE: What percent of 8 is 6?

SOLUTION:
Use the formula $R = \frac{P}{B}$. Divide $\frac{6}{8} = 6 \div 8 = 0.75$. Change the decimal to a percent: $0.75 = 75\%$.

EXAMPLE: 18 is what percent of 90?

SOLUTION:
Use the formula $R = \frac{P}{B}$, and then divide $\frac{18}{90} = 18 \div 90 = 0.20$. Change the decimal to a percent: $0.20 = 20\%$.

PRACTICE:

1. What percent of 18 is 3?
2. 30 is what percent of 240?
3. 5 is what percent of 60?
4. What percent of 20 is 18?
5. What percent of 110 is 60?

SOLUTIONS:

1. $3 \div 18 = 0.16\overline{6} = 16.\overline{6}\%$
2. $30 \div 240 = 0.125 = 12.5\%$
3. $5 \div 60 = 0.08\overline{3} = 8.\overline{3}\%$
4. $18 \div 20 = 0.9 = 90\%$
5. $60 \div 110 = 0.54\overline{54} = 54.\overline{54}\%$

TYPE 3: FINDING THE BASE

Type 3 problems can be stated as follows:

16 is 20% of what number?
20% of what number is 16?

In Type 3 problems, you are given the rate and the part, and you are asked to find the base. Use the formula $B = \frac{P}{R}$.

EXAMPLE: 52% of what number is 416?

SOLUTION:
Use the formula $B = \frac{P}{R}$. Change 52% to 0.52 and divide: $416 \div 0.52 = 800$.

EXAMPLE: 45 is 30% of what number?

SOLUTION:
Use the formula $B = \frac{P}{R}$. Change 30% to 0.30 and divide: $45 \div 0.30 = 150$.

PRACTICE:

1. 6% of what number is 90?
2. 250 is 20% of what number?
3. 35 is 70% of what number?
4. 40% of what number is 200?
5. 19.2% of what number is 115.2?

SOLUTION:

1. $90 \div 0.06 = 1500$
2. $250 \div 0.20 = 1250$
3. $35 \div 0.70 = 50$
4. $200 \div 0.40 = 500$
5. $115.2 \div 0.192 = 600$

Word Problems

Percent word problems can be solved by identifying what you need to find and selecting the correct formula.

In order to solve a percent problem

1. Read the problem.
2. Identify the base, rate (%), and part. One of these will be unknown.
3. Select the correct formula.
4. Substitute the values in the formula and evaluate.

EXAMPLE: On a test consisting of 60 questions, a student received a grade of 85%. How many problems did the student answer correctly?

SOLUTION:
The base is 60 and the rate is 85%. The number of correct answers is the part. Since you need to find the part, use the formula $P = R \times B$. Change 85% to 0.85 and multiply: $0.85 \times 60 = 51$. Hence, the student got 51 problems correct.

EXAMPLE: A basketball team won 12 of its 20 games. What percent of the games played did the team win?

SOLUTION:
The base or total is 20 and the part is 12. The percent is the rate. Since you need to find the rate, use the formula $R = \frac{P}{B}$. Divide $12 \div 20 = 0.60 = 60\%$. Hence, the team won 60% of its games.

EXAMPLE: The sales tax rate in a certain state is 6%. If the sales tax on an automobile was $1350, find the price of the automobile.

SOLUTION:
The rate is 6% and the part is $1350. Since you need to find the base, use the formula $P = \frac{B}{R}$. Change the 6% to 0.06 and divide: $\$1350 \div 0.06 = \$22,500$. Hence the price of the automobile was $22,500.

Another percent problem you will often see is the percent increase or percent decrease problem. In this situation, always remember that the *old* or *original* number is used as the base.

EXAMPLE: The cost of a suit that was originally $300 was reduced to $180. What was the percent of the reduction?

SOLUTION:
Find the amount of reduction $300 − $180 = $120. Use $120 as the part and $300 as the base since it is the original price. Since you are being asked to find the percent or rate of reduction, use the formula $R = \frac{P}{B}$. Divide $120 \div 300 = 0.4$ or 40%. Hence the cost was reduced 40%.

PRACTICE:
1. A home was sold for $80,000. If the salesperson's commission was 7%, find the amount of the person's commission.
2. If a merchant purchased a clock for $30 and sold it for $50, find the rate of the markup based on the price that the merchant paid for the clock.
3. If the regular price of a picture frame is $25 and the price tag is marked 30% off, find the sale price.
4. On a 60-question examination, a student answered 45 questions correctly. What percent did she get correct?
5. The sales tax on a television set is $30.10. Find the cost of the television set if the tax rate is 7%.
6. A person saves $100 a month. If her annual income is $24,000, what percent of her income is she saving?
7. There are 40 students enrolled in Business Math 101. If 15% of the students were absent on a certain day, how many were absent?
8. Last August, the Martin family paid $75 for electricity. In February, they paid $54. What is the percent of decrease?
9. A railroad inspector inspects 360 railcars. If 95% passed, how many cars passed the inspection?
10. An instructor announced that 25% of his students received an A on the last test. If 8 students received an A, how many students took the test?

SOLUTIONS:
1. $0.07 \times \$80,000 = \$5600$
2. $\$50 − \$30 = \$20; \$20 \div \$30 = 0.66\overline{6} = 66.\overline{6}\%$
3. $0.30 \times \$25 = \$7.50; \$25 − \$7.50 = \$17.50$
4. $45 \div 60 = 0.75 = 75\%$
5. $\$30.10 \div 0.07 = \$430$

6. $100 \times 12 = \$1200; \$1200 \div \$24,000 = 0.05 = 5\%$
7. $0.15 \times 40 = 6$
8. $\$75 - \$54 = 21; 21 \div 75 = 0.28 = 28\%$
9. $0.95 \times 360 = 342$
10. $8 \div 0.25 = 32$

Quiz

1. Write 8% as a decimal.
    (a) 8.0
    (b) 0.8
    (c) 0.08
    (d) 0.008

2. Write 37.6% as a decimal.
    (a) 37.6
    (b) 3.76
    (c) 0.376
    (d) 0.0376

3. Write 145% as a decimal.
    (a) 0.145
    (b) 1.45
    (c) 14.5
    (d) 145

4. Write 0.55 as a percent.
    (a) 55%
    (b) 5.5%
    (c) 0.55%
    (d) 550%

5. Write 0.341 as a percent.
    (a) 0.341%
    (b) 0.00341%
    (c) 3.41%
    (d) 34.1%

6. Write 7 as a percent.
    (a) 700%
    (b) 70%
    (c) 7%
    (d) 0.77%

7. Write $\dfrac{3}{10}$ as a percent.
    (a) 3%
    (b) 300%
    (c) 0.3%
    (d) 30%

8. Write $\dfrac{5}{8}$ as a percent.
    (a) 6.25%
    (b) 62.5%
    (c) 0.625%
    (d) 625%

9. Write $2\dfrac{3}{4}$ as a percent.
    (a) 27.5%
    (b) 2.75%
    (c) 0.275%
    (d) 275%

10. Write 48% as a reduced fraction.
    (a) $\dfrac{12}{25}$
    (b) $4\dfrac{8}{10}$
    (c) $\dfrac{1}{48}$
    (d) $\dfrac{18}{25}$

11. Write 2% as a fraction.
    (a) $\dfrac{1}{2}$
    (b) $\dfrac{1}{50}$
    (c) $\dfrac{1}{5}$
    (d) $\dfrac{1}{20}$

12. Write 145% as a fraction.
    (a) $1\frac{3}{8}$

    (b) $1\frac{8}{25}$

    (c) $1\frac{9}{20}$

    (d) $1\frac{3}{4}$

13. Find 15% of 360.
    (a) 54
    (b) 5.4
    (c) 540
    (d) 0.54

14. 9 is what percent of 36?
    (a) 50%
    (b) 40%
    (c) 400%
    (d) 25%

15. 9% of what number is 54?
    (a) 60
    (b) 600
    (c) 6
    (d) 6000

16. 38% of 92 is what number?
    (a) 34.96
    (b) 242
    (c) 130
    (d) 54.6

17. A person earned a commission of $1720 on a home that was sold for $43,000. Find the rate.
    (a) 4%
    (b) 40%
    (c) 400%
    (d) 0.4%

18. A person bought a house for $87,000 and made a 15% down payment. How much was the down payment?
    (a) $6430
    (b) $13,050

(c) $1305
(d) $643

19. If the sales rate is 3% and the sales tax on a calculator is $0.60, what is the cost of the calculator?
(a) $18
(b) $60
(c) $20
(d) $24

20. A salesperson sold a sofa for $680 and a chair for $200. If the commission rate is 12.5%, find the person's commission.
(a) $90
(b) $85
(c) $25
(d) $110

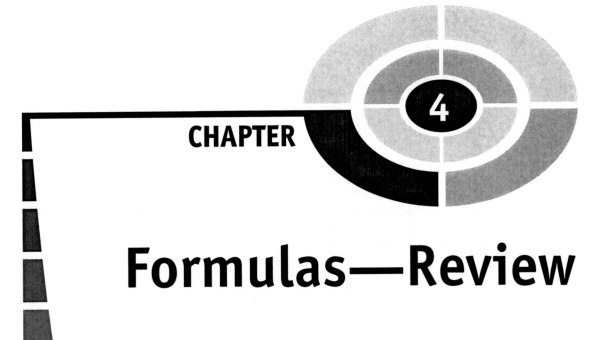

Formulas—Review

Introduction

In mathematics we use *formulas* to solve problems. A **formula** is a rule for expressing the relationship of variables in order to solve a problem. For example, to find the perimeter (i.e., the distance around the outside) of a rectangle, you use the formula $P = 2l + 2w$. In this case, the letter P means perimeter, l stands for the length, and w stands for the width. So in order to find the amount of fencing you need to put around a rectangular field that is 525-ft long and 275-ft wide, you would substitute in the formula:

$$
\begin{aligned}
P &= 2l + 2w \\
&= 2(525\text{ft}) + 2(275\text{ft}) \\
&= 1050 + 550 \\
&= 1600 \text{ ft}
\end{aligned}
$$

Formulas are used quite extensively in business mathematics and in this book. In order to evaluate formulas correctly, you need to know some basic algebra.

Exponents

When the same number is multiplied by itself, the indicated product can be written in **exponential notation**. For example, 4×4 can be written as 4^2 (4 squared). The 4 is called the **base** and the 2 is called the **exponent**. The expression 4^2 can also be read as "4 to the second power." The exponent tells how many times the base is multiplied by itself. Now

$$4^2 = 4 \times 4 = 16$$
$$5^3 = 5 \times 5 \times 5 = 125$$
$$2^6 = 2 \times 2 \times 2 \times 2 \times 2 \times 2 = 64$$

5^3 can be read as "5 cubed" or "5 to the third power." After that, expressions containing exponents are read as follows: 2^6 is "2 to the sixth power." When no exponent is written, it is understood to be 1. For example, $5 = 5^1$.

EXAMPLE: Find 6^4.

SOLUTION:

$$6^4 = 6 \times 6 \times 6 \times 6 = 1296$$

EXAMPLE: Find 2^3.

SOLUTION:

$$2^3 = 2 \times 2 \times 2 = 8$$

PRACTICE:
Find each:
1. 3^6
2. 9^2
3. 7^5
4. 8^1
5. 4^7

Calculator Tip

Most scientific calculators have an exponent key. It is usually the y^x or x^y key. Check the instruction manual to see how it is used.

SOLUTIONS:

1. $3^6 = 3 \times 3 \times 3 \times 3 \times 3 \times 3 = 729$
2. $9^2 = 9 \times 9 = 81$
3. $7^5 = 7 \times 7 \times 7 \times 7 \times 7 = 16{,}807$
4. $8^1 = 8$
5. $4^7 = 4 \times 4 \times 4 \times 4 \times 4 \times 4 \times 4 = 16{,}384$

Order of Operations

Mathematics uses what is called an **order of operations**. This order is used in evaluating formulas and solving equations. You will need this procedure later on in the book to help you evaluate formulas.

ORDER OF OPERATIONS

1. Perform all operations inside parentheses first.
2. Perform all operations with exponents.
3. Perform all operations involving multiplication and division from left to right.
4. Perform all operations involving addition and subtraction from left to right.

Now let's see how to use the order of operations.

EXAMPLE: Simplify $8 + 5 \cdot 6$.

SOLUTION:
In this case, there are two operations: addition and multiplication. Looking at the order of operations rules, you will see two things. First, there are no parentheses or exponents, and we do all multiplications before additions since multiplication and division are done in Step 3. The solution is

$$8 + 5 \cdot 6 = 8 + 30 = 38$$

EXAMPLE: : Simplify $15 - 10 + 5$.

SOLUTION:

Step 4 tells us that addition and subtraction are done as they are written in the problem from left to right. The solution is

$$15 - 10 + 5 = 5 + 5 = 10$$

EXAMPLE: Simplify $7 \cdot 4^3$.

SOLUTION:

Exponentiation is done before multiplication. The solution is

$$7 \cdot 4^3 = 7 \cdot 64$$
$$= 448$$

When an expression contains parentheses, perform the operations inside the parentheses in the same order as Steps 2 to 4.

EXAMPLE: Simplify $4 + (8 - 5)^2$.

SOLUTION:

$$
\begin{aligned}
4 + (8 - 5)^2 &= 4 + (3)^2 && \text{parentheses} \\
&= 4 + 9 && \text{exponents} \\
&= 13 && \text{addition}
\end{aligned}
$$

EXAMPLE: Simplify $136 - 9\,(8 - 2^3)$.

SOLUTION:

$$
\begin{aligned}
136 - 9(8 - 2^3) &= 136 - 9(8 - 8) && \text{parentheses/exponents} \\
&= 136 - 9(0) && \text{parentheses/subtraction} \\
&= 136 - 0 \\
&= 136
\end{aligned}
$$

Note: There are several ways to represent multiplication. One method is the "$\times$" sign. For example, $3 \times 2 = 6$. Another way is to use a dot. For example, $3 \cdot 2 = 6$. Finally, when no sign is written between numbers in parentheses, it means to multiply. For example, $3(2) = 6$, $(3)2 = 6$, or $(3)(2) = 6$. When a number is written in front of parentheses, it means to multiply. For example, $5(6 + 11) = 5(17) = 85$. Finally, in formulas where no sign is written, it means to multiply. For example, $I = PRT$ means to multiply the value for P times the value for R times the value for T.

When grouping symbols are included inside other grouping symbols, start with the innermost and work out.

EXAMPLE: Simplify $5 + \{36 - [4(2 + 1)]\}$.

SOLUTION:

$$5 + \{36 - [4(2 + 1)]\} = 5 + \{36 - [4 \cdot 3]\}$$
$$= 5 + \{36 - 12\}$$
$$= 5 + 24$$
$$= 29$$

When an expression is a fraction, perform all operations in the numerator and denominator and then divide.

EXAMPLE: : Simplify $\dfrac{8 \times 5}{12 - 2}$

SOLUTION:

$$\frac{8 \times 5}{12 - 2} = \frac{40}{10} = 4$$

Calculator Tip

When performing the order of operations on a scientific calculator, key in the expression exactly as written. Also, when no multiplication sign is used in an expression, you need to use one when you use the calculator. For example, the expression $5(6 + 8)$ has to be done as follows:

1. Press 5
2. Press $\times$
3. Press (
4. Press 6
5. Press $+$
6. Press 8
7. Press)
8. Press $=$

Calculator Tip

When an expression has brackets and braces, use the parentheses symbol on the calculator for both brackets and braces. For example, the expression $2\{3 + [4 + (5 + 6)]\}$ can be done on the calculator as follows:

1. Press 2
2. Press ×
3. Press (
4. Press 3
5. Press +
6. Press (
7. Press 4
8. Press +
9. Press (
10. Press 5
11. Press +
12. Press 6
13. Press)
14. Press)
15. Press)
16. Press =

PRACTICE:
Simplify each:

1. $7 + 5(6 - 2)$
2. $53 - 2^3 + 7 \cdot 4$
3. $7(43 - 3^3) + 5 \cdot 2$
4. $18 + 6[4 + 3(2 + 6)]$
5. $9 \cdot 6 + 8 \cdot 4^3 + 3 \cdot 7$
6. $15 + \{3 + 7[9 + 4(8 - 2)]\}$
7. $4 \cdot 8 - 6 \div 2 + 5 \cdot 3$
8. $\dfrac{18 - 9}{3^3 - 3^2}$
9. $\dfrac{3 \cdot (6 + 2)}{18 - 6}$
10. $\dfrac{18 + 6 - 2^2}{5 \cdot 2}$

SOLUTIONS:

1. $7 + 5(6 - 2) = 7 + 5(4) = 7 + 20 = 27$
2. $53 - 2^3 + 7 \cdot 4 = 53 - 8 + 7 \cdot 4 = 53 - 8 + 28 = 45 + 28 = 73$
3. $7(43 - 3^3) + 5 \cdot 2 = 7(43 - 27) + 5 \cdot 2 = 7(16) + 5 \cdot 2 = 112 + 10$
    $= 122$
4. $18 + 6[4 + 3(2 + 6)] = 18 + 6[4 + 3(8)] = 18 + 6[4 + 24] =$
    $18 + 6[28] = 18 + 168 = 186$
5. $9 \cdot 6 + 8 \cdot 4^3 + 3 \cdot 7 = 9 \cdot 6 + 8 \cdot 64 + 3 \cdot 7 = 54 + 512 + 21 =$
    $566 + 21 = 587$
6. $15 + \{3 + 7[9 + 4(8 - 2)]\} = 15 + \{3 + 7[9 + 4(6)]\} = 15 + \{3 +$
    $7[9 + 24]\} = 15 + \{3 + 7[33]\} = 15 + \{3 + 231\} = 15 + \{234\} =$
    249
7. $4 \cdot 8 - 6 \div 2 + 5 \cdot 3 = 32 - 6 \div 2 + 5 \cdot 3 = 32 - 3 + 5 \cdot 3 =$
    $32 - 3 + 15 = 29 + 15 = 44$
8. $\dfrac{18 - 9}{3^3 - 3^2} = \dfrac{18 - 9}{27 - 9} = \dfrac{9}{18} = \dfrac{1}{2}$
9. $\dfrac{3 \cdot (6 + 2)}{18 - 6} = \dfrac{3 \cdot (8)}{12} = \dfrac{24}{12} = 2$
10. $\dfrac{18 + 6 - 2^2}{5 \cdot 2} = \dfrac{18 + 6 - 4}{5 \cdot 2} = \dfrac{20}{10} = 2$

Formulas

As stated previously, a formula is a rule for expressing the relationship of variables in order to solve a problem. The variables in most formulas are the letters of the alphabet. In order to **evaluate** a formula, substitute the values for the variables in the formula and simplify the answer using the order of operations.

EXAMPLE: : Find the value for I in the formula $I = PRT$ when $P = \$2000$, $R = 0.06$, and $T = 5$.

SOLUTIONS:
Substitute for P, R, and T and multiply as shown:

$$I = PRT$$
$$= (\$2000)(0.06)(5)$$
$$= \$600$$

When the formula is a fraction, evaluate the numerator first, then the denominator, and then divide the two values.

EXAMPLE: Find the value for P in the formula $P = \frac{I}{RT}$ when $I = 30$, $R = 0.05$, and $T = 3$.

SOLUTION:

$$P = \frac{I}{RT}$$

$$= \frac{30}{0.05(3)}$$

$$= \frac{30}{0.15} \quad \text{(Multiply the values in the denominator.)}$$

$$= 200$$

EXAMPLE: Find the value for PV using the formula $PV = \frac{FV}{(1 + R)^N}$ when $FV = \$2400$, $R = 0.02$, and $N = 3$.

SOLUTION:

$$PV = \frac{FV}{(1 + R)^N} = \frac{2400}{(1 + 0.02)^3} = \frac{2400}{(1.02)^3} = \frac{2400}{1.061208}$$

$$= 2261.57 \text{ (rounded)}$$

PRACTICE:
Evaluate each formula. You will be using these formulas in later chapters. Round the answers to two decimal places if necessary.

1. $I = PRT$, when $P = 875$, $R = 0.075$, and $T = 6$
2. $S = C + M$, when $C = 350$ and $M = 75$
3. $T = RL$, when $R = 0.07$ and $L = 585$
4. $N = (1.00 - R)L$, when $R = 0.11$ and $L = 600$
5. $R = \frac{I}{PT}$, when $P = 5250$, $I = 1680$, and $T = 4$
6. $FV = P(1 + R)^N$, when $P = 1735$, $R = 0.02$, and $N = 4$
7. $T = \frac{I}{PR}$, when $I = 1200$, $P = 6000$, and $R = 0.04$
8. $R = \frac{L}{T}$, when $L = 875$ and $T = 96.25$

9. $PV = \dfrac{FV}{(1 + R)^N}$, when FV $= 7250$, $R = 0.03$, and $N = 2$

10. $I = P \left(1 + \dfrac{R}{12}\right)^N$, where $R = 0.12$, $P = 500$, and $N = 2$

SOLUTION:

1. $I = PRT$
    $= 875(0.075)(6) = 393.75$

2. $S = C + M$
    $= 350 + 75 = 425$

3. $T = RL$
    $= 0.07(585) = 40.95$

4. $N = (1.00 - R)L$
    $= (1.00 - 0.11)600 = (0.89)600 = 534$

5. $R = \dfrac{I}{PT}$
    $= \dfrac{1680}{5250(4)}$
    $= \dfrac{1680}{21000}$
    $= 0.08$

6. $FV = P(1 + R)^N$
    $= 1735 (1 + 0.02)^4$
    $= 1735 (1.02)^4$
    $= 1735 (1.08243216)$
    $= 1878.02$ (rounded)

7. $T = \dfrac{I}{PR}$
    $= \dfrac{1200}{6000(0.04)}$
    $= \dfrac{1200}{240}$
    $= 5$

8. $R = \dfrac{L}{T}$
    $= \dfrac{875}{96.25}$
    $= 9.09$ (rounded)

9. $PV = \dfrac{FV}{(1+R)^N}$

   $= \dfrac{7250}{(1+0.03)^2}$

   $= \dfrac{7250}{1.0609}$

   $= 6833.82$ (rounded)

10. $I = P\left(1 + \dfrac{R}{12}\right)^N$

   $= 500\left(1 + \dfrac{0.12}{12}\right)^2$

   $= 500\,(1 + 0.01)^2$

   $= 500\,(1.01)^2$

   $= 500\,(1.0201)$

   $= 510.05$

Quiz

1. Find 3^8.
   (a) 24
   (b) 38
   (c) 512
   (d) 6561

2. Find 4^3.
   (a) 64
   (b) 12
   (c) 81
   (d) 43

3. Simplify $25 - 10 \cdot 2$.
   (a) 2
   (b) 5
   (c) 10
   (d) 30

4. Simplify $3(8 + 2)^2$.
   (a) 204
   (b) 60
   (c) 36
   (d) 300

5. Simplify $27 + 2(18 - 4.3)$.
   (a) 174
   (b) 51.2
   (c) 54.4
   (d) 207

6. Simplify $42 - [20 - (6 + 8)]$.
   (a) 24
   (b) 14
   (c) 38
   (d) 36

7. Simplify $\dfrac{17 - 5}{6 - 2}$.
   (a) 3
   (b) 0
   (c) 4
   (d) 8

8. Simplify $\dfrac{8 + 3 \cdot 6}{5 \cdot 8 - 38}$.
   (a) 13
   (b) 33
   (c) 22
   (d) 15

9. What is the value for I in the formula $I = PRT$ when $P = 3275$, $R = 0.06$, and $T = 7$?
   (a) 196.5
   (b) 1375.5
   (c) 0.42
   (d) 1425.5

10. What is the value for T in the formula $T = \dfrac{I}{PR}$ when $I = 910$, $P = 2800$, and $R = 0.05$?
    (a) 3.8
    (b) 5.2

(c) 7.3
(d) 6.5

11. What is the value for R in the formula $R = \dfrac{I}{PT}$ when $I = 600$, $P = 6000$, and $T = 5$?
(a) 0.04
(b) 0.03
(c) 0.02
(d) 0.05

12. What is the value for R in the formula $R = \dfrac{L}{T}$ when $L = 860$ and $T = 5$?
(a) 183
(b) 155
(c) 164
(d) 172

13. What is the value for N in the formula $N = (1.00 - R)L$ when $R = 0.09$ and $L = 1200$?
(a) 1092
(b) 107
(c) 1322
(d) 1416

14. What is the value for the FV in the formula $FV = P(1 + R)^N$ when $P = 1800$, $R = 0.06$, and $N = 2$?
(a) 6480.21
(b) 3126.55
(c) 2022.48
(d) 8214.23

15. What is the value (rounded to two decimal places) for PV in the formula $PV = \dfrac{FV}{(1 + R)^N}$ when $FV = 20{,}000$, $R = 0.02$, and $N = 3$?
(a) 23,021.62
(b) 16,347.43
(c) 15,972.23
(d) 18,846.45

CHAPTER 5

Checking Accounts

Introduction

When it is time for people to pay for something, many people write a **check**. In order to write checks, a person needs to establish a **checking account** at a bank. There are several types of checking accounts, and a bank can explain each type. The person or business that the check is made out to is called the **payee**. When the payee cashes the check, the bank then gives the payee his or her money.

There are two major advantages of having a checking account. First, you can keep a financial record of all of your transactions, and second, you have a receipt of your payments (the cancelled check, a photocopy of the check, or a statement identification of the check).

Recording the Transactions

In order to keep your checking account accurate, you need to keep an accurate recording of all of the transactions. This can be done by using the **account register** that comes with your checkbook.

There are two types of transactions that are commonly associated with a checking account. When you put money into your checking account or collect interest on the money that you have in your account, the transaction is called a **credit transaction**. When you write a check or take money out of your account, the transaction is called a **debit transaction**. The amount of money that you currently have in your checking account is called the **balance**. When you complete a credit transaction, you add the amount of the transaction to your balance. When you complete a debit transaction, you subtract the amount of the transaction from the current balance.

EXAMPLE: On July 1, you deposit your payroll check in the amount of $872.43 into your checking account. Previously the balance was $375.60. During the week, you write the following checks:

Date	Check number	Payee	Amount
7/1	130	Bob's Auto	$18.79
7/3	131	Corner Grocery	$83.15
7/4	132	Jones Hardware	$127.65
7/4	133	Health Club	$40.00
7/5		Deposit	$100.00

Show the transactions on the register.

SOLUTION:

Record the balance, check number, and date in the appropriate columns. When the transaction is a credit transaction, add the amount to the balance. When the transaction is a debit transaction, subtract the amount from the balance.

Number	Date	Transaction	Debit	Credit	Balance
					$375.60
	7/1	Deposit		$872.43	$1248.03
130	7/1	Bob's Auto	$18.79		$1229.24
131	7/3	Corner Grocery	$83.15		$1146.09
132	7/4	Jones Hardware	$127.65		$1018.44
133	7/4	Health Club	$40.00		$978.44
	7/5	Deposit		$100.00	$1078.44

The new balance is $1078.44.

PRACTICE:

1. The balance in a checking account was $2473.12. The following trans-
    actions were made:

Date	Check number	Payee	Amount
5/1	986	Nail Salon	$29.00
5/6	987	Groceries At Home	$56.12
5/8		Deposit	$53.00
5/15	988	Hair In Place	$28.00
5/21	989	Book Club	$38.95
5/22		Deposit	$75.00

   Show these transactions on an account register.

2. On June 1, the balance in a checking account was $785.14. The following
    transactions were made during the month:

Date	Check number	Payee	Amount
6/1		Deposit	$1715.00
6/3	1411	Greenwood Gas	$75.14
6/3	1412	Ellen's Eatery	$15.12
6/10	1413	Brightlight Electric	$53.50
6/15		Deposit	$750.00
6/16	1415	Hunter Oil Company	$98.15

   Show these transactions on an account register.

3. On March 1, the balance in a checking account was $2763.12. The fol-
    lowing transactions were made during March:

Date	Check number	Payee	Amount
3/20	449	James Robinson, DDS	$128.00
3/20	452	Liberty Repair Service	$89.95
3/28		Deposit	$960.00
3/28	453	Community College	$432.00
3/30	454	Yates Conference Center	$215.00

   Show these transactions on an account register.

4. On January 1, the balance in a checking account was $436.19. During the month, the following transactions were made:

Date	Check number	Payee	Amount
1/15	614	Sam's Soccer Store	$53.12
1/15	615	Borough Water Company	$33.15
1/20	616	Link Cable Company	$52.97
1/20		Deposit	$386.00
1/28	617	Toys & Games, Inc	$112.16
1/29	618	Springtime Travel Agency	$250.00
2/3		Deposit	$150.00

Show the transactions on an account register.

5. The balance in a checking account on August 1 was $12,863.19. During the month, the following transactions were made:

Date	Check number	Payee	Amount
8/19	1073	Joan Smith, MD	$125.00
8/19	1074	Exercise Unlimited	$48.00
8/23	1075	Eastwood Golf Club	$515.00
8/27		Deposit	$432.00
8/29	1076	Adelle Auto Repair	$217.83
8/31	1077	Karl's Kat Kennel	$88.53
9/3		Deposit	$75.00

Show the transactions on an account register.

SOLUTIONS:

1.

Number	Date	Transaction	Debit	Credit	Balance
					$2473.12
986	5/1	Nail Salon	$29.00		$2444.12
987	5/6	Groceries At Home	$56.12		$2388.00
	5/8	Deposit		$53.00	$2441.00
988	5/15	Hair In Place	$28.00		$2413.00
989	5/21	Book Club	$38.95		$2374.05
	5/22	Deposit		$75.00	$2449.05

2.

Number	Date	Transaction	Debit	Credit	Balance
					$ 785.14
	6/1	Deposit		$1715.00	$2500.14
1411	6/3	Greenwood Gas	$75.14		$2425.00
1412	6/3	Ellen's Eatery	$15.12		$2409.88
1413	6/10	Brightlight Electric	$53.50		$2356.38
	6/15	Deposit		$750.00	$3106.38
1415	6/16	Hunter Oil Company	$98.15		$3008.23

3.

Number	Date	Transaction	Debit	Credit	Balance
					$2763.12
449	3/20	James Robinson	$128.00		$2635.12
452	3/20	Liberty Repair	$89.95		$2545.17
	3/28	Deposit		$960.00	$3505.17
453	3/28	Community College	$432.00		$3073.17
454	3/30	Yates Conf Center	$215.00		$2858.17

4.

Number	Date	Transaction	Debit	Credit	Balance
					$436.19
614	1/15	Sam's Soccer Store	$53.12		$383.07
615	1/15	Borough Water Co	$33.15		$349.92
616	1/20	Link Cable Co	$52.97		$296.95
	1/20	Deposit		$386.00	$682.95
617	1/28	Toys & Games, Inc	$112.16		$570.79
618	1/29	Springtime Travel	$250.00		$320.79
	2/3	Deposit		$150.00	$470.79

5.

Number	Date	Transaction	Debit	Credit	Balance
					$12,863.19
1073	8/19	Joan Smith, MD	$125.00		$12,738.19
1074	8/19	Exercise Unlimited	$48.00		$12,690.19
1075	8/23	Eastwood Golf Club	$515.00		$12,175.19
	8/27	Deposit		$432.00	$12,607.19
1076	8/29	Adelle Auto Repair	$217.83		$12,389.36
1077	8/31	Karl's Kat Kennel	$88.53		$12,300.83
	9/3	Deposit		$75.00	$12,375.83

Reconciling a Bank Statement

Every month the bank sends a **statement** of the transactions to its checking account customers. The purpose of this statement is to enable you to make sure that your account is **balanced**. If it is not balanced, then you must reconcile any differences in the statement and in your account register.

In addition to your transactions, other fees or credits may appear on your bank statement. One credit you may receive is the **interest** you get on your money. Some checking accounts pay interest and others do not. There may also be **service charges**. These could include a monthly maintenance fee or a charge for each check that you write. If you order new checks, the cost is usually deducted from your balance. Finally, you might be charged for **insufficient funds** or for an **overdrawn account**. If you cash a check from a friend or business, and he/she or the business does not have enough money in his/her or the business account to cover the amount of the check, the amount will be deducted from your account. This is called a **returned check**. You may also be charged a fee for a returned check. If you write a check and do not have enough money in your account to cover it, you will be charged an **insufficient funds fee**. (Of course, after you complete this chapter, you won't have to worry about this unless you make a mistake in your computations.)

The problem with reconciling a bank statement is that not all of the information on the bank statement is in your account register and vice versa; for example, the interest you get and the fees that the bank charges you are not

in your account register. In addition, some of the checks you wrote may not
have been cashed before the statement was sent. Finally, some of your deposits
may not have been recorded in the statement since they were made after the
statement was issued. Therefore it is necessary to reconcile the statement after
you receive it by following these steps:

STEPS IN RECONCILING A BANK STATEMENT

1. Verify the dates of transactions, checking account numbers, and deposits.
2. Check off the matching transactions that appear on the bank statement and in your account register.
3. Write in your account register the transactions that appear on the bank statement and do not appear in your register, and update your account register. Check these off on the bank statement.
4. Using your account register, add up the values of all deposits that you made that do not appear on the bank statement. The sum is called the **outstanding credit transactions**.
5. Using your account register, add up the values of all checks that you wrote that do not appear on the bank statement. The sum is called the **outstanding debit transactions**.
6. Use the following formula to adjust the bank statement balance:

Adjusted balance = Bank statement balance + The total of the

outstanding credit transactions − The total of the

outstanding debit transactions.

This amount should match the amount of the balance in your account register.

EXAMPLE: Using the information in the preceding example for your account register (on page 62) and the information given on the bank statement shown, reconcile your checking account.

Financial statement

Previous balance	$ 375.60
Deposits total	+ 872.43
Withdrawals total	− 141.94
New balance	$1106.09

Financial transactions

Date	Check number	Amount
7/1	130	$18.79
7/3	131	83.15
7/4	133	40.00
Total		$141.94

SOLUTION:
Notice that the balance on the bank statement is $1106.09 while the balance in your financial account in the previous example is $1078.44. (Look back on page 62.)

1. Check off the matched transactions. They are check numbers 130, 131, and 133 and the $872.43 deposit.
2. Since no fees or interest has been accrued, omit this step here.
3. Find the sum of all unaccounted-for deposits. In this case, the $100.00 deposit made on July 5 does not appear on the bank's financial statement. This is the value of the outstanding credit transactions.
4. Find the sum of all unaccounted-for checks. In this case, check number 132 for the amount of $127.65 is an outstanding debit.
5. Substitute in the formula: Adjusted balance = Bank statement balance + Total of the outstanding credit – The total of the outstanding debit.

Adjusted balance = $1106.09 + $100.00 – $127.65 = $1078.44

Since this matches the balance in your account register, you have successfully reconciled or balanced your checkbook. *Viola!*

PRACTICE:

1. For the transactions in Exercise 1 of the last section, reconcile the bank statement shown and find the adjusted balance.

Bank statement

Previous balance	$4473.12
Deposits total	53.00
Withdrawals total	124.07
New balance	$2402.05

Financial transactions

Date	Check number	Amount
5/1	986	$29.00
5/6	987	56.12
5/29	989	38.95
Total		$124.07

2. For the transactions in Exercise 2 of the last section, reconcile the bank statement shown and find the adjusted balance.

Bank statement

Previous balance	$785.14
Deposits total	1715.00
Withdrawals total	128.64
New balance	$2371.50

Financial transactions

Date	Check number	Amount
6/3	1411	$89.95
6/10	1413	53.50
Total		$128.64

3. For the transactions shown in Exercise 3 of the previous section, reconcile the bank statement shown and find the adjusted balance.

Bank statement

Previous balance	$2763.12
Deposits total	960.00
Withdrawals total	521.95
New balance	$3201.17

Financial transactions

Date	Check number	Amount
3/20	452	$89.95
3/28	453	432.00
Total		$521.95

4.   For the transactions shown in Exercise 4 of the previous section, reconcile the bank statement shown and find the adjusted balance.

Bank statement

Previous balance	$436.19
Deposits total	386.00
Withdrawals total	218.25
New balance	$603.94

Financial transactions

Date	Check number	Amount
1/15	614	$53.12
1/20	616	52.97
1/28	617	112.16
Total		$218.25

5. For the transactions shown in Exercise 5 of the previous section, reconcile the bank statement shown and find the adjusted balance.

Bank statement

Previous balance	$12,863.19
Deposits total	432.00
Withdrawals total	390.83
New balance	$12,904.36

Financial transactions

Date	Check number	Amount
8/19	1073	$125.00
8/19	1074	48.00
8/29	1076	217.83
Total		$390.83

SOLUTIONS:

1. Adjusted balance = Bank statement balance + Total of outstanding credit − Total of the outstanding debit

   $2449.05 = $2402.05 + $75.00 − $28.00

2. Adjusted balance = Bank statement balance + Total of outstanding credit − Total of the outstanding debit

   $3008.23 = $2371.50 + $750 − ($15.12 + $98.15)

3. Adjusted balance = Bank statement balance + Total of outstanding credit − Total of the outstanding debit

   $2858.17 = $3201.17 + 0 − ($128.00 + $215.00)

4. Adjusted balance = Bank statement balance + Total of outstanding credit − Total of the outstanding debit

   $470.79 = $603.94 + $150.00 − ($33.15 + $250.00)

5. Adjusted balance = Bank statement balance + Total of outstanding credit − Total of the outstanding debit

   $12,375.83 = $12,904.36 + $75.00 − ($515.00 + $88.53)

Summary

Many businesses and individuals pay their bills with checks. A cancelled check provides a record of the payment. In order to keep account of the transactions, an account register is used. Here all of the deposits and check amounts are recorded. In order to make sure that there is enough money to cover the checks, the account register must be balanced. This chapter presented a method to balance a checkbook registry.

Quiz

1. The person or business that a check is made out to is called the
   (a) maker
   (b) owner
   (c) payee
   (d) teller

2. In order to keep track of the transactions you make on your checking account, you should record them in
   (a) an account register
   (b) a transaction recorder
   (c) a notebook
   (d) a record

3. The amount of money that you currently have in your checking account is called the
   (a) debit
   (b) credit
   (c) transaction
   (d) balance

4. The summary of your transactions obtained from the bank is called the
   (a) bank balance
   (b) deposits total
   (c) transactions total
   (d) bank statement

5. In order to balance your checkbook, the amount of money in the account register should equal the
   (a) new balance
   (b) adjusted balance

(c) total of the financial transactions
(d) previous balance

Use the following information for Questions 6 to 10.

Accounts register

Number	Date	Transaction	Debit	Credit	Balance
					$653.29
156	7/5	Mary Jones	$32.80		$620.49
157	7/12	Hot Water Company	$156.16		$464.33
158	7/17	Sure Lawn Care	$32.00		$432.33
	7/19	Deposit		$500.00	$932.33
159	7/23	Keystone Baking	$50.00		$882.33
160	7/31	Norton Plumbing	$327.62		$554.71
	8/2	Deposit		$200.00	$754.71

Bank statement

Previous balance	$653.29
Deposits total	500.00
Withdrawals total	238.96
New balance	$914.33

Financial transactions

Date	Check number	Amount
7/5	156	$32.80
7/12	157	156.16
7/23	159	50.00
Total		$238.96

6. The previous balance amount is
    (a) $914.33
    (b) $754.71
    (c) $238.96
    (d) $653.29

7. The outstanding credit amount is
    (a) $500.00
    (b) $200.00
    (c) $914.33
    (d) $238.96

8. The outstanding debit amount is
    (a) $238.96
    (b) $500.00
    (c) $359.62
    (d) $200.00

9. The bank balance amount is
    (a) $914.33
    (b) $700.00
    (c) $359.62
    (d) $754.71

10. The adjusted balance amount is
    (a) $914.33
    (b) $754.71
    (c) $653.29
    (d) $359.62

Payroll and Commission

Introduction

There are many different ways an employee can be paid by his or her employer. This chapter explains the different methods that are used to determine a wage earner's salary. In addition, many people work on commission and the different ways to determine a person's commission are also explained. Finally, employers are often required to withhold part of an employee's salary for taxes, insurance, Social Security, dues, and benefits. The last section explains payroll deductions.

Yearly Salary

A person's earnings before deduction is called the **gross pay**. When a person earns a yearly salary, he or she can be paid **monthly** (12 times a year),

semimonthly or twice a month (24 times a year), **biweekly** or every other week (26 times a year), or **weekly** (52 times a year).

In order to find the amount of a person's gross pay based on a yearly salary, divide the yearly salary by

> 12 if the person is paid monthly
> 24 if the person is paid semimonthly
> 26 if the person is paid biweekly
> 52 if the person is paid weekly

EXAMPLE: If a person earns $54,000 a year, find the gross amount the person receives if he is paid monthly.

SOLUTION:
$$\$54,000 \div 12 = \$4500$$

EXAMPLE: If a person earns $40,560 a year, find the person's salary if the person is paid weekly.

SOLUTION:
$$\$40,560 \div 52 = \$780.00$$

EXAMPLE: Find a person's gross pay if she earns $23,140 yearly and is paid biweekly.

SOLUTION:
$$\$23,140 \div 26 = \$890.00$$

EXAMPLE: Find a person's gross pay if he is paid semimonthly and earns $72,000 per year.

SOLUTION:
$$\$72,000 \div 24 = \$3000.00$$

PRACTICE:

1. Find Jane Gilchrist's gross pay if she earns $32,000 a year and is paid monthly.
2. Find Nebo Shah's gross pay if she has a yearly salary of $20,544 and is paid semimonthly.
3. Find Chad Bolic's gross pay if he earns $112,346 a year and is paid biweekly.
4. Find Melodie Smith's gross pay if she is paid weekly and earns $19,448 a year.
5. Find Ying Pan's gross pay if he is paid biweekly and earns a yearly salary of $74,800.

6. Angelo Ureakis's yearly salary is $142,000. Find her gross pay if she is paid monthly.
7. Todd Williams' yearly salary is $68,400. Find his gross pay if he is paid weekly.
8. Vittorio Romeraz earns $156,300 a year. Find his gross pay if he is paid semimonthly.
9. Yolando Lin's yearly salary is $98,376. Find her gross pay if she is paid biweekly.
10. Darnell Tipston makes $34,372 a year. Find her gross pay if she is paid weekly.

SOLUTIONS:

1. $32,000 ÷ 12 = $2666.67
2. $20,544 ÷ 24 = $856.00
3. $112,346 ÷ 26 = $4321.00
4. $19,448 ÷ 52 = $374.00
5. $74,800 ÷ 26 = $2876.92
6. $142,000 ÷ 12 = $11,833.33
7. $68,400 ÷ 52 = $1315.38
8. $156,300 ÷ 24 = $6512.50
9. $98,376 ÷ 26 = $3783.69
10. $34,372 ÷ 52 = $661.00

Hourly Wages

Many people work for an **hourly wage** or an **hourly rate**. In this case, 40 hours per week is considered the standard workweek. In most cases, any hours over 40 per week is considered **overtime**. The overtime rate per hour is often one and a half times the hourly rate. For example, if a person earns $12.00 an hour and is paid one and a half his hourly rate, his overtime rate would be $12.00 × 1.5 or $12.00 × $1\frac{1}{2}$ = $18.00. Sometimes, depending on the contract, employees are paid double time for working on Sundays.

In order to find the person's gross pay per week based on an hourly rate:

1. Multiply the number of hours worked up to and including 40 by the hourly rate.
2. If a person works more than 40 hours per week, multiply the number of hours over 40 that the person has worked by the overtime rate and add it to the answer obtained in Step 1.

EXAMPLE: An employee earns $15.00 per hour. If the person works 47 hours per week, find his gross pay for the week if he is paid at an overtime rate of $1\frac{1}{2}$ times the hourly salary.

SOLUTION:
In this case, the employee worked $47 - 40 = 7$ hours overtime. His pay then would be
   Regular pay: $40 \times \$15.00 = \$600$
   Overtime: $7 \times \$15.00 \times 1.5 = \$157.50$
   Gross pay: $\$600 + \$157.50 = \$757.50$

EXAMPLE: An employee earns $12.75 per hour and is paid one and a half times her hourly rate for any hours that she works over 40 hours per week. Find her pay if she works the following hours:

M	T	W	T	F	S
8	10	6	12	8	5

SOLUTION:
Find the total number of hours that the person worked: $8 + 10 + 6 + 12 + 8 + 5 = 49$ hours. Hence, she worked 9 hours overtime, and so her pay is
   Regular pay: $40 \times \$12.75 = \$510.00$
   Overtime pay: $9 \times \$12.75 \times 1.5 = \$172.13$
   Gross pay: $\$510 + \$172.13 = \$682.13$

EXAMPLE: If a person earned $584 last week and worked 40 hours, find his hourly wage.

SOLUTION:
In this case, divide the gross pay by the number of hours that the person worked to get his hourly wage: $\$584 \div 40 = \$14.60$. Hence the person earns $14.60 per hour.

PRACTICE:

1. Bill Burke worked 46 hours last week. If he earns $8.75 per hour and gets time and a half for all hours he works in excess of 40, find his gross pay.
2. Mary Carlson worked the following hours last week:
   Monday—8; Tuesday—11; Wednesday—10; Thursday—8; Friday—2; Saturday—5.

If she gets $12.60 per hour and time and a half for all hours she works over 40, find her gross pay.

3. If a person's gross pay for a week is $618 and the person worked 40 hours, find her hourly wage.

4. Sean Young earns $6.50 per hour and gets time and a half for all hours he works over 40. If his gross pay last week was $318.50, how many hours overtime did he work?

5. Su Lee earns $9.60 per hour and gets double time for all hours over 40 that she works per week. If she received an $80.00 bonus last week and worked 47 h, find her gross pay.

SOLUTIONS:

1. Regular pay: $40 \times \$8.75 = \$350$
   Overtime pay: $6 \times \$8.75 \times 1.5 = \$78.75$
   Gross pay: $\$350 + \$78.75 = \$428.75$

2. Total hours worked: $8 + 11 + 10 + 8 + 2 + 5 = 44$ hours
   Regular pay: $40 \times \$12.60 = \$504.00$
   Overtime pay: $4 \times \$12.60 \times 1.5 = \$75.60$
   Gross pay: $\$504.00 + \$75.60 = \$579.60$

3. $\$618 \div 40 = \$15.45$

4. His pay for working 40 hours is $40 \times \$6.50 = \$260.00$
   His overtime pay is $\$318.50 - \$260 = \$58.50$
   His overtime rate is $\$6.50 \times 1.5 = \$9.75$
   The number of hours he worked overtime is $\$58.50 \div \$9.75 = 6$ hours

5. Regular pay: $40 \times \$9.60 = \$384.00$
   Overtime pay: $7 \times \$9.60 \times 2 = \$134.40$
   Gross pay: $\$384.00 + \$134.40 + \$80.00 = \$598.40$

Piecework Wages

Sometimes workers are paid on the basis of the number of acceptable items they make. For example, agricultural workers may be paid for the number of baskets of peaches they can pick. A garment maker may be paid on the number of skirts he is able to sew.

There are two types of rates paid to these workers. One type is called a **straight piecework** rate. In this case, the worker is paid a specific amount for each acceptable item made. The second type is called a **differential piece** rate. Here the worker is paid a rate that increases as the number of acceptable items he or she produces increases. For example, the worker may be paid $0.80 for the first 200 items produced, $0.85 for each item produced over 200 up to 400, and $0.90 for each item produced over 400 items per week.

In order to find the worker's gross pay, find the number of items produced in each category, multiply these numbers by the corresponding rates, and find the sum.

EXAMPLE: Find a worker's gross pay if the worker is paid a straight piecework rate of $2.57 for each engraved plaque the worker makes. For this week, the person engraved 378 plaques.

SOLUTION:
Multiply $378 \times \$2.57 = \$971.46$. The worker's gross pay is $971.46.

EXAMPLE: A worker is paid weekly for each rocking chair he or she assembles at the rate of

1 to 50	$2.00
51 to 100	$3.00
101 and over	$4.00

If the person assembled 105 rocking chairs last week, find the person's gross pay.

SOLUTION:
Find the number of chairs assembled in each category and multiply by the corresponding rate for that category. Add the answers as shown:
First 50 items: $50 \times \$2.00 = \$100$
Items 51 to 100: $50 \times \$3.00 = \$150$
Items over 100: $5 \times \$4.00 = \$20$
Gross pay: $\$100 + \$150 + \$20 = \$270$

PRACTICE:

1. Mike Hamilton earns $50 for each child's rocking horse he assembles. Find his gross pay if he assembled 72 rocking horses last week.
2. Beth James assembles charm bracelets. She is paid $0.35 for each bracelet she assembles up to 50 per week. She receives $0.55 for each bracelet over 50 she assembles. Yesterday she assembled 62 bracelets. What was her gross pay?
3. Carrie Williams took a part time job of picking corn. She gets $0.11 for each dozen she picks. Last week, she picked 87, 62, 48, 71, and 54 dozens. Find her gross pay.

4. Margie Scott packages an assortment of teas for mail-order customers. Last week, she made up 171 boxes. Find her gross pay if she is paid a differential piece rate of

1 to 99	$1.05 per box
100 to 199	$1.25 per box
200 and over	$1.40 per box

5. Janice Bolger conducts surveys at a local mall. She is paid $0.25 for every survey she completes. Last week, she completed 327 surveys. Find her gross pay.

SOLUTIONS:

1. $72 \times \$50 = \$3600$
2. $50 \times \$0.35 + 12 \times \$0.55 = \$24.10$
3. $87 + 62 + 48 + 71 + 54 = 322; 322 \times \$0.11 = \$35.42$
4. $99 \times \$1.05 + 72 \times \$1.25 = \$193.95$
5. $327 \times \$0.25 = \$81.75$

Commission

Often employees are paid on *commission*. A **commission** is an amount based on a percentage of sales that is paid to a person. If a person is paid only on commission, it is referred to as a **straight commission**. Sometimes a person receives a salary and a commission. The purpose of a commission is to encourage the person to make more sales. To find the commission, multiply the amount of sales by the commission rate.

EXAMPLE: A real-estate salesperson receives a 3% commission on all the sales he makes. Find his commission if he sells a home for $146,000.

SOLUTION:
Multiply $3\% \times \$146,000 = 0.03 \times \$146,000 = \$4380$.
His commission is $4380.

EXAMPLE: A salesperson is paid a weekly salary of $840 and a 6% commission on all weekly sales over $1000. If the total of his sales is $1546, find his gross pay.

SOLUTION:
First, find the amount of sales over $1000: $\$1546 - \$1000 = \$546$.
Second, find his commission on that amount: $6\% \times \$546 = 0.06 \times 546 = \$32.76$.

Third, add his salary and commission to get his gross pay: $840 + $32.76 = $872.76. His gross pay is $872.76.

EXAMPLE: A salesperson receives a commission for her sales based on the following scale:

   8% on all sales
   5% on all sales between $100,000 and $200,000
   3% on all sales over $200,000

If her total sales were $320,000, find her gross pay.

SOLUTION:
First, find 8% of $320,000: 8% × $320,000 = 0.08 × $320,000 = $25,600.
   Next, find 5% over $100,000: 5% × $100,000 = 0.05 × 100,000 = $5000.
   Then find 3% of the amount over $200,000: $320,000 − $200,000 = $120,000; 3% × $120,000 = $3600.
   Finally, find the sum: $25,600 + $5000 + $3600 = $34,200. Hence her gross pay is $34,200.
   In the previous example, you were asked to find the commission or gross pay. When a person is paid a straight commission and you know the amount of the commission, you can find the rate if you are given the total sales or you can find the total sales if you are given the rate. In these problems, you can use the same formulas as in the three types of percent problems (see Chapter 3). In this case, the base is the total amount of the sales, the rate is the percent, and the commission is the part. The three formulas are

$$P \text{ (commission)} = B \text{ (total sales)} \times R \text{ (rate)}$$
$$R \text{ (rate)} = \frac{P \text{ (commission)}}{B \text{ (total sales)}}$$
$$B \text{ (total sales)} = \frac{P \text{ (commission)}}{R \text{ (rate)}}$$

EXAMPLE: If a real-estate agent receives a 2% commission of $1120, what was the price of the house that she sold?

SOLUTION:
In this case, you need to find the base, and so $B = \frac{P}{R}$ or total sales $= \frac{\text{commission}}{\text{rate}} = \frac{1120}{2\%} = \frac{1120}{0.02} = \$56,000$. The house was sold for $56,000.

EXAMPLE: A furniture salesperson sold a living room suite for $6520 and received a commission of $847.60. What was the commission rate?

SOLUTION:

In this case, you need to find the rate, and so $R = \frac{P}{B}$ or rate $= \frac{\text{commission}}{\text{total sales}} = \frac{\$847.60}{\$6520}$ $= 0.13$ or 13%. Hence the salesperson was paid a 13% commission rate on the item.

PRACTICE:

1. Ming Lang receives a weekly salary of $850 plus a 3% commission on all sales. If he sold $4325 last week, find his gross pay.
2. Brandi Wilson receives a 5% commission on sales up to $10,000 and an 8% commission on sales over $10,000. If she sold $13,350 worth of merchandise last week, find her gross pay.
3. Ted Williams receives a 10% commission on all sales less returns. If he sold $18,256 worth of merchandise last week and $475 worth of merchandise was returned, find his gross pay.
4. Anita Lopez receives $1200 a month plus 4% of all sales over $9000. If she sold $15,230 of merchandise last week, find her gross pay.
5. Hector Rodriguez receives a commission based on the following scale:

   6% on all sales
   4% on all sales over $5000 up to $10,000
   2% on all sales over $10,000

   If he sold $18,275 worth of merchandise last week, find his gross pay.
6. Maura O'Riley receives a commission based on the following scale:

   5% on all sales up to and including $10,000
   7% on all sales over $10,000 up to and including $20,000
   9% on all sales over $20,000

   If she sold $24,300 worth of merchandise, find her gross pay.
7. Ti Lu receives a regular salary of $500 a week plus a $6\frac{1}{2}$% commission on all sales. If she sold $2623 worth of merchandise, find her gross pay.
8. Shawn McMurry earns a 5% commission on all sales. Last week his gross pay was $326.15. How much merchandise did he sell?
9. Tiffany Jenkins sold a home for $64,875. If her commission was $1816.50, find the rate.
10. Jose Hernandez earns a commission of $12\frac{1}{2}$%. If his gross pay was $7227.50, how much did he sell?

SOLUTIONS:

1. Commission: $4325 \times 0.03 = \$129.75$
   Gross pay: $850 + \$129.75 = \$979.75$

2. $10,000 \times 0.05 + \$3350 \times 0.08 = \$768$
3. $\$18,256 - \$475 = \$17,781$
    $\$17,781 \times 0.10 = \$1778.10$
4. $\$15,230 - \$9000 = \$6230$
    $\$6230 \times 0.04 = \$249.20$
    $\$1200 + \$249.20 = \$1449.20$
5. $\$18,275 \times 0.06 = \$1096.50$
    $\$5000 \times 0.04 = \$200$
    $\$8275 \times 0.02 = \$165.50$
    $\$1096.50 + \$200 + \$165.50 = \$1462$
6. $\$10,000 \times 0.05 = \$500$
    $\$10,000 \times 0.07 = \$700$
    $\$4300 \times 0.09 = \$387$
    $\$500 + \$700 + \$387 = \$1587$
7. $\$2623 \times 0.065 = \$170.50$
    $\$1500 + \$170.50 = \$1670.50$
8. $\$326.15 \div 0.05 = \$6523.00$
9. $\$1816.50 \div \$64,875.00 = 0.028 = 2.8\%$
10. $\$7227.50 \div 0.125 = \$57,820.00$

Payroll Deductions

When you work for another person, you seldom receive a paycheck for your gross pay. Employers are required by law to withhold a certain amount of money for tax purposes. Your employer pays this amount to the government for you. These withholdings are called *payroll deductions*. They include federal income tax, Social Security contributions, Medicare, state income tax, and local wage tax. In addition, employers can withhold money for union dues, medical and dental insurance, unemployment, and retirement contributions.

The amount of money withheld for federal income tax is based on a person's salary and the number of dependents he or she claims. In order to determine the amounts withheld, the government has several IRS publications such as *Publications 15, 17,* and *505.* These publications give procedures for determining the amount of money that is withheld and should be used by the employer.

At the time of this writing, the amount withheld for Social Security is 6.2% of a person's salary. Medicare is computed at 1.45% of the gross salary. Other deductions depend on the state and local municipality taxes and various contributions for medical insurance, union dues, etc.

After the payroll deductions are determined, they are subtracted from a person's gross pay. What is left is called the *net pay.*

EXAMPLE: A person receives a weekly salary of $510. The income tax on that amount is $128.52. Social Security is 6.2%, and Medicare is 1.45%. Find the person's net pay.

SOLUTION:
Find the Social Security deduction: $510 × 0.062 = $31.62.
Find the Medicare deduction: $510 × 0.0145 = $7.40.
Find the sum of the deductions: $128.52 + $31.62 + $7.40 = $167.54.
Find the net pay: Net pay = Gross pay − Sum of deductions = $510.00 −$167.54 = $342.46. Hence the person receives a check for $342.46.

EXAMPLE: A person earned $1689.60 last month. The federal income tax deduction was $337.92. Find the net pay if Social Security, Medicare, and $97.60 for health insurance were deducted.

SOLUTION:
Social Security deduction: $1689.60 × 0.062 = $104.76
Medicare deduction: $1689.60 × 0.0145 = $24.50
Total deductions: $337.92 + $104.76 + $24.50 + $97.60 = $564.78
Net pay: $1689.60 − $564.78 = $1124.82

PRACTICE:

1. Albert Lesko earned $574.00 last week. The federal income tax deducted was $86.10. Find his net pay if Social Security and Medicare were also deducted.
2. Sandra Meloski earned $1104.00 last week. The federal income tax deducted was $253.92. Find her net pay if Social security, Medicare, and $5.00 union dues were deducted.
3. Mark Seager earns $8.65 an hour. Last week he worked 36 hours. The federal income tax deducted was $62.20. Find his net pay if Social security and Medicare are deducted.
4. Harriet Johnson earns $48,000 a year. The federal income tax withheld for last month was $810. Find her net monthly pay if Social Security and Medicare are deducted.
5. Richard Todd earns $9.70 an hour. The following deductions are made:

Federal income tax	20%
Social Security	6.2%
Medicare	1.45%
State income tax	2%

Local tax   1%

Find his net pay if he works 40 hours per week.

SOLUTIONS:

1. Social Security: $574 \times 0.062 = \$35.59$
    Medicare: $574 \times 0.0145 = \$8.32$
    Net pay: $574 - \$86.10 - \$35.59 - \$8.32 = \$443.99$
2. Social Security: $\$1104.00 \times 0.062 = \$68.45$
    Medicare: $\$1104.00 \times 0.0145 = \$16.01$
    Net pay: $\$1104.00 - \$253.92 - \$68.45 - \$16.01 - \$5.00 = \$760.62$
3. Gross pay: $\$8.65 \times 36 = \$311.40$
    Social Security: $\$311.40 \times 0.062 = \$19.31$
    Medicare: $\$311.40 \times 0.0145 = \$4.52$
    Net pay: $\$311.40 - \$62.20 - \$19.31 - \$4.52 = \$225.37$
4. Monthly gross pay: $\$48,000 \div 12 = \$4000$
    Social Security: $\$4000 \times 0.062 = \$248$
    Medicare: $\$4000 \times 0.0145 = \$58$
    Net pay: $\$4000 - \$810 - \$248 - \$58 = \$2884$
5. Gross pay: $\$9.70 \times 40 = \$388$
    Federal income tax: $\$388 \times 0.2 = \$77.60$
    Social Security: $\$388 \times 0.062 = \$24.06$
    Medicare: $\$388 \times 0.0145 = \$5.63$
    State income tax: $\$388 \times 0.02 = \$7.76$
    Local tax: $\$388.00 \times 0.01 = \$3.88$
    Net pay: $\$388.00 - \$77.60 - \$24.06 - \$5.63 - \$7.76 - \$3.88 = \$269.07$

Summary

When a business has employees, it must determine the wages that its employees earn. There are several ways to determine a person's salary. Some people get a salary for a year, and it is usually paid monthly, semimonthly, biweekly, or weekly. Others are paid by the hour. Sometimes a person is paid by the number of items he or she produces. This is called piecework. Many people are paid on a commission; that is, they get a percentage of what they sell. Finally, a business is required to withhold part of a person's salary for tax purposes or benefits or union dues.

Quiz

1. A person's earnings before deductions is called the
    (a) net pay
    (b) nondeduction pay
    (c) gross pay
    (d) total pay

2. If a person's yearly salary is $51,036, her monthly salary is
    (a) $2126.50
    (b) $1962.92
    (c) $981.46
    (d) $4253.00

3. If a person's yearly salary is $34,992 and he is paid semimonthly, his gross pay is
    (a) $1458.00
    (b) $1345.85
    (c) $672.92
    (d) $2916.00

4. If a person's yearly salary is $49,920.00, her weekly gross pay is
    (a) $4160.00
    (b) $1920.00
    (c) $960.00
    (d) $2080.00

5. If a person's yearly salary is $17,888.00 and he is paid biweekly, his gross biweekly pay is
    (a) $688.00
    (b) $1490.67
    (c) $745.33
    (d) $344.00

6. Sheila Medic earns $14.32 per hour. If she works 32 hours per week, her gross pay is
    (a) $572.80
    (b) $458.24
    (c) $515.52
    (d) $429.60

7. Adam Smith earns $13.65 an hour and gets time and one half for each hour he works over 40. Last week he worked 47 hours. His gross pay is

   (a) $546.00
   (b) $689.33
   (c) $641.55
   (d) $819.00

8. Maria Hernandez earned $661.96 last week. If she worked 38 hours, find her hourly pay.
    (a) $16.55
    (b) $14.32
    (c) $17.42
    (d) $18.39

9. If a worker is paid $1.75 for each set of car mats he personalizes, find his gross pay if he completes 43 sets.
    (a) $62.85
    (b) $70.45
    (c) $68.95
    (d) $75.25

10. Carol Smith assembles earrings. She is paid the following rates:

1 to 30	$2.50
31 to 50	$3.00
51 and over	$3.25

    If she assembles 62 earrings, find her gross pay.
    (a) $155.00
    (b) $174.00
    (c) $186.00
    (d) $201.50

11. Harriett Johnson receives a commission of $4\frac{1}{4}\%$ on her sales. If she sold a home for $84,600, her commission is
    (a) $3595.50
    (b) $3384.00
    (c) $3360.00
    (d) $3722.40

12. If a salesperson is paid a weekly salary of $650 and receives a 3% commission on all sales over $8000, find his gross pay if he sold $9324 worth of merchandise last week.
    (a) $929.75
    (b) $689.72
    (c) $299.25
    (d) $739.50

13. If a person sold $15,375 worth of merchandise and she is paid on the following rate:

    5% on all sales
    7% on all sales over $10,000

    Her gross pay is
    (a) $1076.25
    (b) $645.00
    (c) $1145.00
    (d) $768.75

14. A person receives a commission of $5\frac{1}{2}\%$. If his gross pay was $196.02, how much did he sell?
    (a) $1078.11
    (b) $3920.40
    (c) $4782.60
    (d) $3564.00

15. If a person is paid $12.35 per hour and worked 40 hours last week, find his net pay if Social Security, Medicare, and $98.80 in federal income tax are deducted.
    (a) $395.20
    (b) $448.55
    (c) $402.65
    (d) $357.41

CHAPTER 7

Markup

Introduction

In order for a person in a business that sells merchandise to make a profit, he or she must sell the merchandise at a price higher than what he or she paid for it. The price that a merchant pays for an item is called the **cost**. The price that the merchant sells the item for is called the **selling price**. The difference between the cost of the item and its selling price is called the **markup**.

The basic formulas for markup are

Selling price $(S) = $ Cost $(C) + $ Markup (M) or $S = C + M$
Markup $(M) = $ Selling price $(S) - $ Cost (C) or $M = S - C$
Cost $(C) = $ Selling price $(S) - $ Markup (M) or $C = S - M$

For example, suppose a merchant bought a wristwatch for \$20 and sold it for \$35. The markup can be found by using the formula: $M = S - C$ or $M = \$35 - \$20 = \$15$. Hence the markup is \$15. Given any two of the three values—cost, selling price, or markup—the third value can be found by using one of the appropriate formulas.

The markup must also cover the expenses of the business in addition to making a profit for the business. Businesses usually have certain methods that they use to determine the markup. There are two basic methods: markup based on the cost of the item and markup based on the selling price of the item.

Markup on Cost

When the markup is a percent of the cost, the cost becomes the base or the 100%. Suppose an item had a 60% markup on cost; then the formula would be

$$\text{Selling price} = \text{Cost} + \text{Markup}$$

$$160\% = 100\% + 60\%$$

In other words, the selling price is 160% of the cost.

The markup is the *part*, the markup percent is the *rate*, and the cost is the *base*. Three additional formulas are used in markup on cost problems. They can be explained by using the circle. The cost is the base (see Figure 7-1).

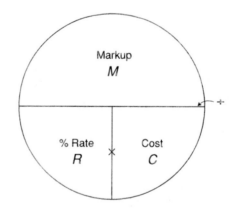

$$\text{Markup } (M) = \text{Rate } (R) \times \text{Cost } (C) \text{ or } M = R \times C$$

$$\text{Rate } (R) = \frac{\text{Markup } (M)}{\text{Cost } (C)} \text{ or } R = \frac{M}{C}$$

$$\text{Cost } (C) = \frac{\text{Markup } (M)}{\text{Rate } (R)} \text{ or } C = \frac{M}{R}$$

Fig. 7-1.

$$\text{Markup } (M) = \text{Rate } (R) \times \text{Cost } (C) \text{ or } M = R \times C$$

$$\text{Rate } (R) = \frac{\text{Markup } (M)}{\text{Cost } (C)} \text{ or } R = \frac{M}{C}$$

$$\text{Cost } (C) = \frac{\text{Markup } (M)}{\text{Rate } (R)} \text{ or } C = \frac{M}{R}$$

Remember to change the percent to a decimal or fraction before multiplying or dividing.

EXAMPLE: Find the markup and selling price on a mailbox that costs $24 if there is a 40% markup on cost.

SOLUTION:
Find the markup.

$$\text{Markup} = \text{Rate} \times \text{Cost or } M = R \times C$$
$$= 0.40 \times \$24$$
$$= \$9.60$$

Find the selling price.

$$\text{Selling price} = \text{Cost} + \text{Markup or } S = C + M$$
$$= \$24 + \$9.60$$
$$= \$33.60$$

(*Note*: The selling price could also be found by multiplying the cost by 140%; i.e., $1.40 \times \$24 = \$33.60$.)
　　Hence the markup is $9.60 and the selling price is $33.60.

EXAMPLE: If an LED nightlight costs $15 and the selling price is $25, find the markup and the rate based on cost.

SOLUTION:
Find the markup.

$$\text{Markup} = \text{Selling price} - \text{Cost or } M = S - C$$
$$= \$25 - \$15$$
$$= \$10$$

Find the rate.

$$\text{Rate} = \frac{\text{Markup}}{\text{Cost}} \text{ or } R = \frac{M}{C}$$

$$= \frac{10}{15}$$

$$= 0.667 \text{ (rounded) or } 66.7\%$$

Hence the markup is $10 and the rate is 66.7% on the cost.

EXAMPLE: If the markup on a label maker is $18 and the markup rate is 30% on cost, find the cost and the selling price of the label maker.

SOLUTION:
Find the cost.

$$\text{Cost} = \frac{\text{Markup}}{\text{Rate}} \text{ or } C = \frac{M}{R}$$

$$= \frac{\$18}{30\%}$$

$$= \$60$$

Find the selling price.

$$\text{Selling price} = \text{Cost} + \text{Markup or } S = C + M$$

$$= \$60 + \$18$$

$$= \$78$$

Hence the cost is $60 and the selling price is $78.

PRACTICE:
1. If a heavy duty stapler costs $32 and there is a 25% markup on cost, find the amount of the markup and the selling price.
2. If an indoor/outdoor vacuum costs $75 and there is a 36% markup on cost, find the amount of the markup and the selling price.
3. If an office suite costs $1000 and there is a 60% markup on cost, find the amount of the markup and the selling price.
4. If a laser printer costs $400 and there is a 48% markup on cost, find the amount of the markup and the selling price.
5. If a FAX machine costs $235 and there is a 70% markup on cost, find the amount of the markup and the selling price.
6. If a scientific calculator costs $50 and sells for $79, find the markup rate based on cost.

7. If a shredder costs \$180 and sells for \$250, find the markup rate based on cost.
8. A conference phone sells for \$700 and the markup is \$250. Find the markup rate on cost.
9. If the markup on a set of two-way radios is \$32 and the markup rate on cost is 48%, find the cost and selling price of the radio.
10. If a notebook computer has a markup of \$300 and the markup rate is 60% on cost, find the cost and selling price of the computer.

SOLUTIONS:

1. $M = R \times C$
   $= 0.25 \times \$32$
   $= \$8$
   $S = C + M$
   $= \$32 + \$8 = \$40$

2. $M = R \times C$
   $= 0.36 \times \$75$
   $= \$27$
   $S = C + M$
   $= \$75 + \$27$
   $= \$102$

3. $M = R \times C$
   $= 0.60 \times \$1000$
   $= \$600$
   $S = C + M$
   $= \$1000 + \$600$
   $= \$1600$

4. $M = R \times C$
   $= 0.48 \times \$400$
   $= \$192$

$$S = C + M$$
$$= \$400 + \$192$$
$$= \$592$$

5. $M = R \times C$
$$= 0.70 \times \$235$$
$$= \$164.50$$

$$S = C + M$$
$$= \$235 + \$164.50$$
$$= \$399.50$$

6. $M = S - C$
$$= \$79 - 50$$
$$= \$29$$

$$R = \frac{M}{C}$$
$$= \frac{29}{50}$$
$$= 0.58 \text{ or } 58\%$$

7. $M = S - C$
$$= \$250 - 180$$
$$= \$70$$

$$R = \frac{M}{C}$$
$$= \frac{70}{180}$$
$$= 0.389 \text{ (rounded)} = 38.9\%$$

8. $C = S - M$
$$= \$700 - \$250$$
$$= \$450$$

$$R = \frac{M}{C}$$

$$= \frac{\$450}{\$700}$$

$$= 0.643 \text{ (rounded)} = 64.3\%$$

9. $C = \dfrac{M}{R}$

$$= \frac{\$32}{0.48}$$

$$= \$66.67$$

$$S = C + M$$

$$= \$66.67 + \$32$$

$$= \$98.67$$

10. $C = \dfrac{M}{R}$

$$= \frac{\$300}{0.60}$$

$$= \$500$$

$$S = C + M$$

$$= \$500 + \$300$$

$$= \$800$$

Markup on Selling Price

Sometimes the markup is based on the selling price. This is often more convenient than determining the markup on cost since the cash register records the transactions based on the selling price. Also, discounts and sales commissions are based on the selling price of the item. When the markup is based on the selling price, the selling price becomes the base or 100%; for example, if there is a 25% markup on the selling price, the formula looks like this:

$$\text{Selling price} = \text{Cost} + \text{Markup}$$

$$100\% = 75\% + 25\%$$

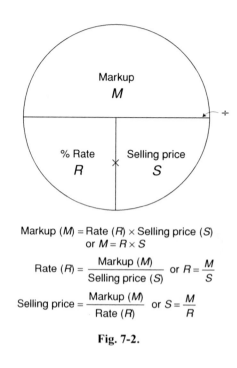

Markup (M) = Rate (R) × Selling price (S)
or $M = R \times S$

Rate (R) = $\dfrac{\text{Markup } (M)}{\text{Selling price } (S)}$ or $R = \dfrac{M}{S}$

Selling price = $\dfrac{\text{Markup } (M)}{\text{Rate } (R)}$ or $S = \dfrac{M}{R}$

Fig. 7-2.

The formulas for markup on selling price problems can be shown by the circle (see Figure 7-2).

$$\text{Markup } (M) = \text{Rate } (R) \times \text{Selling price } (S) \text{ or } M = R \times S$$

$$\text{Rate } (R) = \frac{\text{Markup } (M)}{\text{Selling price } (S)} \text{ or } R = \frac{M}{S}$$

$$\text{Selling Price } (S) = \frac{\text{Markup } (M)}{\text{Rate } (R)} \text{ or } S = \frac{M}{R}$$

EXAMPLE: An air purifier sells for $150. If there is a 40% markup on the selling price, find the cost and the amount of markup.

SOLUTION:
Find the amount of the markup.

$$\text{Markup} = \text{Rate} \times \text{Selling Price or } M = R \times S$$

$$= 0.40 \times \$150$$

$$= \$60$$

Find the cost.

$$C = S - M$$
$$= \$150 - \$60$$
$$= \$90$$

Hence the markup amount is $60 and the cost is $90.

EXAMPLE: If the markup on a scrapbook kit is $6 and the markup rate is 30% of the selling price, find the selling price and the cost of the scrapbook.

SOLUTION:
Find the selling price.

$$\text{Selling price} = \frac{\text{Markup}}{\text{Rate}} \text{ or } S = \frac{M}{R}$$
$$= \frac{\$6}{0.30}$$
$$= \$20$$

Find the cost.

$$\text{Cost} = \text{Selling price} - \text{Markup or } C = S - M$$
$$= \$20 - \$6$$
$$= \$14$$

Hence the cost is $14 and the selling price is $20.

EXAMPLE: An oak jewelry chest costs $56 and has a markup of $16. Find the rate of the markup on the selling price.

SOLUTION:
Find the selling price.

$$\text{Selling price} = \text{Cost} + \text{Markup or } S = C + M$$
$$= \$56 + \$16$$
$$= \$72$$

Find the rate based on the selling price.

$$\text{Rate} = \frac{\text{Markup}}{\text{Selling price}} \text{ or } R = \frac{M}{S}$$

$$= \frac{\$16}{\$72}$$

$$= 0.222 \text{ (rounded)} = 22.2\%$$

PRACTICE:

1. A diamond ring sells for $800. If there is a 70% markup on the selling price, find the cost and the amount of the markup.
2. If a diamond bracelet sells for $300 and there is a 50% markup on the selling price, find the amount of the markup and the cost.
3. If a wrist watch sells for $450 and there is a 75% markup on the selling price, find the amount of the markup and the cost.
4. If a pair of men's work boots sells for $60 and there is a 30% markup on the selling price, find the amount of the markup and the cost.
5. If a self-cleaning oven sells for $650 and there is a 45% markup on the selling price, find the amount of the markup and the cost.
6. A cordless drill set has a markup of $40. The markup on the selling price is 20%. Find the cost and the selling price of the drill set.
7. An air compressor costs $100 and sells for $180. Find the rate of markup on the selling price.
8. An outdoor patio set costs $225 and has a markup of $150. Find the markup rate on the selling price.
9. A blender sells for $50 and costs $32. Find the markup rate on the selling price.
10. If the markup on a pair of sports shoes is $10 and the markup rate is 60% on the selling price, find the selling price and the cost of the shoes.

SOLUTIONS:

1. $M = R \times S$

$$= 0.70 \times \$800$$

$$= \$560$$

$$C = S - M$$

$$= \$800 - \$560$$

$$= \$240$$

2. $M = R \times S$

    $= 0.50 \times \$300$

    $= \$150$

    $C = S - M$

    $= \$300 - \$150$

    $= \$150$

3. $M = R \times S$

    $= 0.75 \times \$450$

    $= \$337.50$

    $C = S - M$

    $= \$450 - \$337.50$

    $= \$112.50$

4. $M = R \times S$

    $= 0.30 \times \$60$

    $= \$18$

    $C = S - C$

    $= \$60 - \$18$

    $= \$42$

5. $M = R \times S$

    $= 0.45 \times \$650$

    $= \$292.50$

    $C = S - M$

    $= \$650 - \$292.50$

    $= \$357.50$

6. $S = \dfrac{M}{R}$

$\quad = \dfrac{\$40}{0.20}$

$\quad = \$200$

$C = S - M$

$\quad = \$200 - \$40$

$\quad = \$160$

7. $M = S - C$

$\quad = \$180 - \$100$

$\quad = \$80$

$R = \dfrac{M}{S}$

$\quad = \dfrac{\$80}{\$180}$

$\quad = 0.444 \text{ (rounded)} = 44.4\%$

8. $M = S - C$

$\quad = \$225 - \$150$

$\quad = \$75$

$R = \dfrac{M}{S}$

$\quad = \dfrac{\$75}{\$225}$

$\quad = 0.333 \text{ (rounded)} = 33.3\%$

9. $M = S - C$

$\quad = \$50 - \$32$

$\quad = \$18$

$R = \dfrac{M}{S}$

$\quad = \dfrac{\$18}{\$50}$

$\quad = 0.36 = 36\%$

10. $S = \dfrac{M}{R}$

$ = \dfrac{\$10}{0.60}$

$ = \$16.67$

$ C = S - M$

$ = \$16.67 - \$10$

$ = \$6.67$

Relationships Between the Markups

If you know the markup rate on the cost, you can find the corresponding markup on the selling price and vice versa. The markup rate on the selling price will always be less than the markup rate on the cost. If you are given the markup rate on the cost and want to find the markup rate on the selling price, follow these steps:

Step 1. Convert the rate to a decimal.
Step 2. Substitute in the formula:

$$\text{Markup rate on selling price} = \frac{\text{Markup rate on cost}}{1 + \text{Markup rate on cost}}$$

Step 3. Convert the answer to a percent (i.e., multiply by 100).

EXAMPLE: If the markup rate on the cost is 15%, find the equivalent markup rate on the selling price.

SOLUTION:

$$\text{Markup rate on selling price} = \frac{\text{Markup rate on cost}}{1 + \text{Markup rate on cost}}$$

$$= \frac{0.15}{1 + 0.15}$$

$$= \frac{0.15}{1.15}$$

$$= 0.130 \text{ (rounded)} = 13\%$$

Hence a markup rate of 15% on cost is approximately equal to a 13% markup on the selling price.

If you are given the markup rate on the selling price, you can find the equivalent markup rate on the cost by following these steps:

Step 1. Convert the rate to a decimal.

Step 2. Substitute in the formula:

$$\text{Markup on cost} = \frac{\text{Markup rate on selling price}}{1 - \text{Markup rate on selling price}}$$

Step 3. Convert the answer to a percent.

EXAMPLE: If the markup rate on the selling price is 20%, find the equivalent markup rate on the cost.

SOLUTION:

$$\text{Markup on cost} = \frac{\text{Markup rate on selling price}}{1 - \text{Markup rate on selling price}}$$

$$= \frac{0.20}{1 - 0.20}$$

$$= \frac{0.20}{0.80}$$

$$= 0.25 = 25\%$$

Hence a markup of 20% on the selling price is equivalent to a 25% markup rate on the cost. This can be verified by considering an item that sells for $80. A markup of 20% on the selling price is

$$20\% \times \$80 = 0.20 \times 0.80$$

$$= \$16$$

Now the cost of the item is $80−$16 = $64. A 25% markup on cost is

$$25\% \times \$64 = 0.25 \times \$64$$

$$= \$16$$

Notice that the markup amount of $16 is the same in both cases.

Knowing how to convert from one markup to the other is helpful when solving a problem when you are given the selling price and the markup rate on the cost or when you are given the cost and the markup rate on the selling price. All you need to do to solve these types of problems is convert the markup rate to the other base and solve as shown in the two previous sections.

EXAMPLE: If the selling price of an item is $120 and the markup rate on cost is 40%, find the markup amount.

SOLUTION:
Since you are given the selling price, it is necessary to convert the markup rate on the cost to the markup rate on the selling price and then find the markup rate.

$$\text{Markup rate on selling price} = \frac{\text{Markup rate on cost}}{1 + \text{Markup rate on cost}}$$

$$= \frac{0.40}{1 + 0.40}$$

$$= \frac{0.40}{1.40}$$

$$= 0.286 \text{ (rounded)} = 28.6\%$$

$$M = R \times S$$

$$= 0.286 \times \$120$$

$$= \$34.32$$

Hence the markup amount is $34.32.

EXAMPLE: The cost of an item is $40. If there is a 50% markup on the selling price, find the amount of the markup.

SOLUTION:
Since you are given the cost and the markup rate on the selling price, it is necessary to convert the markup rate on the selling price to a markup rate on cost and then find the markup amount.

$$\text{Markup on cost} = \frac{\text{Markup rate on selling price}}{1 - \text{Markup rate on selling price}}$$

$$= \frac{0.50}{1 - 0.50}$$

$$= \frac{0.50}{0.50}$$

$$= 1 \text{ or } 100\%$$

$$\text{Markup} = \text{Rate} \times \text{Cost}$$
$$= 100\% \times \$40$$
$$= \$40$$

Hence the markup is $40.

Markdown and Shrinkage

Most retail businesses at one time or another have sales. Here the sale price of the merchandise is reduced in order to get rid of it. There are many reasons for reducing the price. For example, summer clothes are reduced in the fall. After Christmas, decorations are reduced so that the store will not have to store them. When the selling price of an item is reduced, it is called a **markdown**. *All markdowns are calculated using the selling price as the base.* The markdown amount is subtracted from the selling price to find the reduced price.

EXAMPLE: A gas grill selling for $110 is reduced by 30% in the fall. Find the reduced price.

SOLUTION:
Find the markdown amount.

$$\text{Markdown} = \text{Rate} \times \text{Selling price}$$
$$= 0.30 \times \$110$$
$$= \$33$$

Find the reduced price.

$$\text{Reduced price} = \text{Selling price} - \text{Markdown}$$
$$= \$110 - \$33$$
$$= \$77$$

Hence the reduced price or sale price is $77.

Sometimes items are marked down for a sale and then the unsold items are marked up after the sale. This could occur several times during the year. This is known as a *series* of markups and markdowns. The first markups could be based on the cost or the selling price of the item. The remaining markdowns and markups use the previous selling price as the base.

EXAMPLE: A weed trimmer was purchased for $40 and was marked up 60% on cost. For a July 4 sale, it was marked down 25%. After the sale, it was marked up 30%. On September 1, it was marked down 20%. Find the final selling price.

SOLUTION:
Find the first markup.

$$\text{Markup} = \text{Rate} \times \text{Cost}$$
$$= 0.60 \times \$40$$
$$= \$24$$
$$S = C + M$$
$$= \$40 + \$24$$
$$= \$64$$

Find the first markdown.

$$\text{Markdown} = \text{Rate} \times \text{Selling price}$$
$$= 0.25 \times \$64$$
$$= \$16$$
$$\text{Reduced price} = \$64 - \$16$$
$$= \$48$$

Find the second markup.

$$\text{Markup} = \text{Rate} \times \text{Reduced price}$$
$$= 0.30 \times \$48$$
$$= \$14.40$$
$$\text{Selling price} = \text{Reduced price} + \text{Markup}$$
$$= \$48 + \$14.40$$
$$= \$62.40$$
$$\text{Markdown} = \text{Rate} \times \text{Selling price}$$
$$= 0.20 \times \$62.40$$
$$= \$12.48$$
$$\text{Reduced price} = \text{Selling price} - \text{Markdown}$$
$$= \$62.40 - \$12.48$$
$$= \$49.92$$

The final selling price is $49.92.

Many times businesspersons must contend with what is called *shrinkage*. **Shrinkage** is generally thought of as the loss of goods before they can be sold. Merchants can lose goods before they are sold by the passage of time. For example, produce sellers might not be able to sell all the fruit they buy before it spoils. Florists know that cut flowers have a limited lifetime. These types of items are called *perishables*.

Other times merchants lose merchandise through shoplifting or breakage. Many times items in jars are broken by customers. (The author knows from experience since he had to clean up the mess when he worked in a grocery store while attending college.)

In order to maintain the profit margin, the retailer must raise the selling price of the items to cover these kinds of losses. In order to account for shrinkage, the adjusted selling price can be found by following these steps:

Step 1. Find the total of the sales by multiplying the total number of items purchased by the selling price of each item.

Step 2. Find the number of items left to sell after shrinkage has been taken into account.

Step 3. Divide the total of the sales by the number of items left to sell.

EXAMPLE: The owner of a toy store purchases 50 superhero models to sell at $15 each. The owner knows from past experience that about 6% of the items will be broken by children playing with them in the store before they can be sold. Find the adjusted selling price to account for shrinkage.

SOLUTION:

Step 1. Find the total of the sales.

$$\text{Total} = 50 \times \$15$$

$$= \$750$$

Step 2. Find the number of items left to sell after shrinkage.

Since 6% are broken, $100\% - 6\% = 94\%$ of the times will be left to sell.

$$\text{Number} = 94\% \times 50 = 0.94 \times 50 = 47 \text{ items}$$

Step 3. Find the adjusted selling price.

$$\text{Adjusted selling price} = \frac{\text{Total sales}}{\text{Number}} = \frac{\$750}{47} = \$15.96$$

Hence the owner must sell the items for $15.96 to account for shrinkage and to maintain the markup on the original number of items.

EXAMPLE: A florist purchases 200 red roses to sell at $2.00 each. From past experience she knows that about 12% will wilt before they can be sold. Find the adjusted selling price to account for shrinkage.

SOLUTION:

Step 1. Find the total of the sales.

$$\text{Total} = 200 \times \$2.00$$
$$= \$400$$

Step 2. Find the number of items left to sell.

$$\text{Number} = (100\% - 12\%) \times 200$$
$$= 88\% \times 200$$
$$= 0.88 \times 200$$
$$= 176$$

Step 3. Find the adjusted selling price.

$$\text{Adjusted selling price} = \frac{\text{Total sales}}{\text{Number}}$$
$$= \frac{\$400}{176}$$
$$= \$2.27 \text{ (rounded)}$$

Hence the adjusted selling price would be $2.27.

PRACTICE:

1. Find the markup rate on the selling price of an item that is equivalent to a 10% markup on cost.
2. Find the markup rate on the cost of an item that is equivalent to a 33% markup on the selling price.
3. Find the markup on the cost of an item that is equivalent to a 45% markup on the selling price.
4. Find the markup on the selling price of an item that is equivalent to a 60% markup on the cost.
5. A lamp sells for $100. If the markup on the cost is 48%, find the cost and the amount of the markup.

6. A jewelry chest costs $84 and has a 20% markup on the selling price. Find the markup amount and the selling price of the chest.
7. A smoothie maker sells for $50. It has just been reduced 40%. Find the reduced price.
8. A digital camera costing $150 was marked up 60% on the cost. For a July 4 sale, it was reduced 25%. After the sale, it was marked up 50%. In September it was reduced 20%. Find the final selling price.
9. A party supply store bought 500 balloons to sell at $0.60 each. The owner knows that approximately 8% will break on inflation. Find the adjusted selling price if the store owner wishes to account for shrinkage.
10. A grocery store sells homemade pizzas for $6.00 each. Each day, 20 are made. The manager knows that 10% of these pizzas might not sell. Find the adjusted selling price to account for shrinkage.

SOLUTIONS:

1. Markup rate on selling price $= \dfrac{\text{Markup rate on cost}}{1 + \text{Markup rate on cost}}$

$$= \frac{0.10}{1 + 0.10}$$

$$= \frac{0.10}{1.10}$$

$$= 0.091 \text{ (rounded)} = 9.1\%$$

2. Markup rate on cost $= \dfrac{\text{Markup rate on selling price}}{1 - \text{Markup rate on selling price}}$

$$= \frac{0.33}{1 - 0.33}$$

$$= \frac{0.33}{0.67}$$

$$= 0.493 \text{ (rounded)} = 49.3\%$$

3. Markup rate on cost $= \dfrac{\text{Markup rate on selling price}}{1 - \text{Markup rate on selling price}}$

$$= \frac{0.45}{1 - 0.45}$$

$$= \frac{0.45}{0.55}$$

$$= 0.818 \text{ (rounded)} = 81.8\%$$

4. Markup rate on selling price $= \dfrac{\text{Markup rate on cost}}{1 + \text{Markup rate on cost}}$

$$= \dfrac{0.60}{1 + 0.60}$$

$$= \dfrac{0.60}{1.60}$$

$$= 0.375 = 37.5\%$$

5. Markup rate on selling price $= \dfrac{\text{Markup rate on cost}}{1 + \text{Markup rate on cost}}$

$$= \dfrac{0.48}{1.48}$$

$$= 0.324 \ (\text{rounded}) = 32.4\%$$

$$\text{Markup} = \text{Rate} \times \text{Selling price}$$

$$= 0.324 \times \$100$$

$$= \$32.40$$

$$C = S - M$$

$$= \$100.00 - \$32.40 = \$67.60$$

6. Markup rate on cost $= \dfrac{\text{Markup rate on selling price}}{1 - \text{Markup rate on selling price}}$

$$= \dfrac{0.20}{1 - 0.20}$$

$$= \dfrac{0.20}{0.80}$$

$$= 0.25 \text{ or } 25\%$$

$$\text{Markup} = \text{Rate} \times \text{Cost}$$

$$= 0.25 \times \$84$$

$$= \$21$$

$$S = C + M$$

$$= \$84 + \$21$$

$$= \$105.00$$

7.   Markdown $= $ Rate $\times$ Selling price

$= 0.40 \times \$50$

$= \$20$

Reduced price $= \$50 - \$20$

$= \$30$

8.   Markup $= $ Rate $\times$ Cost

$= 0.60 \times \$150$

$= \$90$

$S = C + M$

$= \$90 + \$150$

$= \$240$

Markdown $= $ Rate $\times$ Selling price

$= 0.25 \times \$240$

$= \$60$

Reduced price $= \$240 - \$60$

$= \$180$

Markup $= $ Rate $\times$ Selling price

$= 0.50 \times \$180$

$= \$90$

$S = C + M$

$= \$180 + \$90$

$= \$270$

Markdown $= $ Rate $\times$ Selling price

$= 0.20 \times \$270$

$= \$54$

Reduced price $= \$270 - \$54$

$= \$216$

9.
$$\text{Total sales} = 500 \times \$0.60$$
$$= \$300$$
$$\text{Number} = 0.92 \times 500$$
$$= 460$$
$$\text{Adjusted selling price} = \frac{\$300}{460}$$
$$= \$0.65$$

10.
$$\text{Total sales} = 20 \times \$6.00$$
$$= \$120.00$$
$$\text{Number} = 0.90 \times 20$$
$$= 18$$
$$\text{Adjusted selling price} = \frac{\$120}{18}$$
$$= \$6.67$$

Summary

In business, in order to make a profit, it is necessary to sell items for more than business owners paid for them. The difference between the cost of an item and the selling price is called the markup. The markup can be a percentage of the cost or a percentage of the selling price.

Sometimes it is necessary to reduce the selling price of an item. In this case, it is called a markdown. Many times items are marked up and then marked down, and so on. This is a series of markups and markdowns. Finally, shrinkage means that items are perishable or they are subject to breaking before they can be sold. In order to maintain the markup rate, an adjusted (somewhat higher) selling price is needed.

Quiz

1. If the cost of a briefcase is $80 and the markup rate on cost is 60%, the markup amount is
   (a) $48
   (b) $32

   (c) $54
   (d) $26

2. If the cost of a calendar is $5 and the selling price is $12, the markup rate on the cost is
   (a) 41.7%
   (b) 58.3%
   (c) 40%
   (d) 140%

3. If the markup rate on the cost of an overhead projector is 48% and the markup is $115.20, the cost is
   (a) $55.30
   (b) $240.00
   (c) $211.54
   (d) $105.60

4. A gold pendant sells for $180. If there is a 45% markup on the selling price, the markup amount is
   (a) $99.00
   (b) $400.00
   (c) $327.27
   (d) $81.00

5. If there is a 40% markup on the selling price and the markup is $320, the selling price is
   (a) $533.33
   (b) $800.00
   (c) $128.00
   (d) $192.00

6. A standard metal file cabinet sells for $120 and has a markup of $40. The markup rate on the selling price is
   (a) 25%
   (b) 66.7%
   (c) 33.3%
   (d) 50%

7. If a microwave oven sells for $50 and the markup is $30, the markup rate on the cost is
   (a) 60%
   (b) 40%
   (c) 150%
   (d) 66.7%

8. A laminator sells for $60. It is marked down 30%. The reduced price is
    (a) $78
    (b) $42
    (c) $18
    (d) $45

9. A computer tax program costs $20. It is marked up 80% on the cost. Around tax time, it is reduced 40%. After April 15, it is marked up 50%. The final selling price is
    (a) $32.40
    (b) $36.00
    (c) $21.60
    (d) $38.00

10. A coffee and doughnut shop makes 600 doughnuts a day. They sell for $0.50 each. About 12% are not sold each day and are discarded. The adjusted sale price is
    (a) $0.60
    (b) $0.62
    (c) $0.57
    (d) $0.54

CHAPTER 8

Discounts

Introduction

Many times manufacturers publish catalogs to sell their merchandise to wholesalers or retailers. Wholesalers also use catalogs to sell merchandise to retailers. These catalogs usually contain a picture of the item, a brief description of the item, and the price of the item. The price of an item in the catalog is called the **list price**. Whenever the price of an item changes or if the manufacturer or wholesaler wishes to sell the items for less than the list price, they can offer a **discount**. The reduction in price is called a **trade discount**. Rather than printing a whole new catalog, the manufacturer or wholesaler can just send one sheet offering trade discounts.

In addition to trade discounts, businesses also offer what are called *cash discounts*. A **cash discount** is a reduction in price of merchandise in order to encourage the buyer to pay the bill promptly. These two types of discounts will be explained in this chapter.

Trade Discounts

As previously stated, a trade discount is a percent reduction in the list price of an item. The formula is

Trade discount (T) = Rate (R) × List price (L) or $T = R \times L$

The **net price** of an item is found by subtracting the trade discount amount from the list price of the item; that is,

Net price (N) = List price (L) − Trade discount amount (T) or $N = L - T$

EXAMPLE: A treadmill has a list price of $600. The manufacturer offers a sporting goods store a trade discount of 40%. Find the amount of the discount and the net price.

SOLUTION:
Find the trade discount.

$$\text{Trade discount} = \text{Rate} \times \text{List price}$$
$$= 0.40 \times \$600$$
$$= \$240$$

Find the net price.

$$\text{Net price} = \text{List price} - \text{Discount}$$
$$= \$600 - \$240$$
$$= \$360$$

The discount amount is $240 and the net price is $360.

EXAMPLE: A manufacturer of tents offers a sporting goods store a trade discount of 35% on a family tent that has a list price of $98. Find the amount of the discount and the net price.

SOLUTION:

$$\text{Trade discount} = \text{Rate} \times \text{List price}$$
$$= 0.35 \times \$98$$
$$= \$34.30$$

$$\text{Net price} = \text{List price} - \text{Trade discount}$$
$$= \$98 - \$34.30$$
$$= \$63.70$$

The discount is $34.30 and the net price is $63.70.

The net price can be found by using the **complement** of the rate. To find the complement of a rate, subtract the rate from 100%; for example, the complement of 60% is $100\% - 60\% = 40\%$. The net price can be found by multiplying the list price by the complement of the trade discount rate or

$$\text{Net price}(N) = (100\% - R\%) \times \text{List price}$$

EXAMPLE: A business mathematics book has a list price of $20.00. The publisher offers a 35% trade discount. Find the net price.

SOLUTION:
Find the complement of 35%.

$$100\% - 35\% = 65\%$$

Find the net price.

$$\text{Net price} = 65\% \times \$20$$
$$= 0.65 \times \$20$$
$$= \$13$$

The net price is $13.

PRACTICE:

1. The list price of an elliptical exercise machine is $300. The manufacturer offers a 48% trade discount. Find the amount of the discount and the net price.
2. The list price of 1 dozen men's polo shirts is $180. If a trade discount of 65% is offered, find the amount of the discount and the net price.
3. The list price of a cultivator is $300. If a trade discount of 35% is offered, find the amount of the discount and the net price.
4. The list price of a gas barbeque grill is $200. If the manufacturer offers a trade discount of 25%, find the amount of the discount and the net price.

5. The list price of a pressure washer is $340. A 30% trade discount is being offered. Find the amount of the discount and the net price.

SOLUTIONS:

1. $T = R \times L$

    $\quad = 0.48 \times \$300$

    $\quad = \$144$

    $N = L - T$

    $\quad = \$300 - \$144$

    $\quad = \$156$

    Alternate solution:

    $N = (100 - 48)\% \times \$300$

    $\quad = 0.52 \times \$300$

    $\quad = \$156$

2. $T = R \times L$

    $\quad = 0.65 \times \$180$

    $\quad = \$117$

    $N = L - T$

    $\quad = \$180 - \$117$

    $\quad = \$63$

    Alternate solution:

    $N = (100 - 65)\% \times \$180$

    $\quad = 0.35 \times \$180$

    $\quad = \$63$

3. $T = R \times L$

    $\quad = 0.35 \times \$300$

    $\quad = \$105$

$$N = L - T$$
$$= \$300 - \$105$$
$$= \$195$$

Alternate solution:

$$N = (100 - 35)\% \times \$300$$
$$= 0.65 \times \$300$$
$$= \$195$$

4. $T = R \times L$
$$= 0.25 \times \$200$$
$$= \$50$$
$$N = L - T$$
$$= \$200 - \$50$$
$$= \$150$$

Alternate solution:

$$N = (100 - 25)\% \times \$200$$
$$= 0.75 \times \$200$$
$$= \$150$$

5. $T = R \times L$
$$= 0.30 \times \$340$$
$$= \$102$$
$$N = L - T$$
$$= \$340 - \$102$$
$$= \$238$$

Alternate solution:

$$N = (100 - 30)\% \times \$340$$
$$= 0.70 \times \$340$$
$$= \$238$$

Trade Discount Series

In order to promote sales, a manufacturer or wholesaler may offer more than one discount on the merchandise; for example, three discounts of 25, 15, and 5% may be offered on an item. These discounts are called a **trade discount series**. On a price sheet, the series would be written as 25/15/5. A trade discount series of 25/15/5 is not equivalent to a 45% discount since the 25% discount is taken off the list price, then the 15% is taken off the net price, and finally, the 5% discount is taken off the second net price. This procedure is shown in the next example.

EXAMPLE: A jewelry set consisting of a ring, a pendant, and earrings is listed at $120. A trade discount series of 20/10/5 is offered. Find the final net price of the set.

SOLUTION:
Compute the first discount (20%), using $120.

$$T = R \times L$$
$$= 0.20 \times \$120$$
$$= \$24$$
$$N = L - T$$
$$= \$120 - \$24$$
$$= \$96$$

Compute the second discount (10%), using $96.

$$T = R \times L$$
$$= 0.10 \times \$96$$
$$= \$9.60$$
$$N = L - T$$
$$= \$96.00 - \$9.60$$
$$= \$86.40$$

Compute the third discount (5%), using $86.40.

$$T = R \times L$$
$$= 0.05 \times \$86.40$$
$$= \$4.32$$
$$N = \$86.40 - \$4.32$$
$$= \$82.08$$

The final net price is $82.08.

A shortcut method can be used by multiplying by the complement of each discount. In the previous example, the complement of 20% is 80%. The complement of 10% is 90%, and the complement of 5% is 95%. Hence the net price can be found as shown:

$$0.80 \times 0.90 \times 0.95 \times \$120 = \$82.08$$

EXAMPLE: A scientific calculator has a list price of $20. A trade discount series of 15/8/4 is offered. Find the net price of the calculator.

SOLUTION:
Find the complement of each discount.

$$100\% - 15\% = 85\%$$
$$100\% - 8\% = 92\%$$
$$100\% - 4\% = 96\%$$

Find the net price.

$$0.85 \times 0.92 \times 0.96 \times \$20 = \$15.01.$$

The net price of the calculator is $15.01.

When calculating the net price after a series of trade discounts, you cannot find the sum of the discounts and then multiply the list price by that sum. In the previous example, the total of the discounts is $20.00 - $15.01 = $4.99. However, the sum of the trade discounts was 15% + 8% + 4% = 27% and 0.27 $\times$ $20 = $5.40. The reason is that in a trade series discount, each discount after the first one is completed by using the previous *net price*. The trade discount series of 15/10/4 is equivalent to a single trade discount of 25%. This can be computed by finding the total discount: $20.00 −

$15.01 = $4.99, then dividing by $20.00 and changing the decimal to a percent:

$$R = \frac{\$4.99}{\$20.00} = 0.2495 \text{ or about } 25\%$$

There is a mathematical procedure to find a single discount that is equivalent to a series of trade discounts. This procedure is shown in the next example.

EXAMPLE: Find a single trade discount that is equivalent to a trade discount series of 25/15/5.

SOLUTION:

Step 1. Find the complements of the trade discounts.
The complement of 25% is 100% − 25% = 75%.
The complement of 15% is 100% − 15% = 85%.
The complement of 5% is 100% − 5% = 95%.
Step 2. Change each complement to a decimal and find the product.
0.75 × 0.85 × 0.95 = 0.606 (rounded)
Step 3. Change the product to a percent and subtract from 100%.
0.606 = 60.6%
100% − 60.6% = 39.4%
Hence a trade discount series of 25/15/5 is equivalent to a single trade discount of 39.4%.

EXAMPLE: Find a single trade discount that is equivalent to a trade discount series of 15/10/5.

SOLUTION:

Step 1. The complement of 15% is 100% − 15% = 85%.
The complement of 10% is 100% − 10% = 90%.
The complement of 5% is 100% − 5% = 95%.
Step 2. 0.85 × 0.90 × 0.95 = 0.727 (rounded)
Step 3. 0.727 = 72.7%
100% − 72.7% = 27.3%
A trade discount series of 15/10/5 is equivalent to a single trade discount of 27.3%.

PRACTICE:

1. A table saw has a list price of $180. A trade discount series of 10/5 is offered. Find the amount of the discount and the net price.

2. A garage door has a list price of $210. A trade discount series of 10/5/3 is offered. Find the amount of the discount and the net price.

3. A woman's handbag has a list price of $30.00. For a sale, a 40% discount is offered followed by a 10% discount. Find the net price and the amount of money that has been saved.

4. Find a single trade discount that is equivalent to a discount series of 12/8.

5. Find a single trade discount that is equivalent to a discount series of 18/12/6.

SOLUTION:

1.
$$T = R \times L$$
$$= 0.10 \times \$180$$
$$= \$18$$
$$N = L - T$$
$$= \$180 - \$18$$
$$= \$162$$
$$T = R \times L$$
$$= 0.05 \times \$162$$
$$= \$8.10$$
$$N = L - T$$
$$= \$162 - \$8.10 = \$153.90$$

Trade discount $= \$18 + \$8.10 = \$26.10$

Shortcut method:
$$N = 0.9 \times 0.95 \times \$180$$
$$= \$153.90$$

2.
$$D = R \times L$$
$$= 0.10 \times \$210$$
$$= \$21$$
$$N = \$210 - \$21$$
$$= \$189$$

$$D = R \times L$$
$$= 0.05 \times \$189$$
$$= \$9.45$$
$$N = \$189 - \$9.45$$
$$= \$179.55$$
$$D = R \times L$$
$$= 0.03 \times \$179.55$$
$$= \$5.39$$
$$N = \$179.55 - \$5.39$$
$$= \$174.16$$
$$\text{Total discount} = \$21.00 + \$9.45 + \$5.39$$
$$= \$35.84$$

Shortcut method:

$$N = 0.90 \times 0.95 \times 0.97 \times \$210$$
$$= \$174.16$$

3. Shortcut method:

$$N = 0.60 \times 0.90 \times \$30.00$$
$$= \$16.20$$
$$D = \$30 - \$16.20$$
$$= \$13.80$$

4. The complement of 12% is 88%.

The complement of 8% is 92%.

$$0.88 \times 0.92 = 0.8096$$
$$0.8096 = 80.96\%$$
$$100\% - 80.96\% = 19.04\%$$

5.

$$100\% - 18\% = 82\% = 0.82$$

$$100\% - 12\% = 88\% = 0.88$$

$$100\% - 6\% = 94\% = 0.94$$

$$0.82 \times 0.88 \times 0.94 = 0.678304 = 67.8304\%$$

$$100\% - 67.8304\% = 32.1696\% \text{ or } 32.17\% \text{ (rounded)}$$

Cash Discounts

As stated in the Introduction, the manufacturer or wholesaler will offer *discounts* to buyers in order to encourage them to pay their bills early. A time limit is given and if the bill is paid before the end of the time limit, the buyer can deduct a percentage of the bill. This discount is called a **cash discount**. The discount will be written on the invoice as follows:

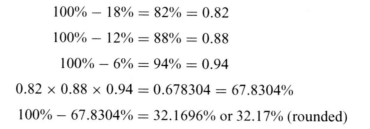

Terms: $\dfrac{3}{10}, \dfrac{n}{30}$

This is read as "three-ten, net thirty." This means that if the bill is paid within 10 days, the buyer can deduct 3%. If the bill is paid anytime after 10 days and up to 30 days, the full amount or net amount must be paid. If the bill is not paid within the 30 days, it becomes *overdue* and an additional charge may be incurred.

Sometimes the cash discount terms are written as follows:

$$\frac{3}{5}, \frac{2}{10}, \frac{n}{30}$$

In this case, a 3% discount can be deducted if the bill is paid within 5 days, a 2% discount is taken if the bill is paid on day 6 through 10, and the full amount is paid from day 11 through 30. After 30 days, the bill is overdue.

Cash discounts are calculated only after trade discounts are deducted. Cash discounts do not apply on any merchandise that is returned and cash discounts do not apply on shipping charges.

In order to determine if a cash discount applies, you will need to know the number of days in each month. See the table on the next page.

EXAMPLE: An invoice has the following terms: $\frac{2}{10}, \frac{n}{30}$. It is dated November 12. How much time does the buyer have to pay in order to get the discount?

	Months with	
31 days	**30 days**	**28 days**
January	April	February*
March	June	
May	September	
July	November	
August		
October		
December		

*Assume February has 28 days unless stated otherwise.

SOLUTION:
In this case, you can add the day of the invoice plus the number of days of the discount—$12 + 10 = 22$. Hence the buyer can pay the bill anytime on or before November 22.

EXAMPLE: An invoice has the following terms: $\frac{3}{15}$, $\frac{n}{30}$. The invoice date is November 24. What is the last day that the invoice can be paid in order to receive the discount?

SOLUTION:
In this case, 15 days from November 24 go into the next month, and so the calculation is slightly different from the one in the previous example.

Step 1. Find the number of days from the invoice date to the end of the month; i.e., November 30.

$$30 - 24 = 6$$

Step 2. Then count 9 days into December, since $15 - 6 = 9$.
Hence the bill should be paid on or before December 9 in order to receive a 3% discount.

Of course if you have a calendar handy, you can always count the days manually. Start counting on the day after the invoice date.

To compute a cash discount, use the same formula as that you used in the previous section.

EXAMPLE: An invoice dated August 18 for 1 dozen belts costing $192 is sent to a retail store with the following terms: $\frac{3}{10}$, $\frac{2}{15}$, $\frac{n}{30}$. If the bill is paid on September 1, how much should the owner pay?

SOLUTION:
Ten days from August 18 is $18 + 10 = 28$ or August 28, and so the owner cannot take advantage of the 3% discount. Since there are $31 - 18 = 13$ days left in August and $15 - 13 = 2$, the last day to get the 2% discount is September 2. Since the bill was paid on September 1, the storeowner can deduct a 2% discount.

$$D = R \times L$$
$$= 0.02 \times \$192$$
$$= \$3.84$$
$$N = L - D$$
$$= \$192 - \$3.84$$
$$= \$188.16$$

Hence the owner should pay $188.16.

Another type of cash discount is called the end-of-month (EOM) discount. For example, the terms might be $\frac{3}{10}$ EOM. In this case, if the bill is paid during the first 10 days of the next month, the buyer receives a 3% discount. For example, if an invoice is dated June 6 and the terms are $\frac{3}{10}$ EOM, the buyer can pay the bill anytime up to and including the 10th of July and still receive a 3% discount.

Furthermore, if the invoice is dated on or after the twenty-sixth day of the month, an additional month is given to make the payment. For example, suppose an invoice is dated June 27 and the terms are $\frac{3}{10}$ EOM. The owner can pay the bill anytime up to and including August 10 and still receive a 3% discount.

EXAMPLE: The Garden Store received a $600 bill for advertisement fliers dated November 6. The terms were $\frac{2}{15}$ EOM. The owner paid the bill on December 9. How much did she pay?

SOLUTION:
The owner has until December 15th to get the 2% discount, and the bill was paid on December 9th, so she is entitled to the discount.

$$D = R \times L$$
$$= 0.02 \times \$600$$
$$= \$12$$

$$N = L - D$$
$$= \$600 - \$12$$
$$= \$588$$

Hence she paid $588 for the fliers.

Another type of cash discount is called the receipt-of-goods discount or ROG. This type of discount would be stated as $\frac{2}{10}$, $\frac{n}{30}$ ROG. Hence the buyer has 10 days after receiving the merchandise to pay the bill and take a 2% discount. The invoice date in this case is ignored.

EXAMPLE: On July 15, the Happy Feet Store received 10 pairs of boots costing $500. The invoice dated June 27 had the terms $\frac{2}{10}$, $\frac{n}{30}$ ROG. If the storeowner paid the bill on July 23, how much did he pay?

SOLUTION:
Since the invoice states ROG, the buyer has 10 days from July 15 to get the discount; therefore, he has until July 25 to get the discount. Because he paid on July 23, he is entitled to a 2% discount.

$$D = R \times L$$
$$= 0.02 \times \$500$$
$$= \$10$$
$$N = L - D$$
$$= \$500 - \$10$$
$$= \$490$$

Hence he paid $490 for the boots.

PRACTICE:

1. If the terms on an invoice are $\frac{2}{15}$, $\frac{n}{30}$ and it is dated July 24, what is the last day the payment can be made in order to get the 2% discount?
2. If the terms on an invoice are $\frac{3}{10}$, $\frac{n}{30}$ EOM and the invoice is dated August 12, what is the last day the payment can be made in order to get the 3% discount?

3. The terms on an invoice are $\frac{5}{10}$, $\frac{n}{30}$ ROG. The invoice is dated May 16 and the merchandise is received on May 22, what is the last day the payment can be made in order to get the 5% discount?

4. The terms on an invoice are $\frac{3}{10}$, $\frac{n}{30}$ EOM. If the invoice is dated January 30, what is the last day the payment can be made in order to get the 3% discount?

5. The terms on an invoice are $\frac{3}{10}$, $\frac{1}{15}$, $\frac{n}{30}$, and the invoice is dated February 18.
   (a) What is the last day the payment can be made in order to get the 3% discount?
   (b) What is the last day the payment can be made in order to get the 1% discount?

6. One dozen duffle bags have a list price of $360. The terms are $\frac{3}{10}$, $\frac{2}{15}$, $\frac{n}{30}$. If the invoice is dated February 19 and the bill is paid on March 2, find the amount of the payment.

7. A carton of men's shirts has a list price of $480. The terms are $\frac{2}{10}$, $\frac{n}{30}$ EOM. If the invoice is dated November 18 and the bill is paid on December 8, find the amount of the payment.

8. Two dozen pairs of women's sandals are received on October 10. The invoice shows a list price of $120 and is dated October 6. If the terms are $\frac{3}{15}$, $\frac{n}{30}$ ROG, find the amount of the payment if the payment was made on October 21.

9. An invoice for $800 was dated July 8. The terms were $\frac{4}{10}$, $\frac{n}{30}$. If the bill was paid on July 20, how much was the payment?

10. An invoice for $83.95 was dated September 29. The terms were $\frac{3}{10}$, $\frac{n}{30}$ EOM. If the bill was paid on November 3, find the payment amount.

SOLUTIONS:

1. There are $31 - 24 = 7$ days in July and 8 days in August, and so the bill must be paid by August 8 in order to get the 2% discount.

2. In order to get the 3% discount the bill must be paid by September 10 since it is an EOM discount.

3. The buyer has 10 days from the receipt-of-goods date to pay in order to get a 5% discount. Hence the bill must be paid by June 1.

4. The buyer has until March 10 to pay the bill since it is dated after the 25th of the month, and the buyer gets an extra month when an EOM discount is given.

5. (a) February 28; (b) March 5.

6. Since the payment was made after 10 days but before the 15-day period, there is a 2% discount; hence,

$$D = R \times L$$
$$= 0.02 \times \$360$$
$$= \$7.20$$
$$N = L - D$$
$$= \$360 - \$7.20$$
$$= \$352.80$$

7. Since the payment was made before December 10th, a 2% discount can be deducted; hence,

$$D = R \times L$$
$$= 0.02 \times \$480$$
$$= \$9.60$$
$$N = L - D$$
$$= \$480 - \$9.60$$
$$= \$470.40$$

8. Since the payment was made within 15 days of the receipt of goods, a 3% discount can be deducted; hence,

$$D = R \times L$$
$$= 0.03 \times \$120$$
$$= \$3.60$$
$$N = L - D$$
$$= \$120 - \$3.60$$
$$= \$116.40$$

9. Since the payment was made after 10 days, the full amount, $800, must be paid.

10. The invoice was dated after the 25th of the month, so an extra month is allowed. Payment was made within the first 10 days of November, so a 3% discount is allowed; hence,

$$D = R \times L$$
$$= 0.03 \times \$83.95$$
$$= \$2.52$$
$$N = L - D$$
$$= \$83.95 - \$2.52$$
$$= \$81.43$$

Discounts and Freight Terms

When a buyer can take advantage of a trade discount and a cash discount, the trade discount is computed first, and then the cash discount is taken on the price *after* the trade discount amount has been deducted.

EXAMPLE: A riding lawn mower costing $1300 was purchased on June 6. A 20% trade discount was given. A cash discount of $\frac{2}{10}, \frac{n}{30}$ was also offered. If the bill was paid on June 10, how much did the buyer pay?

SOLUTION:
Find the net price after the trade discount.

$$D = R \times L$$
$$= 0.20 \times \$1300$$
$$= \$260$$
$$N = L - D$$
$$= \$1300 - \$260$$
$$= \$1040$$

Since the bill was paid within 10 days, deduct 2%.

$$D = R \times L$$
$$= 0.02 \times \$1040$$
$$= \$20.08$$

$$N = L - D$$
$$= \$1040 - \$20.08$$
$$= \$1019.92$$

Hence the purchaser paid $1019.92.

In addition to understanding the nature of discounts, the merchant must understand the freight terms. The freight terms are designated on what is called the **bill of loading**. If the bill of loading states **free on board (FOB) shipping point**, the buyer pays the freight costs directly to the freight company. If the bill of loading states **FOB destination**, then the seller pays the freight charges to the freight company, and there is no charge to the buyer. If the bill of loading is marked **prepay and add**, then the buyer pays the freight charges to the seller, and the seller will pay the freight company. Trade and cash discounts do *not* apply to the freight charges.

EXAMPLE: The bill of loading on the riding lawn mower stated "FOB destination," and the charge was $45. How much does the buyer pay for freight?

SOLUTION:
The buyer does not pay anything for freight.

PRACTICE:

1. On an invoice of $350 a trade discount of 15% is offered. The terms are $\frac{3}{10}$, $\frac{n}{30}$. If the bill is paid within 10 days, what amount should be paid?
2. An invoice of $12,600 has a trade discount series of 20/10/5. If the terms are $\frac{2}{10}$, $\frac{n}{30}$ ROG and the buyer pays the bill within 10 days of the receipt of goods, what amount should be paid?
3. An invoice of $790 has terms of $\frac{5}{10}$, $\frac{n}{30}$. The freight cost of $49 is marked "prepay and add." How much should be paid if the buyer pays within 10 days?
4. An invoice of $300 for an inflatable pool has a 20% trade discount. The terms are $\frac{1}{15}$, $\frac{n}{30}$. The freight charge of $12 is marked "FOB shipping point." What is the total cost of the pool if the bill is paid within 15 days?
5. An invoice of $250 for five boxes of tumblers has a trade discount series of 15/5. The terms are $\frac{3}{15}$, $\frac{n}{30}$. The freight cost is $8.00 and is marked "FOB destination." How much should be paid if the payment is made within 15 days?

SOLUTION:

1. $D = R \times L$
    $= 0.15 \times \$350$
    $= \$52.50$

    $N = L - D$
    $= \$350 - \$52.50$
    $= \$297.50$

    $D = R \times L$
    $= 0.03 \times \$297.50$
    $= \$8.93$

    $N = \$297.50 - \$8.93$
    $= \$288.57$

2. $N = 0.80 \times 0.90 \times 0.95 \times \$12,600$
    $= \$8618.40$

    $D = 0.02 \times \$8618.40$
    $= \$172.37$

    $N = \$8618.40 - \$172.37$
    $= \$8446.03$

3. $D = R \times L$
    $= 0.05 \times \$790$
    $= \$39.50$

    $N = L - D$
    $= \$790 - \$39.50$
    $= \$750.50$

    The buyer must also pay the seller for the freight charges.

    $\$750.50 + \$49 = \$799.50$

4. $D = R \times L$

$\quad = 0.20 \times \$300$

$\quad = \$60$

$N = L - D$

$\quad = \$300 - \$60$

$\quad = \$240$

$D = R \times L$

$\quad = 0.01 \times \$240$

$\quad = \$2.40$

$N = \$240 - \$2.40$

$\quad = \$237.60$

The buyer must also pay the freight operator $12.

5. $N = 0.85 \times 0.95 \times \$250$

$\quad = \$201.88$

$D = R \times L$

$\quad = 0.03 \times \$201.88$

$\quad = \$6.06$

$N = L - D$

$\quad = \$201.88 - \$6.06$

$\quad = \$195.82$

There is no freight charge for the buyer since the seller pays the freight costs.

Summary

In order to encourage people to purchase merchandise, manufacturers and retailers offer discounts. A trade discount is a reduction of the list price of an item. In order to encourage the buyer to pay in a timely manner, a cash discount is sometimes offered. Sometimes the buyer pays the freight or shipping costs and sometimes the seller pays the freight costs.

Quiz

1. A carton containing puzzles has a list price of $59. If a 30% trade discount is offered, find the net price.
   (a) $17.70
   (b) $76.70
   (c) $100.30
   (d) $41.30

2. Find the net price of a chair that has a list price of $375 if a trade discount series of 10/5/3 is offered.
   (a) $311.01
   (b) $63.99
   (c) $67.50
   (d) $307.50

3. Find the single trade discount that is equivalent to a trade discount series of 20/10/5.
   (a) 0.1%
   (b) 68.4%
   (c) 31.6%
   (d) 35%

4. Juan Arillo received a bill dated October 6 for $445. The terms were $\frac{3}{10}$, $\frac{2}{15}$, $\frac{n}{30}$. Juan paid the bill on October 19. How much did he pay?
   (a) $445.00
   (b) $431.65
   (c) $436.10
   (d) $422.75

5. Find the amount of a cash discount on an invoice of $88 that is dated March 26 with terms of $\frac{2}{10}$ EOM. The bill was paid on May 3.
   (a) $88
   (b) $86.24
   (c) $1.76
   (d) $85.06

6. An invoice dated June 10 has the terms $\frac{3}{10}$ ROG. The merchandise was received on June 16. What is the date of the last day the bill can be paid in order to receive the 3% discount?
   (a) June 26
   (b) July 10

(c) June 16

(d) July 1

7. An invoice for $62.50 was dated September 21 and had the terms $\frac{3}{10}$, $\frac{2}{20}$, $\frac{n}{30}$. If it was paid on October 12, what should be paid?

(a) $60.63

(b) $61.25

(c) $62.00

(d) $62.50

8. A 15% trade discount was offered on a clock costing $98. The terms of sale were $\frac{3}{15}$, $\frac{n}{30}$. Find the amount of the payment if the bill was paid within 15 days.

(a) $83.30

(b) $82.70

(c) $80.80

(d) $95.06

9. When an invoice is marked "FOB destination,"

(a) the buyer pays the seller for the freight charge

(b) the seller pays the freight operator the freight charge

(c) the buyer pays the freight operator the freight charge

(d) the seller pays the buyer for the freight charge

10. If an invoice is marked "prepay and add,"

(a) the buyer pays the seller for the freight charge

(b) there is no freight charge for the buyer

(c) the buyer pays the shipper for the freight charge

(d) the seller pays the buyer for the freight charge

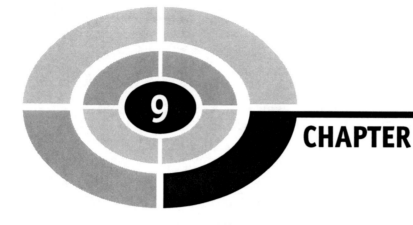

CHAPTER

9

Simple Interest and Promissory Notes

Introduction

Interest is a fee charged for the use of money. For example, if you place money in a savings account or buy a savings bond or purchase a certificate of deposit, the bank, the US government, or some other organization will pay you money to use your money for its purposes. On the other hand, if you borrow money or use a credit card to purchase an item, you must pay the bank, store, or other lending institution a fee (interest) for the use of its money.

There are two ways to compute the time period when money is borrowed. One way is called *exact time*. **Exact time** is based on the calendar (i.e., 365 days in a year and 366 days in a leap year). The other way is called *ordinary time*. **Ordinary time** uses 30 days in a month and 360 days in a year.

Sometimes when you borrow money, you are required to sign a *promissory note*. A **promissory note** is a legal document, promising to pay back a sum of money that is borrowed. It is a legal and binding contract between people or businesses. There are two types of promissory notes: *interest bearing* and *noninterest bearing* notes. Promissory notes can be sold or cashed in. When this occurs, it is called *discounting*.

   This chapter will explain the basic concepts of interest and promissory notes.

Simple Interest

The interest explained in this chapter is called **simple interest**, which is used when a loan or investment is paid back in a lump sum at the end of the borrowing period. Another type of interest called **compound interest** is explained in the next chapter.

   In order to compute interest, three figures (amounts) are needed. They are the principal, the rate, and the time. The amount of money that is borrowed or placed in some type of investment (i.e., government bond, certificate of deposit, savings account, etc.) is called the **principal**. The percent of interest is called the **rate**. The number of days, months, or years for which the money is borrowed or invested is called the **time** or the **term**. The amount of a loan or the amount of the investment plus the interest is called the **maturity value** or the **future value**.

   The basic formula for computing the interest uses the principal, rate, and time as follows:

$$\text{Interest} = \text{Principal} \times \text{Rate} \times \text{Time} \quad \text{or} \quad I = PRT$$

$$\text{Maturity value or Future value} = \text{Principal} + \text{Interest or } MV = P + I$$

   The first example shows how to compute the interest and maturity value when the time is given in whole years.

EXAMPLE: Find the interest on a loan of $3600 for 3 years at a rate of 8%.

SOLUTION:
Change the rate to a decimal and substitute in the formula $I = PRT$: $8\% = 0.08$

$$I = PRT$$
$$= \$3600 \times 0.08 \times 3$$
$$= \$864$$

The interest on the loan is $864.

EXAMPLE: Find the maturity value for the loan in the previous problem.

SOLUTION:

Substitute in the formula: $MV = P + I$.

$$MV = P + I$$
$$= \$3600 + \$864$$
$$= \$4464$$

When the time of a loan or investment is given in months, it must be changed to years by dividing the number of months by 12.

EXAMPLE: United Ceramics, Inc needed to borrow $2000 at 4% for 3 months. Find the interest that had to be paid.

SOLUTION:

Change 3 months to years by dividing by 12.

$$\frac{3}{12} = 0.25$$

Change the rate to a decimal.

$$4\% = 0.04$$

Substitute in the formula $I = PRT$.

$$I = \$2000 \times 0.04 \times 0.25$$
$$= \$20$$

The interest is $20.

EXAMPLE: Admiral Chauffeur Services borrowed $600 at 9% for $1\frac{1}{2}$ years to repair a limousine. Find the interest.

SOLUTION:

Change $1\frac{1}{2}$ years to 1.5 years and 9% to 0.09, and substitute in the formula: $I = PRT$.

$$I = PRT$$
$$= \$600 \times 0.09 \times 1.5$$
$$= \$81$$

The interest is $81.

Sometimes a simple interest loan is paid off in monthly installments. To find the monthly payment, divide the maturity value of the loan by the number of months given to pay off the loan.

EXAMPLE: Using the information in the previous example, Admiral Chauffeur Services decided to repay its loan in monthly installments. Find the monthly payments.

SOLUTION:

Step 1. Find the interest. In this case, it is $81 (see the previous example).
Step 2. Find the maturity value of the loan.

$$MV = P + I$$
$$= \$600 + \$81$$
$$= \$681$$

Step 3. Divide the maturity value of the loan by the number of months. Since $1\frac{1}{2}$ years $= 18$ months, divide $681 by 18 to get $37.83. The monthly payment is $37.83.

PRACTICE:

1. Ace Auto Parts borrowed $6000 at 6% for 5 years to enlarge its display area. Find the interest and maturity value of the loan.
2. Sam's Sound Shack borrowed $13,450 at 8% for 3 years to remodel its existing store. Find the interest and maturity value of the loan.
3. King's Cellular Service borrowed $19,000 at 8.5% for 3 years to purchase a van. Find the interest and maturity value of the loan as well as the monthly payment.
4. Ron's Detailing Service borrowed $435 at 3.75% for 6 months to purchase new equipment. Find the interest and maturity value of the loan and the monthly payment.
5. The Express Delivery borrowed $1535 at 4.5% for 3 months to purchase safety equipment for its employees. Find the interest and maturity value of the loan and the monthly payment.
6. Benson Electric borrowed $1800 at 12% for 1 year from a local bank. Find the interest and maturity value of the investment and the monthly payment.
7. Clark Cycle borrowed $2400 at $12\frac{1}{2}$% for 5 years to purchase new children's tricycles. Find the interest and maturity value of the loan.

8. Cool Air-conditioning Company borrowed $950 at $9\frac{1}{2}$% for 5 months to replace worn-out equipment. Find the interest and maturity value of the loan.

9. Squirrel Hill Tree Service borrowed $25,000 at 10% for $4\frac{1}{2}$ years for new pick up trucks. Find the interest and maturity value of the loan.

10. Cranberry Landscaping, Inc borrowed $6500 at $6\frac{3}{4}$% for $3\frac{1}{2}$ years for lawn mowers. Find the interest and maturity value of the loan.

SOLUTIONS:

1. $I = PRT$

   $= \$6000 \times 0.06 \times 5$

   $= \$1800$

   $MV = P + I$

   $= \$6000 + \$1800$

   $= \$7800$

2. $I = PRT$

   $= \$13,450 \times 0.08 \times 3$

   $= \$3228$

   $MV = P + I$

   $= \$13,450 + \$3228$

   $= \$16,678$

3. $I = PRT$

   $= \$19,000 \times 0.085 \times 3$

   $= \$4845$

   $MV = P + I$

   $= \$19,000 + \$4845$

   $= \$23,845$

   $\text{Monthly payment} = \dfrac{\$23,845}{36} = \$662.36$

4.
$$I = PRT$$
$$= \$435 \times 0.0375 \times \frac{6}{12}$$
$$= \$8.16$$
$$MV = P + I$$
$$= \$435 + \$8.16$$
$$= \$443.16$$
$$\text{Monthly payment} = \frac{\$443.16}{6}$$
$$= \$73.86$$

5.
$$I = PRT$$
$$= \$1535 \times 0.045 \times \frac{3}{12}$$
$$= \$17.27$$
$$MV = P + I$$
$$= \$1535 + \$17.27$$
$$= \$1552.27$$
$$\text{Monthly payment} = \frac{\$1552.27}{3}$$
$$= \$517.42$$

6.
$$I = PRT$$
$$= \$1800 \times 0.12 \times 1$$
$$= \$216$$
$$MV = P + I$$
$$= \$1800 + \$216$$
$$= \$2016$$
$$\text{Monthly payment} = \frac{\$2016}{12}$$
$$= \$168$$

7. $I = PRT$

$= \$2400 \times 0.125 \times 5$

$= \$1500$

$MV = P + I$

$= \$2400 + \$1500$

$= \$3900$

8. $I = PRT$

$= \$950 \times 0.095 \times \dfrac{5}{12}$

$= \$37.60$

$MV = P + I$

$= \$950 + \$37.60$

$= \$987.60$

9. $I = PRT$

$= \$25,000 \times 0.10 \times 4.5$

$= \$11,250$

$MV = P + I$

$= \$25,000 + \$11,250$

$= \$36,250$

10. $I = PRT$

$= \$6500 \times 0.0675 \times 3.5$

$= \$1535.63$

$MV = P + I$

$= \$6500 + \$1535.63$

$= \$8035.63$

Finding the Principal, Rate, and Time

In addition to finding the interest and maturity value for a loan or an investment, the principal, the rate, and the time can also be found. Figure 9-1 shows the circle and the related formulas.

Formula for finding the principal:

$$P = \frac{I}{RT}$$

Formula for finding the rate:
(*Note*: Be sure to change the decimal to a %.)

$$R = \frac{I}{PT}$$

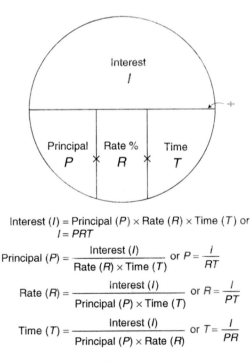

Interest (I) = Principal (P) × Rate (R) × Time (T) or
$$I = PRT$$

Principal $(P) = \dfrac{\text{Interest } (I)}{\text{Rate } (R) \times \text{Time } (T)}$ or $P = \dfrac{I}{RT}$

Rate $(R) = \dfrac{\text{Interest } (I)}{\text{Principal } (P) \times \text{Time } (T)}$ or $R = \dfrac{I}{PT}$

Time $(T) = \dfrac{\text{Interest } (I)}{\text{Principal } (P) \times \text{Rate } (R)}$ or $T = \dfrac{I}{PR}$

Fig. 9-1.

Formula for finding the time:

$$T = \frac{I}{PR}$$

To find one of the variables when the values of the other three variables are given, substitute the given values in the appropriate formula and perform the indicated operations. The next three examples show how to find the principal, rate, and time.

EXAMPLE: Phillips Beauty Spa is replacing one of its workstations. The interest on a loan secured by the spa was $93.50. The money was borrowed at 5.5% for 2 years. Find the principal.

SOLUTION:

Substitute in the formula $P = \dfrac{I}{RT}$ and solve for P.

$$P = \frac{I}{RT}$$
$$= \frac{93.50}{0.055 \times 2}$$
$$= \$850$$

The amount of the loan is $850.

Calculator Tip

When using a calculator, be sure to place the values and operations in the denominator of the formula in parentheses. In the previous example, you would use $\$93.50 \div (0.055 \times 2) =$

EXAMPLE: R and S Furnace Company invested $15,250 for 10 years and received $9150 in interest. What rate did the investment pay?

SOLUTION:

Substitute in the formula $R = \dfrac{I}{PT}$ and solve for R.

$$R = \frac{I}{PT}$$

$$= \frac{9150}{15{,}250 \times 10}$$
$$= 0.06 = 6\%$$

When finding the rate, always change the decimal to a percent.

EXAMPLE: Pryor Furnace Company borrowed $4500 at $8\frac{3}{4}\%$ to upgrade its equipment. The company had to pay $2756.25 interest. Find the term of the loan.

SOLUTION:

Substitute in the formula $T = \dfrac{I}{PR}$ and solve for T.

$$T = \frac{I}{PR}$$
$$= \frac{2756.25}{4500 \times 0.0875}$$
$$= 7$$

The term of the loan is 7 years.

PRACTICE:

1. To purchase a refrigerated showcase, Georgetown Florists borrowed $8000 for 6 years. The interest is $4080. Find the rate.
2. Wayward Singing Telegrams borrowed $15,000 for 12 years to pay for a new vehicle. The interest is $18,000. Find the rate.
3. To take advantage of a going-out-of-business sale at another novelty store, Pleasant Valley Novelty had to borrow some money to buy some stock. They paid $150 interest on a 6-month loan at 12%. Find the principal.
4. To purchase two new industrial ovens, the Oak Tree Bakery paid $1350 interest on a 9% loan for 3 years. Find the principal.
5. To train employees on how to use new equipment, Williams Muffler Repair had to borrow $4500 at $9\frac{1}{2}\%$. The company paid $1282.50 interest. Find the term of the loan.
6. Berger Car Rental borrowed $8650 at 6.8% interest to cover the increasing cost of auto insurance. Find the terms of the loan if the interest expense was $2941.
7. To pay for new supplies, Pleasant Photo Company borrowed $9235 at 8% and paid $2955.20 in interest. Find the term of the loan.

8. Mary Beck earned $216 interest on a savings account at 8% over 2 years. Find the principal.

SOLUTIONS:

1. $R = \dfrac{I}{PT}$

   $= \dfrac{\$4080}{\$8000 \times 6}$

   $= 0.085 = 8.5\%$

2. $R = \dfrac{I}{PT}$

   $= \dfrac{\$18,000}{\$15,000 \times 12}$

   $= 0.10 \times 10\%$

3. $P = \dfrac{I}{RT}$

   $= \dfrac{\$150}{0.12 \times 0.5}$

   $= \$2500$

4. $P = \dfrac{I}{RT}$

   $= \dfrac{\$1350}{0.09 \times 3}$

   $= \$5000$

5. $T = \dfrac{I}{PR}$

   $= \dfrac{\$1282.50}{\$4500 \times 0.095}$

   $= 3 \text{ years}$

6. $T = \dfrac{I}{PR}$

   $= \dfrac{\$2941}{\$8650 \times 0.068}$

   $= 5 \text{ years}$

7. $T = \dfrac{I}{PR}$

    $= \dfrac{\$2955.20}{\$9235 \times 0.08}$

    $= 4$ years

8. $P = \dfrac{I}{RT}$

    $= \dfrac{\$216}{0.08 \times 2}$

    $= \$1350$

Exact and Ordinary Time

Banks and other lending institutions use two methods to compute interest. One method uses what is called *ordinary time*, and the other method uses what is called *exact time*. **Ordinary time** assumes that each month has 30 days and each year has 360 days. A 90-day loan dated March 12 will be due on June 12 since 90 days are equivalent to three months when ordinary time is used. When you count 90 days from March 12 on the calendar, you will find the date to be June 10. But this fact is ignored when using ordinary time. When finding the due dates using ordinary time, simply count the months using 30 days for 1 month to get the month that the loan is due. Then use the same day number on which the loan was made to get the day of the month that the loan is due. The next example illustrates this.

EXAMPLE: A loan was dated February 18 and was due in 120 days. Find the due date using ordinary time.

SOLUTION:

    Step 1. Divide 120 days by 30 to get 4 months.
    Step 2. Count 4 months from February to get the month that the loan is due. In this case, it is June.
    Step 3. Use 18 as the date of the month that the loan is due since the loan was made on the 18th of February. Hence the loan is due on June 18.

    Ordinary time ignores the fact that February has 28 days and 29 days in a leap year, and it also ignores the 31st of the month unless the loan falls due on the day in a month that has 31 days. For example, a loan taken out on May 31 and due in 2 months would be repaid on July 31.

EXAMPLE: A loan was made on January 31 for 60 days. Find the due date using ordinary time.

SOLUTION:

Step 1. Divide 60 by 30 to get 2 months.
Step 2. Two months from January is March.
Step 3. The loan is due on March 31.

If a loan is due to mature at the end of a month that has fewer days than the month in which the loan is made, then use the last day of the month that the loan is due.

EXAMPLE: A loan was made on October 31 for 120 days. Find the due date using ordinary time.

SOLUTION:

Step 1. Divide 120 by 30 to get 4 months.
Step 2. Four months from October is February.
Step 3. The loan is due on February 28 or February 29 in a leap year, since February does not have 31 days.

When computing interest using ordinary time, use 360 days for 1 year. This method is called the **ordinary time/ordinary interest method**.

EXAMPLE: Find the interest on an $800 loan at 9% for 28 days using ordinary time.

SOLUTION:
Use the formula $I = PRT$ and 1 year $= 360$ days.

$$I = PRT$$
$$= \$800 \times 0.09 \times \frac{28}{360}$$
$$= 5.6$$

The interest is $5.60.

When computing the due date of a loan using **exact time**, count the exact number of days on the calendar corresponding to the term of the loan to find the due date.

EXAMPLE: A loan for 120 days is made on May 18. Find the due date using exact time.

SOLUTION:

Step 1. Find the number of days left in May. May has 31 days and so $31 - 18 = 12$.

Step 2: Make a list of months as shown.

May	12 days
June	30 days
July	31 days
August	31 days
September	?
Total	120 days

Step 3. Find the 120-day due date in September. Add the days shown and subtract from 120: $12 + 30 + 31 + 31 = 104$; $120 - 104 = 16$. Hence the loan is due on September 16.

EXAMPLE: A loan was made on September 4 for 180 days. Find the due date using exact time.

SOLUTION:

Step 1. Find the number of days left in September. There are 30 days in September, and so $30 - 4 = 26$.

Step 2. Make a list as shown:

September	26 days
October	31 days
November	30 days
December	31 days
January	31 days
February	28 days
March	?
Total	180 days

Step 3. Find the due date in March.
$26 + 31 + 30 + 31 + 31 + 28 = 177$; $180 - 177 = 3$.
Hence the loan is due on March 3.

Sometimes a loan is repaid before the due date. In this case, it is necessary to find the number of days between two specific dates.

EXAMPLE: A loan is made on March 6 and repaid on August 11. How many days was the term of the loan? Use exact time.

SOLUTION:

Step 1. Find the number of days left in March: $31 - 6 = 25$.
Step 2. Make a list as shown:

March	25 days
April	30 days
May	31 days
June	30 days
July	31 days
August	11 days
Total	158 days

Hence the time of the loan is 158 days.

EXAMPLE: A loan was made on November 9 and repaid on February 26. Find the term of the loan using exact time.

SOLUTION:

Step 1. Find the number of days left in November: $30 - 9 = 21$.
Step 2. Make a list as shown:

November	21 days
December	31 days
January	31 days
February	26 days
Total	109 days

Hence the term of the loan is 109 days.

When computing interest on a loan using exact time, use 365 days for 1 year. Use 366 days if a leap year is specified. If no year is specified, assume it is *not* a leap year. This method is called the **exact time/exact interest method**.

EXAMPLE: A loan of $9270 was made on April 6 and repaid on August 10. Find the interest if the rate is 12% and exact time is used.

SOLUTION:

Step 1. Find the term of the loan in days using the method shown previously.

April	24 days
May	31 days
June	30 days
July	31 days
August	10 days
Total	126 days

Step 2. Use $I = PRT$

$$= \$9270 \times 0.12 \times \frac{126}{365}$$

$$= \$384.01$$

The interest is $384.01.

If the year of the loan includes February of a leap year (every fourth year after 2000), use 29 days for February. If the last two digits of the year are divisible by 4, the year is a leap year. For example, 2004 is a leap year since the last two digits, 0 and 4, are divisible by 4.

A third method of computing interest uses exact time and ordinary interest. This method is called the **banker's rule**. In other words, find the exact time for the loan and use 360 in the formula for the number of days of the year.

EXAMPLE: A $5000 loan is made on July 15 and is paid back on November 6. Find the interest using the banker's method if the rate is 9%.

SOLUTION:
Find the exact number of days from July 15 to November 6.

July	16 days
August	31 days
September	30 days
October	31 days
November	6 days
Total	114 days

Find the interest.

$$I = P \times R \times T$$

$$= \$5000 \times 0.09 \times \frac{114}{360}$$

$$= \$142.50$$

The interest is $142.50.

As shown, there are three common ways to compute interest. They are

1. ordinary time/ordinary interest
2. exact time/exact interest
3. exact time/ordinary interest (banker's rule)

Each is used in different situations. For example, Method 1 is sometimes used in personal loans when monthly payments are made. Method 2 is sometimes used for short-term loans, and Method 3 is sometimes used for business loans. It all depends on the type of loan and the lending institution.

PRACTICE:

1. Sue's loan of $5000 was made on May 6 at 6% interest and was repaid on December 31. Find the interest using exact interest/exact time.
2. Find the interest on a $1000, 90-day, 5% loan that was granted on October 12. Use ordinary time/ordinary interest.
3. A $3500 loan was made at 13% on April 16 and repaid on September 15. Find the interest. Use the banker's rule.
4. Find the interest on a $575, 150-day, 7.5% loan. Use ordinary time/ordinary interest.
5. A $1500, 120-day, 12% loan was granted on June 1. Find the interest and due date. Use the banker's rule.
6. What is the interest on a $7200, 9%, 90-day loan? Use exact time/exact interest.
7. A 30-day, $300 loan was granted to John at 12% on July 21. Find the interest and the due date using ordinary time/ordinary interest.
8. A $400 loan was granted to Joan for 45 days at 11.75%. Find the interest using exact time/exact interest.
9. Fast Wind Karate Academy borrowed $8000 for 21 days at 12.75%. Find the interest using the banker's rule.
10. Bill borrowed $3200 at 11.5% for 60 days to make repairs on his truck. Find the interest using ordinary time/ordinary interest.

SOLUTIONS:

1. Find the term of the loan.
    For May $31 - 6 = 25$ days

June	30 days
July	31 days
August	31 days
September	30 days
October	31 days
November	30 days
December	31 days

$25 + 30 + 31 + 31 + 30 + 31 + 30 + 31 = 239$ days

$I = PRT$

$= \$5000 \times 0.06 \times \dfrac{239}{365}$

$= \$196.44$

2. $I = PRT$

$= 1000 \times 0.05 \times \dfrac{90}{360}$

$= \$12.50$

3. Find the term.
    For April $30 - 16 = 14$ days

May	31 days
June	30 days
July	31 days
August	31 days
September	15 days

$14 + 31 + 30 + 31 + 31 + 15 = 152$ days

$I = PRT$

$= \$3500 \times 0.13 \times \dfrac{152}{360}$

$= \$192.11$

4. $I = PRT$

$= \$575 \times 0.075 \times \dfrac{150}{360}$

$= \$17.97$

5. $I = PRT$

$$= \$1500 \times 0.12 \times \frac{120}{360}$$

$$= \$60$$

For June $30 - 1 = 29$ days
July   31 days
August   31 days
September   ?

Total   120 days

$29 + 31 + 31 = 91$ $120 - 91 = 29$
The loan is due on September 29.

6. $I = PRT$

$$= \$7200 \times 0.09 \times \frac{90}{365}$$

$$= \$159.78$$

7. $I = PRT$

$$= \$300 \times 0.12 \times \frac{30}{360}$$

$$= \$3.00$$

The due date is August 21 since 30 days is 1 month in ordinary time.

8. $I = PRT$

$$= \$400 \times 0.1175 \times \frac{45}{365}$$

$$= \$5.79$$

9. $I = PRT$

$$= \$8000 \times 0.1275 \times \frac{21}{360}$$

$$= \$59.50$$

10. $I = \$3200 \times 0.115 \times \frac{60}{360}$

$$= \$61.33$$

Promissory Notes and Discounting

A **promissory note** is a legal document promising to pay back at some future date a sum of money that has been borrowed. It is a signed contract between two parties. There are two kinds of promissory notes: **interest bearing** and **noninterest bearing**.

When a note is interest bearing, the person borrowing the money must not only pay back the amount of money borrowed but must also pay back any interest accumulated according to the terms of the note. When the note is noninterest bearing, the person pays back only the amount of money borrowed.

The **maker** is the person, company, or institution that has borrowed the money and is obliged to pay the money back. The **payee** is the person, company, or institution that has loaned the money. The **face value** of a note is the amount of money that has been borrowed, symbolized by F (same as the principal for a simple interest loan). The **term of a note** is the time period of the note. The **maturity value** of a note is the face value plus the interest, if any. The **maturity date** is the date the money is to be repaid. Figure 9-2 shows a promissory note.

Computation for promissory notes uses the basic interest formulas; however, the principal is known as the face value of a note. The formulas are

$$\text{Interest}(I) = \text{Face value}(F) \times \text{Rate}(R) \times \text{Time}(T) \quad \text{or} \quad I = F \times R \times T$$

and

$$\text{Maturity value (MV)} = \text{Face value}(F) + \text{Interest}(I) \quad \text{or} \quad MV = F + I$$

Ordinary time/ordinary interest is generally used to find the maturity value.

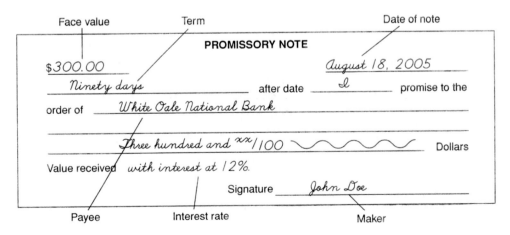

Fig. 9-2.

EXAMPLE: A loan of $9000 was made to Mary Richards on June 27 for 90 days. The promissory note specified that the interest was 12%. Using ordinary time/ordinary interest, find the maturity value of the note.

SOLUTION:
Use the formula $I = F \times R \times T$ to find the interest.

$$I = F \times R \times T$$
$$= 9000 \times 0.12 \times \frac{90}{360}$$
$$= 270$$

The interest is $270.
  Next, find the maturity value of the note using $MV = F + I$.

$$MV = F + I$$
$$= \$9000 + \$270$$
$$= \$9270$$

The maturity value of the note is $9270.
  If the note had been noninterest bearing, the maturity value would have been $9000 since no interest was charged for the use of the money.
  If a person or business (payee) is holding a note and needs the cash before the maturity date of the note, then that person or business can sell or cash in the note to a third party. The third party, however, may charge the payee a sum of money for purchasing the note. When this occurs, it is called **discounting** the note. The third party keeps the note until the maturity date, and the third party receives the maturity value of the note from the maker. The time from when the note is cashed until the maturity date is called the **discount period**. The amount of money that is paid to the original payee is called the **proceeds**, which is the maturity value of the note minus the fee charged to cash the note. The fee is called the **discount** or **discount** amount. The formulas for discounting notes are

Discount amount (DA) = Maturity value (MV) × Rate (R) × Time (T) or

$$DA = MV \times RT$$

(The time is the length of the discount period.)

Proceeds (P) = Maturity value (MV) − Discounted amount (DA) or

$$P = MV - DA$$

Before showing the calculations for discounting a promissory note, the next example shows how to find the discount period.

EXAMPLE: The note in the previous example was written on June 27 for 90 days. It was discounted on July 25. Find the number of days in the discount period using exact time.

SOLUTION:

Step 1. Find the due date.
For June 30 − 27 = 3 days

July	31 days
August	31 days
September	?
Total	90 days

$3 + 31 + 31 = 65$ $90 - 65 = 25$
The maturity date is September 25.

Step 2. Find the number of days in the discount period. That is the number of days between July 25 and September 25.
For July 31 − 25 = 6 days

August	31 days
September	25 days
Total	62 days

Hence the length of the discount period is 62 days.

When computing the discount amount and the proceeds, the banker's rule is generally used. The next example shows how to do this.

EXAMPLE: Using the promissory note in the first example in this section, find the discount amount and the proceeds when the discount rate is 9%.

SOLUTION:
The maturity value of the note was $9270 and the length of the discount period was 62 days (see the two previous examples). Find the discount amount.

$$DA = MV \times R \times T$$
$$= \$9270 \times 0.09 \times \frac{62}{360}$$
$$= \$143.69$$

Find the proceeds.

$$P = MV - DA$$
$$= \$9270 - \$143.69$$
$$= \$9126.31$$

Hence the payee receives $9126.31, and the maker pays the third party $9720.
Promissory notes are used when money is borrowed or merchandise is bought and the buyer agrees to pay the bill sometime in the future.

PRACTICE:
Use this information for Questions 1 to 5:
A promissory note for $8000 was written on June 25 for 90 days at 10% interest. It was discounted on July 5 at 12%.

1. Find the maturity value of the note.
2. Find the maturity date of the note.
3. Find the term of the discount.
4. Find the discount amount.
5. Find the proceeds.

Use the following information for Questions 6 to 10:
A promissory note for $12,500 was written on February 9 for 120 days at 7%. It was discounted on May 15 at 11.5%.

6. Find the maturity value of the note.
7. Find the maturity date of the note.
8. Find the term of the discount.
9. Find the discount amount.
10. Find the proceeds.

Use the following information for Questions 11 to 15.

A promissory note for $3750 was made on March 9 for 180 days at 6.5%. It was discounted on August 2 at 9%.

11. Find the maturity value of the note.
12. Find the maturity date of the note.
13. Find the term of the discount.
14. Find the discount amount.
15. Find the proceeds.

SOLUTIONS:

1. $I = F \times R \times T$

$$= \$8000 \times 0.10 \times \frac{90}{360}$$

$$= \$200$$

$MV = F + I$

$$= \$8000 + \$200$$

$$= \$8200$$

2. For June $30 - 25 = 5$ days

July	31 days
August	31 days
September	?
Total	90 days

$5 + 31 + 31 = 67$ $90 - 67 = 23$

The due date is September 23.

3. For July $31 - 5 = 26$ days

August	31 days
September	23 days
Total	80 days

4. $DA = MV \times R \times T$

$$= \$8200 \times 0.12 \times \frac{80}{360}$$

$$= \$218.67$$

5. $P = MV - DA$

$= \$8200 - \$218.67$

$= \$7981.33$

6. $I = F \times R \times T$

$= \$12{,}500 \times 0.07 \times \dfrac{120}{360}$

$= \$291.67$

$MV = F + I$

$= \$12{,}500 + \$291.67$

$= \$12{,}791.67$

7.   For February $28 - 9 = 19$ days

March	31 days
April	30 days
May	31 days
June	?
Total	120 days

$19 + 31 + 30 + 31 = 111$ $120 - 111 = 9$

The maturity date is June 9.

8.   For May $31 - 15 = 16$ days

June	9 days
Total	25 days

9. $DA = MV \times R \times T$

$= \$12{,}791.67 \times 0.115 \times \dfrac{25}{360}$

$= \$102.16$

10. $P = MV - DA$

$= \$12{,}791.67 - \$102.16$

$= \$12{,}689.51$

11. $I = F \times R \times T$

$$= \$3750 \times 0.065 \times \frac{180}{360}$$

$$= \$121.88$$

$\text{MV} = F + I$

$$= \$3750 + \$121.88$$

$$= \$3871.88$$

12.   For March $31 - 9 = 22$ days

April	30 days
May	31 days
June	30 days
July	31 days
August	31 days
September	?
Total	180 days

$22 + 30 + 31 + 30 + 31 + 31 = 175$ $180 - 175 = 5$

The maturity date is September 5.

13.   For August $31 - 2 = 29$ days

September	5 days
Total	34 days

14. $\text{DA} = \text{MV} \times R \times T$

$$= \$3871.88 \times 0.09 \times \frac{34}{360}$$

$$= \$32.91$$

15. $P = \text{MV} - \text{DA}$

$$= \$3871.88 - \$32.91$$

$$= \$3838.97$$

Summary

This chapter explained simple interest and promissory notes. Interest is the amount of money a lending institution charges for the use of its money or the amount of money the institution pays you to keep your money in a savings account. To calculate simple interest, it is necessary to multiply the principal by the rate and by the time (expressed in years) for which the money is borrowed. Given any three of the variables, it is possible to find the other one by using one of the four formulas. In banking, interest can be computed using exact time (1 year = 365 days or 366 days in leap year) or ordinary time (1 year = 360 days).

A promissory note is a legal written contract specifying the amount of money a person borrows, the interest rate if there is one, and the term of the note. Promissory notes can be cashed in or sold before the maturity date if the payee needs cash before the term is up. This is called discounting.

Quiz

1. Pete borrowed $750 at $9\frac{3}{4}$% for 2 years. The interest is
   (a) $146.25
   (b) $135.00
   (c) $142.75
   (d) $139.00

2. A person borrowed $5600 at 12% and paid $2688 in interest. The time of the loan in years is
   (a) 2 years
   (b) 4.5 years
   (c) 4 years
   (d) 3.5 years

3. Mary borrowed $4750 for 6 years. If the interest was $1710, the interest rate is
   (a) 5.5%
   (b) 4%
   (c) 7.75%
   (d) 6%

4. The interest on a loan is $126 and the time is 3 years. If the rate is 7%, the principal is
   (a) $725
   (b) $600

(c) $675
(d) $550

5. $1825 was borrowed at 8%. If the interest was $1022, the number of years was
    (a) 7 years
    (b) 6.8 years
    (c) 3.5 years
    (d) 9 years

6. A loan was made on January 5 for 45 days. Using exact time, the repayment date is
    (a) February 18
    (b) February 19
    (c) February 20
    (d) February 16

7. A loan was made on May 16 for 90 days. The repayment date using ordinary time is
    (a) August 15
    (b) August 16
    (c) August 17
    (d) August 18

8. A loan was secured on April 12 for 180 days. Find the repayment date using exact time.
    (a) October 10
    (b) October 9
    (c) October 12
    (d) October 11

9. The exact number of days between November 19 and May 10 is
    (a) 172 days
    (b) 170 days
    (c) 168 days
    (d) 174 days

    Use the following information to answer Questions 10 to 14:
    On December 3, a promissory note for $5250 was written at 7.8%. The term of the note was 60 days. On January 10, the note was discounted at 12.5%.
10. The maturity value of the note is
    (a) $68.25
    (b) $5318.25

(c) $67.32
(d) $5317.32

11. The maturity date of the note is
(a) January 30
(b) January 31
(c) February 1
(d) February 3

12. The term of discount is
(a) 22 days
(b) 21 days
(c) 23 days
(d) 20 days

13. The discounted amount of the note is
(a) $40.63
(b) $39.81
(c) $42.37
(d) $41.81

14. The proceeds are
(a) $5278.21
(b) $5275.03
(c) $5277.62
(d) $5276.70

Compound Interest

Introduction

Simple interest was explained in the last chapter. This chapter explains what is known as **compound interest**. When loans are made for a short term, simple interest is usually used; however, for long-term loans, the interest is usually compounded. Simple interest is computed only on the principal whereas compound interest is computed not only on the principal but also on any previous interest accrued. Compound interest is collected on savings accounts and other investments such as certificates of deposit and so on.

Compound Interest

Interest is compounded *annually* (once a year), *semiannually* (twice a year), *quarterly* (four times a year), *monthly* (12 times a year), *daily* (365 times a year), and *continuously* (all the time). When computing compound interest, the first thing to do is find what is called the **period interest rate**.

The period interest rate is computed by dividing the yearly interest rate by the number of periods per year that the interest is compounded. The symbol r will be used for the period interest rate and the symbol n will be the number of times the interest is computed per year. Then the period interest rate is

$$\text{Period interest rate} = \frac{\text{Yearly interest rate}}{\text{Number of interest periods per year}} \text{ or } r = \frac{R}{n}$$

To find the period interest rate when interest is compounded

yearly: divide the yearly interest rate by 1;
semiannually: divide the yearly interest rate by 2;
quarterly: divide the yearly interest rate by 4;
monthly: divide the yearly interest rate by 12;
daily: divide the yearly interest rate by 365.

EXAMPLE: Find the period interest rate if the annual interest rate is 8% and the interest is compounded quarterly.

SOLUTION:
If the interest is compounded quarterly, then the number of interest payments per year is 4; hence,

$$\text{Period interest rate} = \frac{8\%}{4} = \frac{0.08}{4} = 0.02 \text{ or } 2\%$$

When the interest rate is compounded annually, the period interest rate is the same as the annual interest rate.

The next example shows the difference between simple interest and compound interest.

EXAMPLE: Find the amount of the simple interest on a $2000 investment at an annual rate of 4% for 3 years. The interest is compounded yearly.

SOLUTION:
For simple interest, use the formula $I = PRT$ when $P = \$2000$, $R = 4\%$, and $T = 3$.

$$I = PRT$$
$$= \$2000 \times 0.04 \times 3$$
$$= \$240$$

The simple interest is $240.

For compound interest, the calculations need to be done three times, one for each year.

For year 1:

$$I = PRT \ (P = \$2000, \ R = 4\%, \text{ and } T = 1)$$

$$= \$2000 \times 0.04 \times 1$$

$$= \$80$$

During the second year, the $80 interest also generates interest, and so the principal is $2000 + $80 = $2080.

For year 2:

$$I = PRT$$

$$= \$2080 \times 0.04 \times 1$$

$$= \$83.20$$

For year 3:

$$I = PRT$$

$$= \$2163.20 \times 0.04 \times 1$$

$$= \$86.53$$

Hence the total compound interest is $80 + $83.20 + $86.53 = $249.73.

When the interest is compounded yearly, you get an additional payment of $9.73. The total amount of the investment or future value is $2000 + $249.73 = $2249.73.

If interest is compounded semiannually, the same problem would require six calculations (two for each year). If interest is compounded quarterly, the problem would require 12 calculations (four for each year). Fortunately, the following formula can be used:

$$FV = P(1 + r)^N$$

where

$$FV = \text{future value}$$
$$P = \text{principal}$$
$$r = \text{period interest rate}$$
$$N = \text{number of periods per year times the number of years}$$

EXAMPLE: Find the future value and compound interest on a $2000 investment at a rate of 4% compounded yearly for 3 years.

SOLUTION:
In this case, the period interest rate is 4% since the interest is compounded yearly and $N = 1 \times 3 = 3$ or once a year for 3 years.

$$FV = P(1 + R)^N$$
$$= \$2000\,(1 + 0.04)^3$$
$$= \$2249.73$$

The amount of the compound interest can be found by subtracting the principal: $2249.73 − $2000 = $249.73. Notice that this is the same result as found in the previous example doing it the long way.

EXAMPLE: Find the future value and compound interest on a $6000 investment at 10% compounded semiannually for 6 years.

SOLUTION:
The period investment rate is $\frac{10\%}{2} = 5\%$ or 0.05. The number of periods is $2 \times 6 = 12$.

$$FV = P(1 + r)^N$$
$$= \$6000\,(1 + 0.05)^{12}$$
$$= \$10{,}775.14$$

The amount of the compound interest is $10775.14 − $6000 = $4775.14.

EXAMPLE: Find the future value and compound interest on a $500 investment at 6% compounded daily for 5 years.

SOLUTION:
The period interest rate is $\frac{6\%}{365}$. The number of periods is $365 \times 5 = 1825$.

$$FV = P(1 + R)^N$$
$$= 500\,(1 + \frac{0.06}{365})^{1825}$$
$$= \$674.91$$

The compounded interest is $674.91 − $500 = $174.91.

Calculator Tip

The following steps will help you evaluate the formula $FV = P(1 + r)^N$ using a scientific calculator:

1. Enter the value for P
2. Press ×
3. Press (
4. Enter 1
5. Press +
6. Enter the value for the period interest rate
7. Press)
8. Press the exponent key
9. Enter the value for the number of periods, N
10. Press =

Note: In this case, it is best not to round the period interest rate but to let the calculator do the division.

PRACTICE:

1. Find the future value and compound interest on an investment account of $700 compounded quarterly at 10% for 3 years.
2. Crystal Smith deposited $4000 in a savings account paying 2% interest compounded daily. Find the future value of the money and the compound interest she earned at the end of 5 years.
3. Matthew Hadley bought a CD for $3000 that pays 6% interest and is compounded semiannually. Find the future value and the interest he earned if he cashed in the CD at the end of 7 years.
4. Leva Lin has a savings account that has a principal of $3250. If she is getting an interest rate of 3% annually, find the future value and the interest earned if she keeps the money in the account for 2 years.
5. Martha Burns invested $14,200 in an account that pays 6% interest compounded monthly. Find the future value and the interest she earned on her investment if she kept it for 8 years.

SOLUTIONS:

1. $r = \dfrac{R}{n} = \dfrac{0.10}{4} = 0.025; \; N = 4 \times 3 = 12$

$$FV = P(1+r)^{12}$$
$$= \$700\,(1 + 0.025)^{12}$$
$$= \$941.42$$

The interest earned is $\$941.42 - \$700 = \$241.42$.

2. $r = \dfrac{R}{n} = \dfrac{0.02}{365}; N = 365 \times 5 = 1825$

$$FV = P(1+r)^N$$
$$= \$4000(1 + \frac{0.02}{365})^{1825}$$
$$= \$4420.67$$

The interest earned is $\$4420.67 - \$4000 = \$420.67$.

3. $r = \dfrac{R}{n} = \dfrac{0.06}{2} = 0.03; N = 2 \times 7 = 14$

$$FV = P(1+r)^N$$
$$= \$3000\,(1 + 0.03)^{14}$$
$$= \$4537.77$$

The interest earned is $\$4537.77 - \$3000 = \$1537.77$.

4. $r = \dfrac{R}{n} = \dfrac{0.03}{1} = 0.03; \ N = 1 \times 2 = 2$

$$= \$3250\,(1 + 0.03)^2$$
$$= \$3447.93$$

The interest earned is $\$3447.93 - \$3250 = \$197.93$.

5. $r = \dfrac{R}{n} = \dfrac{0.06}{12} = 0.005; \ N = 12 \times 8 = 96$

$$= \$14{,}200\,(1 + 0.005)^{96}$$
$$= \$22{,}920.83$$

The interest earned is $\$22{,}920.83 - \$14{,}200 = \$8720.83$.

Effective Rate

When the interest is compounded more than once a year, it is sometimes necessary to determine an equivalent simple interest rate. For example, suppose a person invested $800 in a savings account for 1 year at a rate of 8% compounded quarterly. The future value would be

$$FV = P(1 + r)^N$$
$$= \$800\,(1 + 0.02)^4$$
$$= \$865.95$$

The total interest is $865.95 − $800.00 = $65.95. Now the comparable simple interest rate is

$$R = \frac{I}{PT}$$
$$= \frac{\$65.95}{\$800 \times 1}$$
$$= 0.0824 \text{ (rounded) or } 8.24\%$$

In other words, if a person invested $800 in a savings account paying 8.24% simple interest for 1 year, he or she would receive $65.95 in interest, which is the same amount as the person investing $800 for 1 year at 8% compounded quarterly.

The actual interest or simple interest rate that is equivalent to a compound interest rate is called the **effective rate**. For a savings account, the effective rate is also called the **annual percentage yield (APY)**, and for a loan, this rate is also called the **annual percentage rate (APR)**.

The effective rate can be computed as shown previously; however, the following formula can also be used:

$$E = (1 + r)^n - 1$$

where

$E =$ effective rate of interest
$r =$ period interest rate $(\frac{R}{n})$
$n =$ the number of periods per year

EXAMPLE: Find the effective rate of interest that is equivalent to an 8% rate compounded quarterly.

SOLUTION:

Since the interest is compounded quarterly, $r = \dfrac{0.08}{4} = 0.02$.

$$E = (1 + r)^n - 1$$
$$= (1 + 0.02)^4 - 1$$
$$= (1.02)^4 - 1$$
$$= 1.0824 \text{ (rounded)} - 1$$
$$= 0.0824 \text{ or } 8.24\%$$

EXAMPLE: Find the effective rate of interest that is equivalent to a 5% rate compounded semiannually.

SOLUTION:

Since the interest is compounded semiannually,

$$r = \frac{R}{n} = \frac{0.05}{2} = 0.025$$
$$E = (1 + r)^n - 1$$
$$= (1 + 0.025)^2 - 1$$
$$= 0.0506 \text{ (rounded) or } 5.06\%$$

PRACTICE:

For Exercises 1 to 5, find the effective rates:

1. 6% compounded quarterly
2. 9% compounded semiannually
3. 3% compounded quarterly
4. 9% compounded monthly
5. 8% compounded daily

SOLUTIONS:

1. $r = \dfrac{R}{n} = \dfrac{0.06}{4} = 0.015$

  $E = (1 + r)^n - 1$

$$= (1 + 0.015)^4 - 1$$
$$= 0.0614 \text{ (rounded) or } 6.14\%$$

2. $r = \dfrac{R}{n} = \dfrac{0.09}{2} = 0.045$

   $E = (1 + r)^n - 1$
   $$= (1 + 0.045)^2 - 1$$
   $$= 0.092 \text{ (rounded) or } 9.2\%$$

3. $r = \dfrac{R}{n} = \dfrac{0.03}{4} = 0.0075$

   $E = (1 + r)^n - 1$
   $$= (1 + 0.0075)^4 - 1$$
   $$= 0.0303 \text{ (rounded) or } 3.03\%$$

4. $r = \dfrac{R}{n} = \dfrac{0.09}{12} = 0.0075$

   $E = (1 + r)^n - 1$
   $$= (1 + 0.0075)^{12} - 1$$
   $$= 0.0938 \text{ (rounded) or } 9.38\%$$

5. $r = \dfrac{R}{n} = \dfrac{0.08}{365}$

   $E = (1 + r)^n - 1$
   $$= (1 + \tfrac{0.08}{365})^{365} - 1$$
   $$= (1 + \tfrac{0.08}{365})^{365} - 1$$
   $$= 0.083 \text{ (rounded) or } 8.3\%$$

Present Value

Businesses have to plan for the future. Since equipment breaks down or wears out, business owners have to have the money to replace the equipment. In addition, money might be set aside for retirement benefits for their employees. Individuals also plan for the future. Some may want to set aside money now for college expenses for their children, their retirement, future vacations, or future purchases.

In order to have the finances for these endeavors, a lump sum of money can be set aside that will collect interest. This amount is called the **present value**. The formula for the present value of a sum of money is

$$PV = \frac{FV}{(1+r)^N}$$

where

        PV = present value
        FV = future value
        r = period interest rate
        N = number of periods that the amount is invested for

EXAMPLE: The owner of Dee Dee's Deli wants to set aside some money to insure that she has enough money to purchase a new delivery van in 5 years. She feels that with her trade-in, she can purchase a new van for $18,000. How much would she have to set aside today if she can get a 5% interest rate compounded quarterly?

SOLUTION:
The future value is FV = $18,000.

The period interest rate is $r = \dfrac{0.05}{4} = 0.0125$.

The number of periods is $N = 5$ years $\times 4$ periods $= 20$.
Then

$$PV = \frac{FV}{(1+r)^N}$$
$$= \frac{\$18,000}{(1+0.0125)^{20}}$$
$$= \$14,040.15$$

Hence in order to have $18,000 in 5 years, she must invest $14,040.15 now at a 5% interest rate compounded quarterly.

The answer can be verified by using the formula for future value. Using $14,040.15 as the principal and substituting in the formula with $r = 0.0125$ and $N = 20$, one gets

$$FV = P(1 + R)^N$$
$$= \$14{,}040.15\,(1 + 0.0125)^{20}$$
$$= \$18{,}000$$

EXAMPLE: The owner of Tee-Time Golf Course plans to add another nine holes to the existing course in 10 years. He estimates that the cost of construction will be $30,000. How much money must he set aside now at 4% interest compounded semiannually in order to have $30,000 in 10 years?

SOLUTION:

$$FV = \$30{,}000$$
$$r = \frac{0.04}{2} = 0.02$$
$$N = 10 \text{ years} \times 2 = 20$$
$$PV = \frac{FV}{(1 + r)^N}$$
$$= \frac{\$30{,}000}{(1 + 0.02)^{20}}$$
$$= \$20{,}189.14$$

Hence $20,189.14 must be invested now at 4% interest compounded semiannually in order to have $30,000 in 10 years.

PRACTICE:

1. Twin Valley Lumber Company's owner feels that he will need a new roof over his lumber bins in about 8 years. He estimates the cost at $4000. How much money must be invested now at 3% compounded semiannually in order to have $4000 in 8 years?
2. The owner of Holt Pharmacy plans to remodel her store in 3 years. She estimates that she will need $15,000 for the project. How much should she set aside at 4% interest compounded quarterly to have $15,000 in 3 years?

3. Monica Boris is planning a vacation in 2 years. She will need $3000 for her trip. How much must she invest now at 2% interest compounded quarterly in order to have $3000 in 2 years?

4. In 5 years, Larry McCoy plans to purchase a boat for about $11,000. How much should be set aside at 10% interest compounded yearly in order to have $11,000 in 5 years?

5. Michael Young wants to set aside some money for his daughter's college education. He estimates that in 15 years, his 3-year-old daughter's college costs will be about $60,000. He can obtain an interest rate of 6.5% compounded semiannually. How much money should he invest now?

SOLUTIONS:

1. $FV = \$4000$

$$r = \frac{0.03}{2} = 0.015$$

$$N = 8 \times 2 = 16$$

$$PV = \frac{FV}{(1+r)^N}$$

$$= \frac{\$4000}{(1+0.015)^{16}}$$

$$= \$3152.12$$

2. $FV = \$15,000$

$$r = \frac{0.04}{4} = 0.01$$

$$N = 3 \times 4 = 12$$

$$PV = \frac{FV}{(1+r)^N}$$

$$= \frac{\$15,000}{(1+0.01)^{12}}$$

$$= \$13,311.74$$

3. $FV = \$3000$

$$r = \frac{0.02}{4} = 0.005$$

$$N = 2 \times 4 = 8$$

$$PV = \frac{FV}{(1+r)^N}$$

$$= \frac{\$3000}{(1+0.005)^8}$$

$$= \$2882.66$$

4. $FV = \$11,000$

$$r = \frac{0.10}{1} = 0.10$$

$$N = 5 \times 1 = 5$$

$$PV = \frac{FV}{(1+r)^N}$$

$$= \frac{\$11,000}{(1+0.10)^5}$$

$$= \$6830.13$$

5. $FV = \$60,000$

$$r = \frac{0.065}{2} = 0.0325$$

$$N = 15 \times 2 = 30$$

$$PV = \frac{FV}{(1+r)^N}$$

$$= \frac{\$60,000}{(1+0.0325)^{30}}$$

$$= \$22,985.26$$

Summary

When interest is compounded only on the principal, it is called simple interest. When interest is compounded on the principal and previously accumulated interest, it is called compound interest. Compound interest can be computed annually, semiannually, quarterly, monthly, and daily. The effective rate of interest is the simple interest rate that is equivalent to a compound interest rate.

When a sum of money is set aside to earn interest for a future amount of money, this sum is called the present value of the money.

Quiz

1. The future value of $1540 invested at 9% compounded semiannually for 6 years is
    (a) $2611.66
    (b) $2371.60
    (c) $2005.48
    (d) $2582.73

2. The future value of $8500 invested at 12% compounded quarterly for 10 years is
    (a) $18,700
    (b) $95,200
    (c) $26,399.71
    (d) $27,727.32

3. The future value of $300 invested at 7% compounded daily for 3 years is
    (a) $363.00
    (b) $367.51
    (c) $370.10
    (d) $653.21

4. The future value of $1400 invested at 4% compounded yearly for 9 years is
    (a) $1992.64
    (b) $1904.00
    (c) $1900.00
    (d) $1985.03

5. The effective rate equivalent to 6% compounded quarterly is
    (a) 6.32%
    (b) 6.02%
    (c) 6.14%
    (d) 6.48%

6. The effective rate equivalent to 10% compounded semiannually is
    (a) 10.34%
    (b) 10.25%

    (c) 10.15%

    (d) 10.30%

7. The effective rate equivalent to 12% compounded yearly is

    (a) 12.65%

    (b) 11.87%

    (c) 12.13%

    (d) 12%

8. The present value of $22,000 invested at 8% compounded semiannually for 10 years is

    (a) $1019.03

    (b) $1486.24

    (c) $9963.59

    (d) $10,040.51

9. The present value of $800 invested at 3% compounded annually for 15 years is

    (a) $656.28

    (b) $513.49

    (c) $524.37

    (d) $519.62

10. The present value of $975 compounded quarterly at 2% for 3 years is

    (a) $918.76

    (b) $768.78

    (c) $918.36

    (d) $814.25

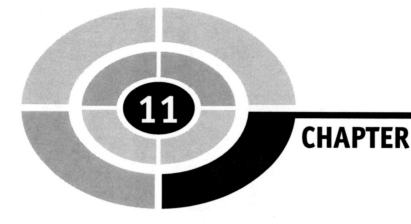

CHAPTER 11

Annuities and Sinking Funds

Introduction

The last two chapters explained how a single lump sum can be borrowed or saved, and how simple or compound interest is accrued. This chapter explains two concepts, *annuities* and *sinking fund payments*. Here the payment of a specific amount of money is made annually, semiannually, quarterly, and sometimes monthly and compound interest is accrued. These types of investments are called **annuities**. A **sinking fund payment** is the payment amount that needs to be made in an ordinary annuity in order to achieve a certain amount of money in the future.

Annuities

There are two types of annuities: an *ordinary annuity* and an *annuity due*. For an **ordinary annuity**, the payment is made at the end of the period. When the payment is made at the beginning of the period, it is called an **annuity due**. Consider the following example:

EXAMPLE: A person purchases an ordinary annuity with a payment of $800 annually and the interest rate of 6%. Find the future value at the end of 3 years.

SOLUTION:
At the end of year 1, a payment of $800 is made. The value of the annuity then is $800. At the end of year 2, the $800 has earned 6% interest. The interest is

$$I = PRT$$
$$= \$800 \times 0.06 \times 1$$
$$= \$48$$

Also a second payment of $800 is made. The value of the annuity then is $800 + $48 + $800 = $1648. At the end of year 3, the $1648 has earned 6% interest. The interest is

$$I = PRT$$
$$= \$1648 \times 0.06 \times 1$$
$$= \$98.88$$

Also another $800 payment is made. The value of the annuity at the end of year 3 is $1648 + $98.88 + $800 = $2546.88.

Now if a person purchased a 5-year annuity and made quarterly payments which earned interest, 5 × 4 or 20 computations would have to be made to find its value at the end of 5 years. Fortunately there is a formula that can be used for ordinary annuities. It is

$$FV = PM \left((1 + r)^N - 1 \right) \div r$$

where

$PM =$ payment amount
$r =$ period interest rate
$N =$ number of years times the number of payments made per year

Using the formula to solve the problem given in the previous example, $PM = \$800$, $r = 1 \times 0.06 = 0.06$, and $N = 3 \times 1 = 3$; hence

$$FV = PM\left((1+r)^{N} - 1\right) \div r$$
$$= \$800\left((1+0.06)^{3} - 1\right) \div 0.06$$
$$= \$2546.88$$

Notice that this is the same answer calculated in the previous example.

Calculator Tip

The following steps will help you evaluate the formula $FV = PM\left((1+r)^{N} - 1\right) \div r$:

1. Enter the value for the payment
2. Press $\times$
3. Press (
4. Press (
5. Press 1
6. Press $+$
7. Enter the value for r
8. Press)
9. Press the exponent key
10. Enter the value for N
11. Press $-$
12. Press 1
13. Press)
14. Press $\div$
15. Enter the value for r
16. Press $=$

EXAMPLE: Tai Yun purchased an ordinary annuity that paid 8% interest quarterly. The payment amount was $50. Find the future value of the annuity in 6 years.

SOLUTION:

$$PM = \$50$$

$$r = \frac{0.08}{4} = 0.02$$

$$N = 6\,\text{years} \times 4\,\text{payments per year} = 24$$

then

$$FV = PM\,((1 + r)^N - 1) \div r$$

$$= \$50\,((1 + 0.02)^{24} - 1) \div 0.02$$

$$= \$1521.09$$

Note: You may think that this is a large sum but remember that Tai is putting $50 into the annuity four times a year. This amounts to $50 × 4 = $200. Now $200 × 6 years = $1200. So the interest earned is $1521.09 − $1200 = $321.09.

The second type of annuity is called an **annuity due**. Recall that in this type of annuity, the payments are made at the beginning of the period. You can see the difference by comparing the next example with the first example in this chapter.

EXAMPLE: A person purchases an annuity due with a payment of $800 annually and an interest rate of 6%. Find the value of the annuity after 3 years.

SOLUTION:
Since the $800 is paid at the beginning of the year, it collects 6% during the year.

$$I = PRT$$

$$= \$800 \times 0.06 \times 1$$

$$= \$48$$

So its value at the beginning of year 2 is $800 + $48 + $800 = $1648. The second $800 was deposited at the beginning of year 2. Now at the end of year 2, the $1648 earns 6% interest.

$$I = PRT$$

$$= \$1648 \times 0.06 \times 1$$

$$= \$98.88$$

At the beginning of year 3, another $800 is deposited so the total is $1648 + $98.88 + $800 = $2546.88. This sum earns 6% interest during year 3.

$$I = PRT$$
$$= \$2546.88 \times 0.06 \times 1$$
$$= \$152.81$$

At the end of year 3, the annuity is worth $2546.88 + $152.81 = $2699.69.

After 3 years, the annuity due is worth $2699.69, while the ordinary annuity is worth $2546.88, a difference of $152.81. The reason is that when payments are made at the beginning of the period, they collect interest for that entire period and furthermore, the interest is then compounded over the remaining periods.

Like the ordinary annuity, there is a formula to find the value of the annuity due. It is

$$FV = PM\left((1+r)^N - 1\right) \div r \times (1+r)$$

EXAMPLE: Use the formula to find the value of the annuity due in the previous example.

SOLUTION:

$$PM = \$800, r = 0.06, N = 3$$
$$FV = PM\left((1+r)^N - 1\right) \div r \times (1+r)$$
$$= \$800\left((1+0.06)^3 - 1\right) \div 0.06 \times (1+0.06)$$
$$= \$2699.69$$

PRACTICE:

1. Fred Carr purchases an ordinary annuity paying 8% quarterly for 6 years. Find the future value of the annuity if the payment is $75.
2. Evelyn Anthony wants to save some money for a vacation in 4 years. She decides to purchase an ordinary annuity paying 5% semiannually. If her payment is $200, find the future value of the annuity in 4 years.
3. Nick Lazar wants to save some money for his daughter's first year of college. If he purchases an ordinary annuity paying 3% yearly and makes a payment of $3000 for 5 years, how much will he save?
4. Jim Linn purchases an annuity due paying 10% quarterly. If his payment is $125, how much will its value be in 2 years?

5. Rosetta Schaffer purchases an annuity due paying 5% semiannually. If her payment is $675, how much will she have saved in 4 years?

Calculator Tip

The following steps will help you calculate the formula $FV = PM ((1 + r)^N - 1) \div r \times (1 + r)$:

1. Enter the value for the payment
2. Press $\times$
3. Press (
4. Press (
5. Press 1
6. Press +
7. Enter the value for r
8. Press)
9. Press the exponent key
10. Enter the value for N
11. Press $-$
12. Press 1
13. Press)
14. Press $\div$
15. Enter the value for r
16. Press $=$
17. Press $\times$
18. Press (
19. Press 1
20. Press +
21. Enter the value for r
22. Press)
23. Press $=$

SOLUTIONS:

1. $PM = \$75; r = \dfrac{0.08}{4} = 0.02; N = 6 \times 4 = 24$

$FV = PM ((1 + r)^N - 1) \div r$

$= \$75 ((1 + 0.02)^{24} - 1) \div 0.02$

$= \$2281.64$

2. $\text{PM} = \$200; r = \dfrac{0.05}{2} = 0.025; N = 4 \times 2 = 8$

$$\begin{aligned} \text{FV} &= \text{PM} \left((1+r)^N - 1 \right) \div r \\ &= \$200 \left((1 + 0.025)^8 - 1 \right) \div 0.025 \\ &= \$1747.22 \end{aligned}$$

3. $\text{PM} = \$3000; r = 0.03; N = 5$

$$\begin{aligned} \text{FV} &= \text{PM} \left((1+r)^N - 1 \right) \div 0.03 \\ &= \$3000 \left((1 + 0.03)^5 - 1 \right) \div 0.03 \\ &= \$15{,}927.41 \end{aligned}$$

4. $\text{PM} = \$125; r = \dfrac{0.10}{4} = 0.025; N = 2 \times 4 = 8$

$$\begin{aligned} \text{FV} &= \text{PM} \left((1+r)^N - 1 \right) \div r \times (1+r) \\ &= \$125 \left((1 + 0.025)^8 - 1 \right) \div 0.025 \times (1 + 0.025) \\ &= \$1119.31 \end{aligned}$$

5. $\text{PM} = \$675; r = \dfrac{0.05}{2} = 0.025; N = 4 \times 2 = 8$

$$\begin{aligned} \text{FV} &= \text{PM} \left((1+r)^N - 1 \right) \div r \times (1+r) \\ &= \$675 \left((1 + 0.025)^8 - 1 \right) \div 0.025 \times (1 + 0.025) \\ &= \$6044.30 \end{aligned}$$

Sinking Funds

If a person wants to purchase an ordinary annuity to guarantee a certain sum of money in the future, that person can determine the amount of the payment by using what is called a **sinking fund payment**. The formula is $\text{PM} = \text{FV} \times r \div ((1+r)^N - 1)$
where

$$\begin{aligned} \text{PM} &= \text{payment} \\ \text{FV} &= \text{future value} \\ r &= \text{period interest rate} \\ N &= \text{the number of periods} \end{aligned}$$

EXAMPLE: The manager of a landscaping service decides that he will need $1800 in 5 years to purchase a new lawn tractor. If he purchases an ordinary annuity that pays 4% semiannually, find the payment.

SOLUTION:

In this case, FV = $1800; $r = \dfrac{0.04}{2} = 0.02$; $N = 5$ years $\times 2 = 10$ periods.

$$
\begin{aligned}
PM &= FV \times r \div ((1 + r)^N - 1) \\
&= \$1800 \times 0.02 \div ((1 + 0.02)^{10} - 1) \\
&= \$164.39
\end{aligned}
$$

In this case, he must pay $164.39 twice a year to get $1800 in 5 years. This can be verified by substituting $164.39 in the formula for an ordinary annuity and seeing if the result is about $1800 for the future value.

EXAMPLE: Country Farms Dairy needs to purchase a new machine to cap the milk bottles in 10 years. The estimated cost is about $9000. Find the sinking fund payment if the dairy can get 6% interest quarterly.

SOLUTION:

$$
FV = \$9000; r = \dfrac{0.06}{4} = 0.015; N = 10 \times 4 = 40
$$

$$
\begin{aligned}
PM &= FV \times r \div ((1 + r)^N - 1) \\
&= \$9000 \times 0.015 \div ((1 + 0.015)^{40} - 1) \\
&= \$165.84
\end{aligned}
$$

PRACTICE:

1. The owner of Vicki's Transmission Service needs to set aside $6000 to purchase new tools in 3 years. Find the sinking fund payment if she can purchase an ordinary annuity that pays 4% quarterly.
2. The manager of the Royal Greeting Card Company decides that he will need two new printers in 5 years. He estimates that the total cost of both printers will be about $12,000 and wants to purchase an ordinary annuity paying 2% quarterly. Find the payment.

Calculator Tip

The following steps will help you evaluate the formula PM = FV $\times$ r $\div$ $((1 + r)^N - 1)$:

1. Enter the future value
2. Press $\times$
3. Enter the value for r
4. Press $\div$
5. Press (
6. Press (
7. Press 1
8. Press +
9. Enter the value for r
10. Press)
11. Press the exponent key
12. Enter the value for N
13. Press $-$
14. Press 1
15. Press)
16. Press =

3. The owner of Clear Window Cleaning wants to purchase an ordinary annuity paying 6% semiannually to buy new ladders in 4 years. He estimates the cost to be $1300. Find the sinking fund payment.

4. Jeannette, owner of Jeanette's Health Club, wants to purchase an ordinary annuity to buy a new pec-deck machine in 3 years. The cost of the machine is $900. Find the sinking fund payment if the annuity pays 10% annually.

5. Leva Linn wants to remodel his game room in 2 years. He estimates the cost to be $10,000. Find the sinking fund payment if he can purchase an ordinary annuity that is paying 5% quarterly.

SOLUTIONS:

1. FV = $6000; $r = \dfrac{0.04}{4} = 0.01$; $N = 3 \times 4 = 12$

$$PM = FV \times r \div ((1 + r)^N - 1)$$

$$= \$6000 \times 0.01 \div ((1 + 0.01)^{12} - 1)$$

$$= \$473.09$$

2. $FV = \$12,000; r = \dfrac{0.02}{4} = 0.005; N = 5 \times 4 = 20$

$PM = FV \times r \div ((1 + r)^N - 1)$

$\quad = \$12,000 \times 0.005 \div ((1 + 0.005)^{20} - 1)$

$\quad = \$572.00$

3. $FV = \$1300; r = \dfrac{0.06}{2} = 0.03; N = 4 \times 2 = 8$

$PM = FV \times r \div ((1 + r)^N - 1)$

$\quad = \$1300 \times 0.03 \div ((1 + 0.03)^8 - 1)$

$\quad = \$146.19$

4. $FV = \$900; r = 0.10; N = 3 \times 1 = 3$

$PM = FV \times r \div ((1 + r)^N - 1)$

$\quad = \$900 \times 0.10 \div ((1 + 0.10)^3 - 1)$

$\quad = \$271.90$

5. $FV = \$10,000; r = \dfrac{0.05}{4} = 0.0125; N = 2 \times 4 = 8$

$PM = FV \times r \div ((1 + r)^N - 1)$

$\quad = \$10,000 \times 0.0125 \div ((1 + 0.0125)^8 - 1)$

$\quad = \$1196.33$

Summary

In addition to savings accounts, certificates of deposits, etc., another way to save money is to purchase an annuity. Here payments of a certain amount are made annually, semiannually, quarterly, or monthly. The money collects compound interest at a certain rate for the life of the annuity. There are two basic types of annuities. They are the ordinary annuity and the annuity due. With the ordinary annuity, the payments are made at the end of the period. With the annuity due, the payments are made at the beginning of the period.

If a person knows in advance or can estimate how much money he or she will need in the future, he or she can purchase an ordinary annuity and determine by a sinking fund payment how much will be required to achieve that amount in the future.

Quiz

1. The payment for an ordinary annuity is $375. The interest rate is 6% semiannually. The future value of the annuity in 4 years is
   (a) $3215.62
   (b) $3478.86
   (c) $3327.11
   (d) $3334.63

2. An ordinary annuity pays 9% quarterly. The payment is $250. The future value of the annuity in 3 years is
   (a) $3217.62
   (b) $3400.56
   (c) $3506.16
   (d) $3437.21

3. The payment for an ordinary annuity is $780. If the interest rate is 3% semiannually, the future value in 5 years will be
   (a) $8348.12
   (b) $8526.07
   (c) $8419.35
   (d) $8286.28

4. The payment on an annuity due is $425. If the interest rate is 12% quarterly, the value of the annuity in 2 years will be
   (a) $4009.40
   (b) $4472.18
   (c) $3892.62
   (d) $3779.24

5. An annuity due is paying 7% annually. If the payment is $700, the value in 7 years will be
   (a) $6317.21
   (b) $6523.76
   (c) $6481.86
   (d) $6443.11

6. An annuity due is paying 8% semiannually. If the payment is $1120, the value of the annuity in 2 years will be
   (a) $4713.72
   (b) $4841.45

(c) $4946.28
(d) $4997.14

7. A person wishes to save $5000 for a vacation in 3 years. If she can purchase an ordinary annuity paying 10% semiannually, the sinking fund payment would be
    (a) $733.91
    (b) $735.09
    (c) $762.15
    (d) $771.22

8. How much sinking fund payment is necessary in order to save $800 if an ordinary annuity paying 5% quarterly for 2 years is purchased?
    (a) $95.71
    (b) $99.43
    (c) $94.26
    (d) $92.57

9. A manager will need $22,000 in 10 years to replace a delivery van. If he can purchase an ordinary annuity paying 9% annually, the sinking fund payment should be
    (a) $1432.56
    (b) $1448.04
    (c) $1426.10
    (d) $1414.43

10. How much more money would a person earn if he purchased an annuity due as opposed to an ordinary annuity paying 6% semiannually, and if a payment of $200 was made every 6 months for 4 years?
    (a) $52.70
    (b) $48.26
    (c) $55.42
    (d) $53.35

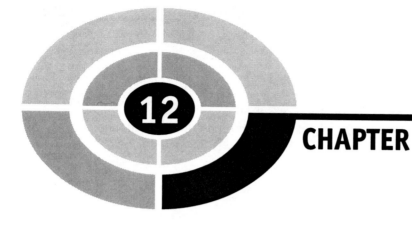

Consumer Credit

CHAPTER 12

Introduction

Many times individuals and businesses make purchases and do not pay the full amount of the costs. Instead they usually make a down payment and then pay off the balance in equal monthly payments for a specific number of months. When this occurs, the person or business is securing what is called an **installment loan**. In other words, the person or business is buying on **credit**.

Today credit cards make it very easy to buy services and merchandise on credit. The buyer must be aware that many installment loans charge interest or a finance charge, and all credit cards charge interest.

Installment Loans

The price of the merchandise that a person is buying is called the **cash price**. If the person pays part of the cash price at the time of purchase, this amount is called a **down payment**. The balance is usually paid off in equal monthly installments and is called the **amount financed**. Installment loans may also include finance charges, interest, and other types of fees. Many businesses set up their own repayment plans so the buyer does not have to secure a loan from a bank or other lending institution. The Truth-In-Lending Law requires all interest, finance charges, and fees be reported to the borrower.

In order to find the total cost of a purchase that is bought using an installment loan, multiply the payment amount by the number of payments and add the down payment.

EXAMPLE: Mary purchased a refrigerator costing $470. She made a 20% down payment and paid $39 a month for 10 months. Find the total amount that she paid for the refrigerator.

SOLUTION:

Step 1. Find the down payment amount.

$$\text{Down payment} = 0.20 \times \$470 = \$94$$

Step 2. Next, find the total amount of the monthly payment.

$$\text{Total of monthly payments} = 10 \times \$39 = \$390$$

Step 3. Add the two values.

$$\$94 + \$390 = \$484$$

In the previous example, Mary paid $484 for a refrigerator that cost $470, so the extra charge or finance charge was $484 − $470 = $14.

The amount of the monthly payment can also be found. The procedure is shown in the next example.

EXAMPLE: Phil Martin purchased a large screen television set for $1560. He made a 15% down payment and paid the balance over 18 months. The store charged 8% interest on the amount financed. Find the monthly payment.

SOLUTION:

Step 1. Find the amount financed.

$$\text{Down payment} = 0.15 \times \$1560$$
$$= \$234$$

$$\text{Amount financed} = \$1560 - \$234$$
$$= \$1326$$

Step 2. Find the interest.
In this case, the interest rate is 8% and 18 months is 1.5 years.

$$I = PRT$$
$$= \$1326 \times 0.08 \times 1.5$$
$$= \$159.12$$

Step 3. Add the amount financed and the interest and divide the sum by 18 months.

$$\text{Monthly payments} = \frac{\$1326 + \$159.12}{18}$$
$$= \frac{\$1485.12}{18}$$
$$= \$82.51 (\text{rounded})$$

Hence the monthly payment is $82.51.

PRACTICE:

1. Barbara Johnson purchased a mattress and box spring set for $500. She made a down payment of 15% and financed the rest for 12 months with payments of $37. Find the total amount she paid for the set.
2. Bob Beam purchased a treadmill costing $800. He made a 10% down payment and financed the rest. His monthly payments were $49.50 for 15 months. Find the total amount he paid for the treadmill.
3. Megan Howard purchased a water softener for $400. She made a down payment of $50 and paid the balance in nine monthly payments. If the store charged 10% interest on the loan, find the monthly payment.
4. Hang Yo bought a washer and dryer for $700. He made a 25% down payment and financed the balance over 12 months. If the interest was 8%, find the monthly payment.
5. Margie bought a room air conditioner for $380. She made a down payment of $30 and obtained an installment loan for 6 months. If the finance charge was $10, find the monthly payment.

SOLUTIONS:

1. Down payment $= 0.15 \times \$500 = \$75$

    Installment payments $= 12 \times \$37 = \$444$

    Total amount paid $= \$444 + \$75 = \$519$

2. Down payment $= 0.10 \times \$800 = \$80$

    Installment payments $= 15 \times \$49.50 = \$742.50$

    Total amount paid $= \$742.50 + \$80 = \$822.50$

3. Amount financed $= \$400 - \$50 = \$350$

    $$I = PRT$$
    $$= \$350 \times 0.10 \times \frac{9}{12}$$
    $$= \$26.25$$
    $$\text{Monthly payment} = \frac{\$350 + \$26.25}{9}$$
    $$= \frac{\$376.25}{9}$$
    $$= \$41.81$$

4. Down payment $= 0.25 \times \$700 = \$175$

    Amount financed $= \$700 - \$175 = \$525$

    $$I = PRT$$
    $$= \$525 \times 0.08 \times 1$$
    $$= \$42$$
    $$\text{Monthly payment} = \frac{\$525 + \$42}{12}$$
    $$= \frac{\$567}{12}$$
    $$= \$47.25$$

5.   Amount borrowed $= \$380 - \$30 + \$10 = \$360$

Monthly payment $= \dfrac{\$360}{6} = \$60$

Annual Percentage Rate

Suppose a person borrowed $1000 for 1 year and the person paid 8% interest on the money. The person would have to pay $\$1000 \times 0.08 = \$80$ in interest. At the end of the year, the person would have to pay $1000 + \$80 or $1080. However, most lending institutions require that the loan be paid back in equal monthly installments of $\$1080 \div 12 = \$90$. When this happens, the person does not have the use of the $1000 for the entire year because each month the principal decreases. Because of this, the interest on the $1000 is actually higher than the stated 8%.

In 1969, the federal government passed the Truth-In-Lending Act requiring lending institutions to tell the borrower the true percent of interest. This true percent is called the *annual percentage rate* or *APR*. It is similar to the effective rate explained in Chapter 10.

In order to find the APR, a table is issued by the federal government and can be used by lending institutions. This table is quite lengthy and so a mathematical formula can be used to find the *approximate APR*. If payments are made monthly, the formula is

$$\text{APR} = \frac{24 \times \text{Total interest}}{\text{Principal} \times (1 + \text{Total number of payments})}$$

or

$$\text{APR} = \frac{24I}{P(T+1)}$$

where

$I =$ total interest

$P =$ principal

$T =$ total number of payments

EXAMPLE: If a person borrowed $8000 for 2 years and paid 8% per year, find the APR for the loan if monthly payments were made.

SOLUTION:
First find the total amount of interest.

$$I = PRT$$
$$= \$8000 \times 0.08 \times 2$$
$$= \$1280$$

Next find the APR. In this case, $I = \$1280$, $P = \$8000$, and $T = 12$ monthly payments $\times 2$ years $= 24$.

$$\text{APR} = \frac{24 \times \$1280}{\$8000 \times (1 + 24)}$$
$$= 0.1536 \text{ or } 15.36\%$$

Remember that this value is only an approximation of the APR.

EXAMPLE: Bob Malone borrowed $2000 for 18 months at $6\frac{1}{2}\%$ per year. Find the APR if the loan was repaid monthly.

SOLUTION:

$$18 \text{ months} = 1.5 \text{ years}$$
$$I = PRT$$
$$= \$2000 \times 0.065 \times 1.5 = \$195$$
$$I = \$195; P = \$2000; N = 18$$
$$\text{APR} = \frac{24 \times \$195}{\$2000 \times (1 + 18)}$$
$$= 0.1232 \text{ (rounded) or } 12.32\%$$

PRACTICE:

1. Mary Bixby borrowed $3000 at 6% for 2 years. Find the APR on the installment loan.
2. Tom Thomas borrowed $4750 at 5% for 18 months. Find the APR on the installment loan.
3. Rudy Johns borrowed $6200 at 12% for 3 years. Find the APR on the installment loan.

Calculator Tip

The following steps will help you evaluate the previous formula:
1. Enter 24
2. Press ×
3. Enter the value for I
4. Press ÷
5. Press (
6. Enter the value for P
7. Press ×
8. Enter (
9. Enter 1
10. Press +
11. Enter the value for T
12. Press)
13. Press)
14. Press =

4. If the amount financed for 2 years on an installment loan was $1875 and the interest was $206.25, find the APR.
5. Brooke Davis purchased a stove for $525. She had no down payment but made 15 monthly payments of $37 each. Find the APR on the installment loan.

SOLUTIONS:

1. $I = PRT$

$$= \$3000 \times 0.06 \times 2 = \$360$$

$$P = \$3000; T = 24 \text{ months (2 years)}$$

$$\text{APR} = \frac{24 \times I}{P(1 + T)}$$

$$= \frac{24 \times \$360}{\$3000 \times (1 + 24)}$$

$$= 0.1152$$

$$= 11.52\%$$

2. $I = PRT$

$\quad = \$4750 \times 0.05 \times \dfrac{18}{12}$

$\quad = \$356.25$

$P = \$4750; T = 18$

$\mathrm{APR} = \dfrac{24 \times \$356.25}{\$4750 \times (1 + 18)}$

$\quad = 0.0947 \,(\text{rounded})$

$\quad = 9.47\%$

3. $I = PRT$

$\quad = \$6200 \times 0.12 \times 3$

$\quad = \$2232$

$P = \$6200; T = 36$

$\mathrm{APR} = \dfrac{24 \times I}{P(1 + T)}$

$\quad = \dfrac{24 \times \$2232}{\$6200\,(1 + 36)}$

$\quad = 0.2335 \,(\text{rounded}) = 23.35\%$

4. $I = \$206.25; P = \$1875; T = 24$

$\mathrm{APR} = \dfrac{24 \times \$206.25}{\$1875\,(1 + 24)}$

$\quad = 0.1056 = 10.56\%$

5. Total amount paid $= 15 \times \$37 = \$555$

$I = \$555 - \$525 = \$30$

$P = \$525, T = 15$

$\mathrm{APR} = \dfrac{24 \times \$30}{\$525 \times (1 + 15)}$

$\quad = 0.0857 \,(\text{rounded}) = 8.57\%$

Rule of 78s

Some installment loans can be paid off early. When this occurs, the borrower can save money on the interest. For example, if a 1-year installment loan is paid off in 6 months, you may think that you should pay only one-half of the interest since you are using the money for half of the term. However, in many institutions this is not what happens since lending institutions use what is called the **rule of 78s** to compute the interest owed when a loan is paid off early.

The rule of 78s requires that the larger amounts of the interest be paid with the earlier payments. Remember though that payments are the same amount each month. The rule of 78s for a 12-month loan requires that

$\frac{12}{78}$ of the interest be paid the first month,

$\frac{11}{78}$ of the interest be paid the second month,

$\frac{10}{78}$ of the interest be paid the third month,

$\frac{9}{78}$ of the interest be paid the fourth month

$\vdots$

$\frac{1}{78}$ of the interest be paid the last (twelfth) month.

(When you add $\frac{12}{78} + \frac{11}{78} + \frac{10}{78} + \cdots + \frac{2}{78} + \frac{1}{78}$, you get 1.)

When loans are secured for longer or shorter periods of time, the rule of 78s is adjusted accordingly as shown in the examples.

The formula that is used to find the refund when a loan is paid off early is Refund = total of interest × refund factor; the refund factor is found by:

$$\text{Refund factor} = \frac{\text{sum of numbers of months remaining}}{\text{sum of numbers for months of loan}}$$

EXAMPLE: An installment loan for 12 months was paid off at the end of the seventh month. Find the refund factor.

SOLUTION:
Since the loan is paid off at the end of the seventh month, there are five months remaining (i.e., $12 - 7 = 5$), so the numerator of the refund factor is $1 + 2 + 3 + 4 + 5 = 15$. The denominator is the sum of the numbers for the entire loan, i.e., 12 months; hence it is $1 + 2 + 3 + 4 + 5 + 6 + 7 + 8 + 9 + 10 + 11 + 12 = 78$. The refund factor then is $\frac{15}{78}$.

EXAMPLE: An installment loan for 10 months is paid off at the end of the third month. Find the refund factor.

SOLUTION:
The duration of the loan is 10 months, so the sum of the digits for the *denominator* is $1 + 2 + 3 = 4 + 5 + 6 + 7 + 8 + 9 + 10 = 55$. Since the loan was paid off at the end of the third month, there are $10 - 3 = 7$ months remaining; hence, the sum of the numbers of the *numerator* is $1 + 2 + 3 + 4 + 5 + 6 + 7 = 28$. The refund factor is $\frac{28}{55}$.

   Rather than adding a sequence of consecutive numbers starting from 1 to n, a mathematical shortcut can be used. It is

$$\text{Sum} = \frac{n(n + 1)}{2}$$

For example, if you want to add the consecutive numbers from 1 to 30, $n = 30$, and so the sum is

$$\frac{30(30 + 1)}{2} = \frac{30(31)}{2} = \frac{930}{2} = 465$$

EXAMPLE: Add the consecutive numbers from 1 to 100 using the shortcut formula.

SOLUTION:
$n = 100$, so the sum is $\dfrac{100(100 + 1)}{2} = \dfrac{100(101)}{2}$

$$= \frac{10{,}100}{2} = 5050.$$

   Now that you know how to find the sum of the consecutive numbers, you can find the interest refund on an installment loan when it is paid off early.

EXAMPLE: Mike Schmidt purchased a lawn tractor for $900. He made a down payment of $100 and financed the rest at 7% for 24 months. He paid off the loan at the end of the fifteenth month. Find the amount of his refund using the rule of 78s.

SOLUTION:

   Step 1. Find the amount of the loan.

$$\$900 - \$100 = \$800$$

Step 2. Find the interest.

$$I = PRT$$

$$= \$800 \times 0.07 \times 2 = \$112$$

Step 3. Find the refund factor.

Since he paid off the loan at the end of the fifteenth month, the number of remaining months is $24 - 15 = 9$. Hence,

$$\text{Refund factor} = \frac{1 + 2 + 3 + \cdots + 8 + 9}{1 + 2 + 3 + \cdots + 23 + 24} = \frac{45}{300}$$

Step 4. Find the refund.
Refund = total interest × refund factor

$$\$112 \times \frac{45}{300} = \$16.80$$

Hence the refund was $16.80.

EXAMPLE: Hazel Harkness purchased a digital camera for $400. She made a down payment of $50 and paid off the rest over 15 months at 6% interest. If she paid off the loan at the end of 9 months, find her refund using the rule of 78s.

SOLUTION:

Step 1. Find the amount of the loan.

$$\$400 - \$50 = \$350$$

Step 2. Find the interest.

$$I = PRT$$

$$= \$350 \times 0.06 \times \frac{15}{12}$$

$$= \$26.25$$

Step 3. Find the refund factor.
$15 - 9 = 6$ months remaining

$$\text{Refund factor} = \frac{1+2+3+4+5+6}{1+2+3\cdots+14+15} = \frac{21}{120}$$

Step 4. Find the refund.

$$\text{Refund} = \text{total interest} \times \text{refund factor}$$

$$= \$26.25 \times \frac{21}{120} = \$4.59$$

Hence the refund is $4.59.

PRACTICE:

1. Pamela Andrews purchased a living room set for $3600. She made a down payment of $400 and financed the rest for 3 years at 4% interest. At the end of 2 years (24 months) she paid off the balance of her loan. Find the amount of the refund using the rule of 78s.
2. Dirk Wilson bought a set of automobile tires for $370. He made a down payment of $50 and financed the rest for 1 year at 10% interest. If he paid off the loan at the end of the ninth month, find his refund using the rule of 78s.
3. Sally French bought an air conditioning unit for $1800. She made a down payment of $600 and financed the rest for 18 months at $6\frac{1}{2}$%. At the end of 11 months she paid off the balance. Find her refund using the rule of 78s.
4. Bill Paxton bought an outdoor gas grill for $435. He made a down payment of $50 and paid off the balance over 9 months at 3% interest. At the end of 6 months, he paid off the balance. Find his refund using the rule of 78s.
5. Wendy Bass purchased an electric water heater for $370. She made a down payment of $60 and financed the rest for 6 months at 10% interest. If she paid off the balance of the loan at the end of the third month, find her refund using the rule of 78s.

SOLUTIONS:

1. Amount financed: $3600 - $400 = $3200

    Interest: $I = PRT$

    $$= \$3200 \times 0.04 \times 3 = \$384$$

Months remaining: $36 - 24 = 12$

Refund factor: $\dfrac{1 + 2 + 3 + \cdots + 12}{1 + 2 + 3 + \cdots + 36} = \dfrac{78}{666}$

Refund amount: $\$384 \times \dfrac{78}{666} = \$44.97$

2. Amount financed: $\$370 - \$50 = \$320$

Interest: $I = PRT$

$$= \$320 \times 0.10 \times 1 = \$32$$

Months remaining: $12 - 9 = 3$

Refund factor: $\dfrac{1 + 2 + 3}{1 + 2 + 3 + \cdots + 12} = \dfrac{6}{78}$

Refund amount: $\$32 \times \dfrac{6}{78} = \$2.46$

3. Amount financed: $\$1800 - \$600 = \$1200$

Interest: $I = PRT$

$$= \$1200 \times 0.065 \times \dfrac{18}{12} = \$117$$

Months remaining: $18 - 11 = 7$

Refund factor: $\dfrac{1 + 2 + 3 + \cdots + 7}{1 + 2 + 3 + \cdots + 18} = \dfrac{28}{171}$

Refund amount: $\$117 \times \dfrac{28}{171} = \$19.16$

4. Amount financed: $\$435 - \$50 = \$385$

Interest: $I = PRT$

$$= \$385 \times 0.03 \times \dfrac{9}{12} = \$8.66$$

Months remaining: $9 - 6 = 3$

Refund factor: $\dfrac{1 + 2 + 3}{1 + 2 + 3 + \cdots + 9} = \dfrac{6}{45}$

Refund amount: $\$8.66 \times \dfrac{6}{45} = \$1.15$

5.   Amount financed: $370 − $60 = $310

Interest: $I = PRT$

$$= \$310 \times 0.10 \times \frac{6}{12} = \$15.50$$

Months remaining: $6 - 3 = 3$

Refund factor: $\dfrac{1 + 2 + 3}{1 + 2 + 3 + 4 + 5 + 6} = \dfrac{6}{21}$

Refund amount: $\$15.50 \times \dfrac{6}{21} = \$4.43$

Credit Cards

Many credit purchases are made using credit cards. Credit cards have a **credit limit**, which is the maximum amount of money that the customer can charge on the account. Interest is usually charged monthly and it is around 18% per year or about 1.5% per month. The interest varies with the brand and the type of card.

   There are two types of credit cards. On the first type of card, the interest is charged on the *unpaid balance*. On the second type of card, the interest is computed on the *average daily balance*. The next example explains the interest on the unpaid balance method.

EXAMPLE: The previous balance on Mike's credit card on May 1 was $280.60. During the month of May he made purchases of $673.29 and he made a payment of $200. The interest rate on his credit card is 1.8% per month. Find the amount of the unpaid balance on June 1.

SOLUTION:

   Step 1. Find the interest on the previous balance.

$$I = \$280.60 \times 0.018 = \$5.05$$

(In this case, the interest rate is calculated per month and so the time is 1 month.)

   Step 2. Add the amount of the previous balance and the amount of the purchases and the interest and subtract the amount of the payment.

$$\$280.60 + \$673.29 + \$5.05 - \$200 = \$758.94$$

The new balance is $758.94.

With this type of credit card, if you pay off the entire balance each month, you will pay no interest and you can use the credit card company's money for free.

The second type of credit card charges interest based on the *average daily balance*. To calculate the **average daily balance**, the sum of the balances for each day is determined, and then this sum is divided by the number of days in the month or billing cycle to get the average daily balance. The next example shows how the interest is computed using this method.

EXAMPLE: Maryanne's transactions on her credit card are shown for the month of July. Find the average daily balance, the interest for the month, and the new balance at the beginning of August. The interest rate is 1.8% per month on the average daily balance.

July 1	Balance	$360.25
July 8	Tom's Auto Service	$673.87
July 12	Apple Market	$32.50
July 20	Payment	$200.00
July 27	Miller Office Supply	$73.87

SOLUTION:

Step 1. Find the number of days for each unpaid balance.
    The balance of $360.25 lasted from July 1 to July 8 or $8 - 1 = 7$ days. Then a purchase of $673.87 was made on July 8, so the new balance was $360.25 + $673.87 = $1034.12, and that lasted from July 8 to July 12 or $12 - 8 = 4$ days. On July 12 a purchase of $32.50 was made, making the new balance $1034.12 + $32.50 = $1066.62. This balance ran from July 12 to July 20 or $20 - 12 = 8$ days. On July 20, a $200 payment was made, so the new balance was $1066.62 - $200.00 = $866.62. (When payments are made, the amount is subtracted from the balance.) This balance went from July 20 to July 27 or $27 - 20 = 7$ days. Finally a purchase of $73.87 was made on July 27, bringing the balance to $866.62 + $73.87 = $940.49, which ran from July 27 through the end of the day on July 31. The number of days is $31 - 27 = 4 + 1 = 5$ days. One day needs to be added since the month ends on July 31 at midnight. That is, July 27, 28, 29, 30, and 31, or 5 days.

The results can be summarized in table form as shown.

Date	Balance	Days
July 1	$360.25 (balance)	7
July 8	$1034.12	4
July 12	$1066.62	8
July 20	$866.62	7
July 27	$940.49	5
Total		31

Step 2. Multiply the unpaid balance by the number of days and find the sum of these products.

$$\$360.25 \times 7 = \$2521.75$$
$$\$1034.12 \times 4 = \$4136.48$$
$$\$1066.62 \times 8 = \$8532.96$$
$$\$866.62 \times 7 = \$6066.34$$
$$\$940.49 \times 5 = \underline{\$4702.45}$$
$$\text{Sum} = \$25,959.98$$

Step 3. Divide the sum by the number of days in the period to get the daily average balance.

$$\text{Daily average balance} = \frac{\$25,959.98}{31} = \$837.42$$

Step 4. Multiply the daily average balance by the interest rate to get the interest.

$$\text{Interest} = \$837.42 \times 0.018 = \$15.07$$

Step 5. Find the new balance by adding the balance on the last day and the interest.

$$\text{New balance} = \$940.49 + \$15.07 = \$955.56$$

PRACTICE:

1. Find the interest and the new balance for the month of November for the following transactions on a credit card that charges 1.5% monthly interest on the unpaid balance.

> Previous balance $1562.06
> Purchases $745.11
> Payments $550.00

2. Find the interest and the new balance for the month of March for the following transactions on a credit card that charges 1.2% monthly interest on the unpaid balance.

> Previous balance $3265.11
> Purchases $1016.23
> Payments $800.00

3. Find the average daily balance, the interest, and the new balance on the following transactions made using a credit card. The interest rate is 1.4% monthly on the average daily balance.

> April 1   Balance $632.81
> April 11   Betty's Transmission Service $1056.32
> April 19   Diamond Jewelry $235.16
> April 22   Payment $300.00
> April 25   The Mailbox Shop $73.20

4. Find the average daily balance, the interest, and the new balance on the following transactions made using a credit card that has a 1.5% monthly interest on the average daily balance.

> June 1   Balance $202.16
> June 8   Clair's Cleaning Service $32.50
> June 16   Payment $100.00
> June 20   Lewis Landscaping $42.50

5. Find the average daily balance, the interest, and the new balance on the following transactions made on a credit card that has a 2% monthly interest rate on the average daily balance.

February 1	Balance	$732.60
February 10	Meyers Hardware	$380.16
February 16	Payment	$350.00
February 22	Knight's Investigations	$250.00

SOLUTIONS:

1. $I = PRT$

    $= \$1562.06 \times 0.015 \times 1$

    $= \$23.43$

    New balance = Previous balance + Purchases + Interest − Payment

    $= \$1562.06 + \$745.11 + \$23.43 - \$550.00$

    $= \$1780.60$

2. $I = PRT$

    $= \$3265.11 \times 0.012 \times 1$

    $= \$39.18$

    New balance $= \$3265.11 + 1016.23 + \$39.18 - \$800.00$

    $= \$3520.52$

3.

Date	Balance	Days
April 1	$632.81	10
April 11	$1689.13	8
April 19	$1924.29	3
April 22	$1624.29	3
April 25	$1697.49	6
Total		30

$632.81 \times 10 = \$6328.10$

$1689.13 \times 8 = \$13,513.04$

$1924.29 \times 3 = \$5772.87$

$1624.29 \times 3 = \$4872.87$

$1697.49 \times 6 = \underline{\$10,184.94}$

Total $= \$40,671.82$

Average daily balance $= \dfrac{\$40,671.82}{30} = \$1355.73$

Interest $= \$1355.73 \times 0.014 = \$18.98$

New balance $= \$1697.49 + \$18.98 = \$1716.47$

4.

Date	Balance	Days
June 1	$202.16	7
June 8	$234.66	8
June 16	$134.66	4
June 20	$177.16	11
Total		30

$202.16 \times 7 = \$1415.12$

$234.66 \times 8 = \$1877.28$

$134.66 \times 4 = \$538.64$

$177.16 \times 11 = \underline{\$1948.76}$

Total $= \$5779.80$

Average daily balance $= \dfrac{\$5779.80}{30} = \$192.66$

Interest $= \$192.66 \times 0.015 = \$2.89$

New balance $= \$177.16 + \$2.89 = \$180.05$

5.

Date	Balance	Days
February 1	$732.60	9
February 10	$1112.76	6
February 16	$762.76	6
February 22	$1012.76	7
Total		28

$732.60 \times 9 = \$6593.40$

$1112.76 \times 6 = \$6676.56$

$762.76 \times 6 = \$4576.56$

$1012.76 \times 7 = \underline{\$7089.32}$

Total $= \$24,935.84$

Average daily balance $= \dfrac{\$24,935.84}{28} = \$890.57$

Interest $= \$890.57 \times 0.02 = \$17.81$

New balance $= \$1012.76 + \$17.81 = \$1030.57$

Summary

When the buyer does not pay the full amount of the purchase price for an item but instead makes a down payment and pays off the balance in monthly installments, he or she is said to be buying on credit. Some businesses offer the buyer an installment loan while others allow the buyer to use a credit card.

The interest on a credit card is charged either on the unpaid balance or on the average daily balance. When a loan is paid off early, the buyer in most cases is entitled to a refund on the interest. Sometimes the refund is computed by the rule of 78s.

Quiz

1. Sam purchased a television set for $50 down and 12 payments of $36 each. The total purchase price of the television set is
    (a) $432
    (b) $382
    (c) $636
    (d) $482

2. Ruby bought a 10-speed bicycle costing $430. She made a down payment of $50 and paid the balance off in 6 monthly installments of $70 each. The finance charge for the loan is
    (a) $470
    (b) $40
    (c) $10
    (d) $420

3. If a person borrowed $3000 for 1 year and paid 5% interest, the monthly payment in 12 equal payments is
    (a) $250.00
    (b) $150.00
    (c) $262.50
    (d) $242.50

4. Ronald borrowed $7500 for 18 months and paid $6\frac{1}{2}$% interest. The annual percentage rate based on 18 equal monthly payments is
    (a) 16.25%
    (b) 12.47%
    (c) 8.55%
    (d) 12.32%

5. The total interest for a 6-month installment loan is $80. If the loan is paid off at the end of 3 months, the interest refund using the rule of 78s will be
    (a) $22.86
    (b) $14.22
    (c) $16.03
    (d) $5.61

6. Wendel borrowed $4000 at 6% interest for 2 years. If he paid off the loan after 20 months, his interest refund using the rule of 78s is
    (a) $80
    (b) $24

(c) $16

(d) $52

7. Bill Hygens made purchases of $347.82 on his credit card in November. His previous balance was $533.85, and he made a payment of $85.00 during the month. If he is charged 1.6% monthly interest on the unpaid balance, his interest will be

(a) $12.75

(b) $4.21

(c) $6.32

(d) $8.54

8. Using the information in Exercise 9, the balance on Bill's credit card at the end of the month is

(a) $796.67

(b) $805.21

(c) $882.67

(d) $743.29

Use the following information for Exercises 9 to 11:

Mary Morgenstern's transactions on her credit card for April were

April 1	Balance	$1256.03
April 10	All Pro Golf Shop	$163.47
April 14	Payment	$800.00
April 22	Heritage Art Center	$435.77

She is charged 1.5% monthly interest on the average daily balance.

9. The average daily balance for the month of April on Mary's charge card is

(a) $943.62

(b) $1093.71

(c) $972.88

(d) $1047.86

10. The interest on Mary's charge card for the month of April is

(a) $13.23

(b) $15.72

(c) $16.21

(d) $14.77

11. The new balance on Mary's charge card at the beginning of May is

(a) $1055.27

(b) $1070.99

(c) $435.77

(d) $862.39

Mortgages

Introduction

In order to purchase a home, many people need to obtain a loan. A loan that is used to pay for a home or building is called a **mortgage**. The value of the home or building less the amount that is owed on the mortgage is called **collateral**. If the buyer does not make regular payments on the mortgage, the lending institution can repossess the home and sell it to get its money back.

There are several types of mortgages available. The most common one is called a **fixed-rate mortgage**. With the fixed-rate mortgage, the interest rate remains the same for the term of the mortgage. Another type of mortgage is called an **adjustable-rate mortgage**. In this case, the interest rate varies with the economy and prime lending rate of the banks. A third type of mortgage is called the **graduated payment mortgage**. Here the homebuyer makes smaller payments at the beginning of the term and larger payments at the end of the term. The reason a homebuyer may choose this option is that the income of the homebuyer may be expected to rise as the person remains in the work force.

Fixed-Rate Mortgage

As stated previously, the most common type of mortgage is the fixed-rate mortgage. With this type of mortgage, the interest rate remains the same for the term of the mortgage. The term could be any number of years; however, the most common terms are 5, 10, 15, 20, 25, and 30 years. Payments are usually made monthly. A lending institution usually requires a down payment on a home before it gives the buyer a mortgage.

EXAMPLE: If a home is sold for $89,000 and the bank requires a 20% down payment, find the amount to be financed.

SOLUTION:

$$
\begin{aligned}
\text{Down payment} &= 20\% \times \$89{,}000 \\
&= 0.20 \times \$89{,}000 \\
&= \$17{,}800
\end{aligned}
$$

The down payment is $17,800, and the amount to be financed is $89,000 − $17,800 = $71,200.

Alternate solution:

Since the down payment is 20%, 100% − 20% or 80% of the purchase price needs to be financed; hence,

$$
\begin{aligned}
\text{Amount to be financed} &= 80\% \times \$89{,}000 \\
&= 0.80 \times \$89{,}000 \\
&= \$71{,}200
\end{aligned}
$$

Sometimes a lending institution may charge **points** to secure a loan. One point is 1% of the amount borrowed and is a one-time payment to the lending institution.

EXAMPLE: In order to obtain a mortgage for $125,000, the buyer must pay 2 points. Find the amount paid to the lending institution.

SOLUTION:
2 points means 2%

$$
\begin{aligned}
2\% \times \$125{,}000 &= 0.02 \times \$125{,}000 \\
&= \$2500
\end{aligned}
$$

Hence, in order to obtain the loan, the homebuyer must pay the lending institution $2500 for the mortgage.

The interest rates for first mortgages are usually between 5 and 10%. Over a long period of time, the amount of interest paid is considerable. Sometimes it can be double or triple the amount that one borrows. The next example shows how to find the total interest that is paid over a long-term mortgage.

EXAMPLE: A person borrowed $150,000 at 7% for the purchase of a home. If his monthly payment is $997.50 on a 30-year mortgage, find the total amount of interest he will pay over the 30-year period.

SOLUTION:
First, find the total amount that will be paid back over 30 years at 12 monthly payments.

$$\text{Total amount} = \$997.50 \times 12 \text{ months} \times 30 \text{ years}$$
$$= \$359,100$$

Second, subtract this amount from the amount borrowed.

$$\text{Total interest} = \$359,100 - \$150,000$$
$$= \$209,100 \text{ The total amount in interest paid is } \$209,100.$$

The next section will show you how to find the monthly payment amount.

PRACTICE:

1.   If a home is purchased for $115,000 and the bank requires a 15% down payment, how much money will the buyer need to borrow?
2.   A home is purchased for $265,000. The bank requires a 10% down payment. How much money will the buyer need to borrow?
3.   If a building is purchased for $435,000 and the buyer puts 18% down payment, what is the amount of the down payment?
4.   On the sale of a $60,000 home, the buyer is required to pay 3 points. How much will the buyer pay?
5.   A buyer purchased a home for $239,000. She was required to pay 2 points. How much did she pay?
6.   A home sold for $182,000. The bank required a 20% down payment and charged 2 points to obtain a mortgage. How much did the buyer have to pay before she could get a mortgage?
7.   A person obtained a $300,000 mortgage. If his monthly payment is $2604, find the total amount of interest he paid over the 20 years.
8.   Mary Young obtained a 15-year mortgage for $170,000. If her monthly payment is $1827.50, find the total amount of interest she would pay over the 15 years.

9. A warehouse was purchased for storage. The buyer was required to borrow $625,000. The monthly payment was $5462.50 for a 25-year mortgage. Find the total amount of interest the buyer paid over the 25 years.

10. Harry Miller obtained a 30-year mortgage for $95,000. If his monthly payment is $941.45, find the total amount of interest he paid over the 30 years.

SOLUTION:

1. Down payment $= 0.15 \times \$115,000$
$= \$17,250$
Amount borrowed $= \$115,000 - \$17,250$
$= \$97,750$
Alternate solution:
Amount borrowed $= 0.85 \times \$115,000$
$= \$97,750$

2. Down payment $= 0.10 \times \$265,000$
$= \$26,500$
Amount borrowed $= \$265,000 - \$26,500$
$= \$238,500$
Alternate solution:
Amount borrowed $= 0.90 \times \$265,000$
$= \$238,500$

3. Down payment $= 0.18 \times \$435,000$
$= \$78,300$

4. Amount $= 3\% \times \$60,000$
$= 0.03 \times \$60,000$
$= \$1800$

5. Amount $= 2\% \times \$239,000$
$= 0.02 \times \$239,000$
$= \$4780$

6. Down payment $= 20\% \times \$182,000$
$= 0.20 \times \$182,000$
$= \$36,400$
Amount of mortgage $= \$182,000 - \$36,400$
$= \$145,600$
2 points $= 2\%$
Point amount $= 0.02 \times \$145,600$
$= \$2912.00$
Total amount $= \$36,400 + \$2912$
$= \$39,312$

7.   Total amount paid $= \$2604 \times 12 \, \text{months} \times 20 \, \text{years}$
$$= \$624,960$$
$$\text{Interest} = \$624,960 - \$300,000$$
$$= \$324,960$$

8.   Total amount paid $= \$1827.50 \times 12 \, \text{months} \times 15 \, \text{years}$
$$= \$328,950$$
$$\text{Interest} = \$328,950 - \$170,000$$
$$= \$158,950$$

9.   Total amount paid $= \$5462.50 \times 12 \, \text{months} \times 25 \, \text{years}$
$$= \$1,638,750$$
$$\text{Interest} = \$1,638,750 - \$625,000$$
$$= \$1,013,750$$

10.   Total amount $= \$941.45 \times 12 \, \text{months} \times 30 \, \text{years}$
$$= \$338,922$$
$$= \$338,922 - \$95,000$$
$$= \$243,922$$

Finding Monthly Payments

Monthly payments for a mortgage can be computed by using a table of values or a formula. Tables are available for various interest rates and terms. A condensed version of a mortgage table is shown:

Table 13-1   Interest factor for mortgage.

Years	Annual interest			
	7%	8%	9%	10%
10	11.61	12.14	12.67	13.22
20	7.75	8.37	9.00	9.66
30	6.65	7.34	8.05	8.78

In order to use the table, divide the amount of the mortgage by 1000 and multiply by the value found in the table for the appropriate interest rate and the term of the mortgage. In other words,

$$\text{Monthly payment} = \frac{\text{Amount of mortgage}}{\$1000} \times \text{Table value}$$

EXAMPLE: Find the monthly payment on a $60,000 mortgage at 8% for 20 years.

SOLUTION:
Look up the value for 20 years at 8% in Table 13-1. It is 8.37. Substitute in the formula:

$$\text{Monthly payment} = \frac{\text{Amount of mortgage}}{\$1000} \times \text{Table value}$$

$$= \frac{\$60,000}{\$1000} \times 8.37$$

$$= \$502.20$$

The monthly payment is $502.20.

EXAMPLE: Find the monthly payment on a $179,000 mortgage at 10% interest for 30 years.

SOLUTION:
The table value for 30 years at 10% interest is 8.67. Substitute in the formula:

$$\text{Monthly payment} = \frac{\text{Amount of mortgage}}{\$1000} \times \text{Table value}$$

$$= \frac{\$179,000}{\$1000} \times 8.78$$

$$= \$1571.62$$

The monthly payment is $1571.62.

The values in the table are limited, but a formula can be used to find the monthly payment for any interest rate and any given term.

$$MP = \frac{P(R/n)}{1 - (1 + R/n)^{-nT}}$$

where
   P = amount of mortgage or principal
   R = interest rate per year
   n = number of payments per year (usually 12)
   T = term in years of mortgage

EXAMPLE: Find the monthly payment on a $179,000 mortgage at 10% for 30 years.

SOLUTION:
In this case, $P = \$179{,}000$, $R = 10\%$, $n = 12$, and $T = 30$.

$$\text{Monthly payment} = \frac{\$179{,}000\left(\dfrac{0.10}{12}\right)}{1 - \left(1 + \dfrac{0.10}{12}\right)^{-12 \times 30}}$$

$$= \frac{\$179{,}000(0.008333)}{1 - (1.008333)^{-360}}$$

$$= \frac{1491.607}{0.94958}$$

$$= \$1570.81$$

Note that this value is close to the value $1571.62 found by using the table. The reason for the difference is that the formula gives more precise values than those values in the tables if you carry the answer to more decimal places. If you let the calculator do all the calculations without rounding, you get $1570.85. The dilemma is which is the correct answer? Actually what happens is that the lending company will round off the answer to the nearest dollar (in this case $1571) and then compute the interest for each month. Finally, when the last payment is made, the lending company will adjust the payment to correct any rounding errors.

PRACTICE:

1. Harry Week obtained a mortgage for $150,000 at 10% for 20 years. Find the monthly payment using Table 13-1.
2. Barbara Shue obtained a mortgage for $235,000 at 7% for 10 years. Using Table 13-1, find her monthly payment.
3. The Johnson family obtained a $70,000 mortgage at $8\frac{1}{2}\%$ for 15 years. Using the formula, find the monthly payment.
4. Sharon Kerr obtained a $132,000 mortgage at 6% for 25 years. Using the formula, find the monthly payment.
5. Joseph Barron purchased a home for $190,000. He made a down payment for 20% and obtained a mortgage for the balance. Find his monthly payment using the formula if the mortgage was $6\frac{3}{4}\%$ for 18 years.

Calculator Tip

In order to evaluate the formula $MP = \dfrac{P(R/n)}{1-(1+R/n)^{-nT}}$ use the following steps:

1. Enter the value for P
2. Press $\times$
3. Enter the value for R
4. Press $\div$
5. Enter the value for n (usually 12)
6. Press $=$
7. Press $\div$
8. Press (
9. Enter 1
10. Press $-$
11. Press (
12. Enter 1
13. Press $+$
14. Enter the value for R
15. Press $\div$
16. Enter the value for n
17. Press)
18. Press the exponent key
19. Press (
20. Enter the value for n
21. Press $\times$
22. Enter the value for T
23. Press $+/-$ (*Note*: On some calculators, you must make the exponent negative before entering the values; i.e., -12.)
24. Press)
25. Press $=$

SOLUTIONS:

1. The table value for 20 years at 10% is 9.66.

$$\text{Monthly payment} = \frac{\text{Amount of mortgage}}{\$1000} \times \text{Table value}$$

$$= \frac{\$150{,}000}{\$1000} \times 9.66$$
$$= \$1449$$

The monthly payment is $1449.

2. The table value for 10 years at 7% is 11.61.

$$\text{Monthly payment} = \frac{\text{Amount of mortgage}}{\$1000} \times \text{Table value}$$
$$= \frac{\$235{,}000}{\$1000} \times 11.61$$
$$= \$2{,}728.35$$

3. $P = \$70{,}000; \ R = 8\frac{1}{2}\%; \ n = 12; \ T = 15$

$$\text{Monthly payment} = \frac{\$70{,}000 \left(\dfrac{0.085}{12}\right)}{1 - \left(1 + \dfrac{0.085}{12}\right)^{-12 \times 15}}$$
$$= \$689.32$$

4. $P = \$132{,}000; \ r = 6\%; \ n = 12; \ T = 25$

$$\text{Monthly payment} = \frac{\$132{,}000 \times \left(\dfrac{0.06}{12}\right)}{1 - \left(1 + \dfrac{0.06}{12}\right)^{-12 \times 25}}$$
$$= \$850.48$$

5. $P = \$190{,}000 \times 0.80 = \$152{,}000; \ r = 6\frac{3}{4}\%; \ n = 12; \ T = 18$

$$\text{Monthly payment} = \frac{\$152{,}000 \times \left(\dfrac{0.0675}{12}\right)}{1 - \left(1 + \dfrac{0.0675}{12}\right)^{-12 \times 18}}$$
$$= \$1217.47$$

Amortization Schedule

A mortgage repaid with equal payments is called **amortization**. Part of the payment is paid on the amount of the mortgage, called the principal, and part of the payment is interest. Lending institutions keep a record of these amounts by using an amortization schedule. An amortization schedule looks like this:

Month	Interest	Amount paid on principal	Balance of principal
1			
2			
3			
.			
.			

The next example shows the steps for making an amortization schedule.

EXAMPLE: A person purchased a home with an $80,000 mortgage at 8% for 20 years. Make an amortization table for the first 3 months.

SOLUTION:

Step 1. Find the monthly payment. From Table 13-1, the value for 20 years at 8% is 8.37. The monthly payment is

$$\text{Monthly payment} = \frac{\$80,000}{\$1000} \times 8.37$$
$$= \$669.60$$

2. Find the interest for the first month: $P = \$80,000; R = 8\%; T = 1$ month $= \frac{1}{12}$.

$$I = PRT$$
$$= \$80,000 \times 0.08 \times \frac{1}{12}$$
$$= \$533.33$$

Place this value in the column labeled "Interest."
3. Find the amount paid on the principal. To find this amount, subtract the interest from the payment amount.

$$\$669.60 - \$533.33 = \$136.27$$

Place this value in the column labeled "Amount paid on the principal."

4. Find the balance of the principal. To find this value, subtract the amount obtained in Step 3 from the previous balance.

$$\$80,000 - \$136.27 = \$79,863.73$$

Place this value in the column labeled "Balance on principal."
For month 2, use $79,863.73 as the new principal. Repeat Steps 2 to 4, as shown:
  Find the interest.

$$I = PRT$$
$$= \$79,863.73 \times 0.08 \times \frac{1}{12}$$
$$= \$532.42$$

Find the amount paid on the principal.

$$\$669.60 - \$532.42 = \$137.18$$

Find the balance on principal.

$$\$79,863.73 - \$137.18 = \$79,726.55$$

Place the values in columns 2, 3, and 4, respectively.
For month 3, use $79,726.55 as the new principal and complete Steps 2 to 4.
Find the interest.

$$I = PRT$$
$$= \$79,726.55 \times 0.08 \times \frac{1}{12}$$
$$= \$531.51$$

Find the amount paid on the principal.

$$\$669.60 - \$531.51 = \$138.09$$

Find the balance of the principal.

$$\$79,726.55 - \$138.09 = \$79,588.46$$

Place these values in columns 2, 3, and 4 respectively.

The completed table is shown here:

Month	Interest	Amount paid on principal	Balance of principal
1	$533.33	$136.27	$79,863.73
2	$532.42	$137.18	$79,726.55
3	$531.51	$138.09	$79,588.46

Note that in the beginning of a mortgage, most of the payment is interest. As the loan is repaid, the amount of the interest goes down and the amount of the principal goes up.

PRACTICE:

Use the following information for Exercises 1—to 5.

Sandra Burns purchased a home for $142,000. She made a 20% down payment and obtained a 9% mortgage for 30 years.

1. Find the amount of the mortgage.
2. Find the monthly payment (use Table 13-1).
3. Find the amortization for month 1.
4. Find the amortization for month 2.
5. Find the amortization for month 3.

SOLUTIONS:

1. The amount of the mortgage (or principal) is

$$0.80 \times \$142,000 = \$113,600$$

2. The value from Table 13-1 for 30 years at 9% is 8.05.

$$\text{Monthly payment} = \frac{\text{Amount of mortgage}}{\$1000} \times \text{Table value}$$

$$= \frac{\$113,600}{\$1000} \times 8.05$$

$$= \$914.48$$

3. For month 1:

$$I = PRT$$

$$= \$113{,}600 \times 0.09 \times \frac{1}{12}$$

$$= \$852$$

Amount paid on the principal $= \$914.48 - \$852 = \$62.48$
Balance after the first payment $= \$113{,}600 - \$62.48 = \$113{,}537.52$
4. For month 2:

$$I = PRT$$

$$= \$113{,}537.52 \times 0.09 \times \frac{1}{12}$$

$$= \$851.53$$

Amount paid on the principal $= \$914.48 - \$851.53 = \$62.95$
Balance after the second payment $= \$113{,}537.52 - \$62.95 = \$113{,}474.57$
5. For month 3:

$$I = PRT$$

$$= \$113{,}474.57 \times 0.09 \times \frac{1}{12}$$

$$= \$851.06$$

Amount paid on principal $= \$914.48 - \$851.06 = \$63.42$
Balance after third payment $= \$113{,}474.57 - \$63.42 = \$113{,}411.15$

Summary

When people purchase homes, buildings, or property, they usually need to borrow money. This type of loan is called a mortgage. There are several types of mortgages available. The type of mortgage explained in this chapter is called a fixed-rate mortgage. The interest rate does not change over the period of the mortgage. This type of mortgage is usually paid off in equal monthly installments over a period of 5, 10, 15, 20, 25, 30, or 40 years. Part of the payment is for the interest and the rest is used to pay off the balance of the mortgage.

Many times a down payment is required and lending institutions usually charge their customers points to obtain a mortgage. One point is 1% of the principal of the mortgage.

In order to keep a record of the payments, lending institutions use an amortization schedule. This schedule is a record of the interest, amount paid on the mortgage principal, and the balance of the mortgage. These can be used for income tax purposes and other situations.

Quiz

1. A home is purchased for $182,500. If the down payment is 20% of the purchase price, the amount of the down payment is
    (a) $144,000
    (b) $146,000
    (c) $36,500
    (d) $145,600

2. If a building is purchased for $540,000 and a 15% down payment is required, what is the amount of the mortgage the owner must obtain?
    (a) $81,000
    (b) $459,000
    (c) $75,000
    (d) $425,000

3. In order to obtain a $75,000 mortgage, the buyer had to pay 3 points. The total amount of the points is
    (a) $2250
    (b) $7275
    (c) $22,500
    (d) $72,750

4. Carrie Hamilton obtained a $60,000 mortgage for 20 years. If her monthly payment is $540, the amount of interest she will pay over the 20 years will be
    (a) $6480
    (b) $129,600
    (c) $108,000
    (d) $69,600

5. The monthly payment for a $48,000 mortgage at 10% for 30 years found by using Table 13-1 is
    (a) $421.44
    (b) $356.87
    (c) $521.63
    (d) $606.22

6. The monthly payment found by using the formula for a $236,000 mortgage at $6\frac{1}{2}$% for 25 years is
   (a) $1584.66
   (d) $1621.34
   (c) $1593.49
   (d) $1611.03

7. The monthly payment found by using the formula for a $93,000 mortgage at 11% for 15 years is
   (a) $977.23
   (b) $1057.04
   (c) $1106.89
   (d) $1062.35

   Use the following information for Questions 8 to 10.
   Tom Walsh obtained a $58,000 mortgage at 9% for 20 years. His monthly payment is $485.46.

8. How much interest did he pay the first month?
   (a) $464.00
   (b) $435.00
   (c) $342.33
   (d) $451.16

9. How much did he pay on the principal the first month?
   (a) $87.66
   (b) $21.46
   (c) $143.13
   (d) $50.46

10. What was his balance after the first month?
    (a) $57,856.87
    (b) $57,978.54
    (c) $57,949.54
    (d) $57,912.34

14

Insurance

Introduction

Most individuals today carry some kind of insurance such as life insurance, medical insurance, automobile insurance, homeowners insurance, etc. Businesses also need to carry insurance to protect them against losses.

This chapter explains some of the basic concepts of automobile insurance, fire insurance, and life insurance. When purchasing insurance, there are many options to consider and it is not possible to cover them all in one chapter, and so only the fundamentals are presented here.

Fire Insurance

Fire insurance protects the owner of a building against damage from a fire. It can also include coverage for damage from smoke and the water needed to put out the fire. The premiums are based on the amount of coverage, the location of the property, the contents of the building, the type of structure (wood, brick, etc.), and the location of the fire hydrants.

Insurance rates are based on an annual amount per $100 in coverage. The amount due is called a **premium**. The annual premium is found by using the following formula:

$$\text{Annual premium} = \frac{\text{Insured value}}{100} \times \text{Rate}$$

EXAMPLE: A homeowner insured his house for $80,000. If the rate is $0.74 per $100, find his annual premium.

SOLUTION:

$$\text{Annual premium} = \frac{\text{Insured value}}{100} \times \text{Rate}$$

$$= \frac{\$80,000}{100} \times 0.74$$

$$= \$592$$

Hence the annual premium is $592.

There is a principle called the **indemnity principle** that states a person cannot collect more money from fire damage than the actual value of the loss. This means that in the event of a fire, the property owner cannot make money from the disaster. The owner can only collect on the actual cost of the replacement. In this case, it does not benefit the person to have more insurance than his or her property is worth.

Another principle that is usually in a fire insurance policy is the **coinsurance principle**. The coinsurance principle states that the insurance company has to pay only a portion of the loss in relationship to the full amount of the loss if the insured carries less than the full amount of insurance for the value of the property. Most companies use the **80% clause**. This means that a property must be insured for at least 80% of its full value.

There are two reasons for insuring property for less than its actual value. The main reason is to save money on the insurance premium. The second reason is that in many cases of fire, the damage is only to part of the structure, and it will usually not result in a total loss.

When using the coinsurance principle, the compensation for the loss is computed using the following formula:

$$\text{Amount received} = \frac{\text{Amount carried}}{\text{Amount required}} \times \text{Loss}$$

EXAMPLE: A person owns a building worth $200,000. He insures it for $150,000. If the loss from a fire is $20,000, how much money would he receive?

SOLUTION:
First find 80% of $200,000.

$$0.80 \times \$200,000 = \$160,000$$

Since this amount is greater than $150,000, the coinsurance principle is used to find the compensation.

$$\text{Amount received} = \frac{\text{Amount carried}}{\text{Amount required}} \times \text{Loss}$$

$$= \frac{\$150,000}{\$160,000} \times \$20,000$$

$$= \$18,750$$

Hence the property owner would receive $18,750.

You may be inclined to think that a property owner would only need to carry insurance of 80% of the value of the property. However, the owner would receive 100% compensation for all damages up to 80% of the property value. If the loss was greater than 80%, the owner would not get anything above 80%. For example, if a building worth $200,000 was insured for 80% of its worth or $160,000, and the fire damage was $180,000, the owner would only receive $160,000.

Another thing to be aware of is that you should not over insure property. For example, if you insure a $200,000 building for $250,000 and then incur a $40,000 loss, you cannot use the formula:

$$\frac{\$250,000}{\$180,000} \times \$40,000 = \$55,555.55$$

and make a profit on your loss. According to the indemnity principle, you would get $40,000.

Another situation that can occur is when a policy is cancelled before its expiration date. In this case, the insured person is due a refund. The amount of the refund can be computed by finding the number of days left on the policy, dividing that number by 365, and multiplying the result by the amount of the premium. In other words,

$$\text{Amount of refund} = \frac{\text{Number of days left}}{365} \times \text{Premium}$$

EXAMPLE: A fire insurance policy on a building was purchased on March 6. The premium was $800. If the building was sold on November 10, find the amount of the refund.

SOLUTION:

Step 1. Find the number of days from November 10 to March 6. Use the method shown in Chapter 9 for exact time.

Number of days in November 30 − 10 = 20	
December	31
January	31
February	28
March	6
Total	116

The total number of days from November 10 to March 6 is 116.

Step 2. Substitute in the formula:

$$\text{Amount of refund} = \frac{\text{Number of days left}}{365} \times \text{Premium}$$

$$= \frac{116}{365} \times \$800$$

$$= \$254.25$$

The amount of the refund is $254.25.

Many companies have a minimum amount to pay, usually 25%. So if a person purchases an insurance policy and cancels it a week later, the person would get a 75% refund.

PRACTICE:

1. Find the annual premium on a $40,000 building if the rate is $0.87 per $100.
2. Find the annual premium on a $65,000 building if the rate is $1.65 per $100.
3. Find the annual premium on a building worth $127,000 if the rate is $1.23 per $100.
4. The owner of a building has $75,000 in insurance on a building worth $150,000. How much can he collect on a loss of $25,000 using the 80% coinsurance principle?

5. Henry's Tavern is worth $205,000. Henry has the building insured for $150,000. How much would the insurance company pay him on a loss of $32,000 if they use the 80% coinsurance principle?

6. The Oak Leaf Community Center building is worth $160,000. It is insured for $128,000. The loss from a recent fire was $26,000. How much did the community center receive if they use the 80% coinsurance principle?

7. Brian King purchased a 1-year fire insurance policy on October 7 having a premium of $1240. He cancelled the policy on June 12. How much of a refund did he receive?

8. June Carson insured her salon for 1 year on January 16. The premium was $540. She cancelled the insurance on August 14. What was the refund?

9. The owner of Bradley's Seafood Joint purchased a 1-year insurance policy on July 6. The premium was $870. If she cancelled the policy on February 8, how much of a refund is she entitled to receive?

10. On May 10, the owner of Tom's Train House insured his store for $140,000. His premium was $0.75 per $100. If he cancelled his policy on January 2, how much was his refund?

SOLUTIONS:

1. $\text{Annual premium} = \dfrac{\text{Insured value}}{100} \times \text{Rate}$

$= \dfrac{\$40,000}{\$100} \times 0.87$

$= \$348$

2. $\text{Annual premium} = \dfrac{\text{Insured value}}{100} \times \text{Rate}$

$= \dfrac{\$65,000}{\$100} \times 1.65$

$= \$1072.50$

3. $\text{Annual premium} = \dfrac{\text{Insured value}}{100} \times \text{Rate}$

$= \dfrac{\$127,000}{\$100} \times 1.23$

$= \$1562.10$

4. $0.80 \times \$150,000 = \$120,000$

$$\text{Amount received} = \frac{\text{Amount carried}}{\text{Amount required}} \times \text{Loss}$$

$$= \frac{\$75,000}{\$120,000} \times \$25,000$$

$$= \$15,625$$

5. $0.80 \times \$205,000 = \$164,000$

$$\text{Amount received} = \frac{\text{Amount carried}}{\text{Amount required}} \times \text{Loss}$$

$$= \frac{\$150,000}{\$164,000} \times \$32,000$$

$$= \$29,268.29$$

6. $0.80 \times \$160,000 = \$128,000$. Since the owner is carrying the required 80%, he will receive $26,000.

7. Days in June $30 - 12 = 18$

July	31
August	31
September	30
October	7
Total	117

$$\text{Amount of refund} = \frac{\text{Number of days left}}{365} \times \text{Premium}$$

$$= \frac{117}{365} \times \$1240$$

$$= \$397.48$$

8. Days in August $31 - 14 = 17$

September	30
October	31
November	30
December	31
January	16
Total	155

$$\text{Amount of refund} = \frac{\text{Number of days left}}{365} \times \text{Premium}$$

$$= \frac{155}{365} \times \$540$$

$$= \$229.32$$

9. Number of days in February $28 - 8 = 20$

March	31
April	30
May	31
June	30
July	6
Total	148

$$\text{Amount of refund} = \frac{\text{Number of days left}}{365} \times \text{Premium}$$

$$= \frac{148}{365} \times \$870$$

$$= \$352.77$$

10. $$\text{Annual premium} = \frac{\text{Insured value}}{100} \times \text{Rate}$$

$$= \frac{\$140,000}{\$100} \times 0.75$$

$$= \$1050$$

Number of days in January $31 - 2 = 29$

February	28
March	31
April	30
May	10
Total	128

$$\text{Amount of refund} = \frac{\text{Number of days left}}{365} \times \text{Premium}$$

$$= \frac{128}{365} \times \$1050$$

$$= \$368.22$$

Automobile Insurance

Businesses need to carry automobile insurance on their vehicles. There are several factors that need to be considered when purchasing automobile insurance. One consideration is **liability**. The owner or driver of an automobile is liable for the safety of passengers and the safety of other drivers and other vehicles as well as property damage that can result from being in an accident. Irresponsible driving can result in monetary compensation for medical bills, pain, and suffering. **Bodily injury** is the result of someone being injured in an accident. **Collision insurance** money is paid to the owner of a vehicle when he is in an accident with damage to his or her vehicle. Finally, **comprehensive insurance** protects the vehicle owner from damages that occur from vandalism, weather, or theft.

The insurance premium that a vehicle owner pays is based on the age of the driver, the driver's record, the type of vehicle, the geographic area where the vehicle is being used, and other related factors.

Most insurances have a **deductible** clause. This means that the owner must pay the first $100, $200, etc. of the repair bill. The higher the deductible, the lower the premium.

EXAMPLE: The damage to Walter Arden's automobile, which was the result of an accident that was his fault, was $4032. If his policy had a $500 deductible clause, how much did his insurance company pay for the damages?

SOLUTION:

$$\$4032 - \$500 = \$3532$$

Hence Walter paid $500, and his insurance company paid $3532.

Automobile insurance policies are written in terms of the amount the company is willing to pay per accident. It is usually stated as 25/50/10. This means that in the event of an accident, the insurance company will pay up to $25,000 for an injury to one person. The company will pay up to $50,000 for injuries to all the people involved in one accident. The last number means that the insurance company will pay up to $10,000 for any property damage. The owner of the automobile is liable for any other damage.

EXAMPLE: Catherine Reno was involved in an automobile accident that resulted in a $32,000 injury. The insurance policy contained a 25/50/10 clause. How much did the insurance company have to pay?

SOLUTION:

The insurance company will pay up to $25,000 for an injury to one person, so $32,000 − $25,000 = $7000. Hence, Catherine Reno must pay $7000.

EXAMPLE: Ping Kim and his wife were involved in an automobile accident. If Ping was awarded $28,000 in damages and his wife was awarded $12,000, how much money did the insurance company have to pay and how much money did the insured pay if his policy contained a 25/50/10 clause?

SOLUTION:
The insurance company will pay Ping $25,000 for one person, so they will pay $25,000 of the $28,000 for Ping's injuries. They will also pay $12,000 for his wife's injury since it is less than the $25,000 per person limit and the total is less than $50,000. Hence the insurance company will pay $25,000 + $12,000 = $37,000, and the insured will have to pay $3000.

EXAMPLE: Sam Johnston is at fault in an automobile accident. He carries 50/100/10 liability. The driver of the car he hit was awarded $52,000. Two passengers in the vehicles were awarded $8000 and $7000 respectively. Damage to Sam's automobile was $5000 and to the car he hit, $8000. How much did his insurance company pay and how much was Sam's liability?

SOLUTION:
The insurance company will pay the other driver $50,000. Sam will pay $2000. The insurance company will pay the passengers $8000 and $7000 respectively since the total of all three is less than the maximum amount of $100,000 for personal injury. The insurance company will pay $5000 for damages to each vehicle, equal to the maximum of $10,000. Sam will pay $3000 for the rest of the damage to his automobile.

PRACTICE:
1. Explain what the 50/100/25 clause means in an automobile insurance policy.
2. If Sam King was at fault in an accident and he had a $2000 deductible in his automobile insurance policy, how much did his insurance company pay if the damage to his car was $8725?
3. Peter Lite was in an automobile accident in which he was at fault. His medical bills amounted to a total of $11,560, and the repairs on his car cost $4385. If his insurance policy states that he had a 10/25/5 clause, how much did his insurance company pay and how much did he have to pay?
4. Hector Avery carries 25/50/10 liability insurance on his automobile. He is in an accident that was his fault. The medical bill for the other driver is $32,300. Hector's medical bill is $18,500. One passenger's medical bill is $8000. How much did his insurance company pay and how much did Hector pay?

5. Keisha Jones has a 50/100/10 liability. She is in an accident in which the damage to her car is $4000, and the damage to the other car is $7250. Her medical bill is $16,175, and the other driver's medical bill is $37,220. How much did Keisha's insurance company pay and how much did Keisha pay?

SOLUTIONS:

1. The first number 50 means that the insurance company will pay up to $50,000 for an injury to one person. The second number 100 means that the insurance company will pay up to a total of $100,000 for injuries to all people involved in an automobile accident. The third number 25 means that the insurance company will pay up to $25,000 for property damage.

2. The insurance company will pay $8725 − $2000 = $6725 for the repair.

3. For the medical bills, the insurance company will pay $10,000. Peter will pay the remaining $1560. For the automobile repair, the insurance company will pay $4385 since this total is less than $5000.

4. The insurance company will pay $25,000 for the other driver's injuries. Hector will pay $32,300 − $25,000 = $7300. The insurance company will pay a maximum of $50,000 of the total of $25,000 + $18,500 + $8000 = $51,500, so Hector will pay an additional $1500.

5. The total of the two medical bills is $16,175 + $37,220 = $53,395. The insurance company will pay both bills since neither exceeded $50,000 and the total is less than $100,000. The total property damage is $4000 + $7250 = $11,250. The insurance company will pay $10,000, so Keisha will have to pay $11,250 − $10,000 = $1250.

Life Insurance

A person can insure his or her life by purchasing life insurance. There are several different types of life insurance:

A **straight life insurance** policy requires the insured to pay premiums for his or her entire life. At the time of his or her death, the face value of the policy is paid to the beneficiary. The policy collects dividends that can add to its face value. This type of policy can also be cashed in or used to borrow money.

A **term life insurance** policy requires the insured to pay premiums for a specific number of years such as 1 year, 5 years, 10 years, or 20 years. If the insured died during the term, the beneficiary receives the face value of the policy. If the insured lives beyond the term, the beneficiary receives nothing and the policy becomes invalid. This type of insurance is the least expensive type of life insurance.

A **limited payment** policy requires that payments be made for a specific number of years, and then the policy is paid up. The beneficiary receives the face value of the policy upon the death of the insured.

An **endowment** policy is paid off in a specific number of years. If the insured dies before the maturity date, the beneficiary receives the face value of the policy. If the insured lives past the maturity date, he receives the face value of the policy.

The premiums paid for life insurance depend on the type of policy, the face value of the policy, the age of the insured, the health of the insured, and the gender of the insured. For the purpose of this section, only a general premium will be used.

EXAMPLE: If a healthy 45-year old female purchased a $100,000 10-year term policy and the premium was $61.80 per month, find the yearly premium and the total amount she would pay for 10 years.

SOLUTION:

For 1 year: $61.80 × 12 = $741.60
For 10 years: $741.60 × 10 = $7416.00

Sometimes rates are given per $1000. To find the annual premium, use the following formula:

$$\text{Annual premium} = \frac{\text{Face value}}{\$1000} \times \text{Rate}$$

EXAMPLE: Byron Simmons purchased a $50,000 straight life insurance policy. If the premium is $23.40 per $1000 for a 35-year old male, what was his annual premium?

SOLUTION:

$$\text{Annual premium} = \frac{\text{Face value}}{\$1000} \times \text{Rate}$$

$$= \frac{\$50,000}{\$1000} \times \$23.40$$

$$= \$1170.00$$

Sometimes people cannot afford to pay large premiums yearly so insurance companies allow the insured to pay semiannually, quarterly, or monthly. However, the premium is somewhat higher due to more paperwork for the company.

EXAMPLE: Debbie Henderson decides to purchase a $30,000 10-year policy. The rate is $5.75 per $1000 for a 32-year-old female. If she decides to pay semiannually, she will pay 52% of the premiums. If she decides to pay quarterly, she will pay 26.5% of the annual premium. If she decides to pay monthly, she will pay 9% of the annual premium. Find the premium if she decides to pay

(a) annually
(b) semiannually
(c) quarterly
(d) monthly

SOLUTION:

(a) Annual premium $= \dfrac{\text{Face value}}{\$1000} \times \text{Rate}$

$\qquad = \dfrac{\$30,000}{\$1000} \times \$5.75$

$\qquad = \$172.50$

(b) Semiannual premium $= 0.52 \times \$172.50$

$\qquad\qquad = \$89.70$

(c) Quarterly premium $= 0.265 \times \$172.50$

$\qquad\qquad = \$45.71$

(d) Monthly premium $= 0.09 \times \$172.50$

$\qquad\qquad = \$15.53$

PRACTICE:

1. Thomas Andrews purchased a $100,000 10-year term insurance policy. If his monthly premium was $64, find the total amount he paid in 1 year.
2. Adrienne Plum purchased a $50,000 10-year term policy and paid the premium monthly. If the total that she paid in 1 year was $477, find her monthly premium.
3. Soo Chung purchased a $250,000 straight life insurance policy. Her premium rate was $28.55 per $1000. Find her annual premium.

4. Priscilla O'Rourke purchased a $75,000 5-year term life insurance policy. The premium rate for her was $8.72 per $1000. Find her annual premium.
5. Leroy Zeff purchased a 10-year term life insurance policy with a face value of $60,000. The rate was $18.32 per $1000. If the monthly premium was 8.5% of the annual premium, find the amount of the monthly premium.

SOLUTIONS:

1. $64 \times 12 = $768

2. $477 \div 12 = $39.75

3. Annual premium $= \dfrac{\text{Face value}}{\$1000} \times \text{Rate}$

   $= \dfrac{\$250,000}{\$1000} \times \$28.55$

   $= \$7137.50$

4. Annual premium $= \dfrac{\text{Face value}}{\$1000} \times \text{Rate}$

   $= \dfrac{\$75,000}{\$1000} \times \$8.72$

   $= \$654.00$

5. Annual premium $= \dfrac{\text{Face value}}{\$1000} \times \text{Rate}$

   $= \dfrac{\$60,000}{\$1000} \times \$18.32$

   $= \$1099.20$

   Monthly premium $= 0.085 \times \$1099.20$

   $= \$93.43$

Summary

Businesses and individuals purchase insurance to cover various losses due to fires, accidents, weather, negligence, and loss of life. An insurance policy has a face value which is the maximum amount of money the company will pay the insured in the event of a loss. In order to pay for the insurance, the person

pays a premium. This premium can be paid yearly, semiannually, quarterly, or monthly.

There are many kinds of insurance policies. The basic concepts of fire insurance, automobile insurance, and life insurance were explained in this chapter.

Quiz

1. Jeff Hansen insured his home for $175,000. If his insurance rate is $0.94 per $100, his annual premium is
   (a) $16,450
   (b) $10,500
   (c) $1505
   (d) $1645

2. A building is worth $275,000, and its owner insured it for $200,000. If a loss due to fire is $82,000, the insurance company would pay the owner the sum of
   (a) $59,636.36
   (b) $74,545.45
   (c) $82,000.00
   (d) $63,246.46

3. A fire insurance policy was purchased on November 10. The premium was $1320. If the policy is cancelled on June 6, the refund will be
   (a) $766.68
   (b) $832.44
   (c) $447.26
   (d) $567.78

4. The repair bill for Byron Simmon's automobile due to an accident that was his fault was $6273. If he had a $500 deductible clause in his automobile insurance policy, the insurance company will pay
   (a) $500
   (b) $6773
   (c) $6273
   (d) $5773

5. Mary Rojohn was at fault in an automobile accident in which she received a personal injury resulting in a $62,500 medical bill. If the automobile policy had a 50/100/25 clause, the insurance company will pay her
   (a) $18,000
   (b) $12,500

(c) $50,000
(d) $13,000

6. Debbie Henderson had a 25/50/10 clause in her automobile insurance policy. She was at fault in an accident in which the total amount of medical expenses was $63,000 with no individual's bill more than $25,000. How much of this bill is she responsible for?
(a) $13,000
(b) $63,000
(c) $50,000
(d) $25,000

7. If a person had a 50/100/10 clause in his automobile policy and the property damage was $24,000, the amount of money the person would pay is
(a) $24,000
(b) $50,000
(c) $14,000
(d) $9000

8. A life insurance policy which is paid off in a specific number of years and if the insured lives beyond the term, the amount of its face value of the policy is returned to the insured is called
(a) a straight life policy
(b) a limited life payment policy
(c) a term life policy
(d) an endowment policy

9. Brianne Johnson purchased a $75,000 straight life insurance policy. If the rate for her age and health conditions was $18.60 per $1000, her annual premium would be
(a) $1428
(b) $1395
(c) $1654
(d) $1487

10. Pierre Lubuto purchased a $150,000 20-year term life insurance policy. If the rate was $9.62 per $1000 and he decided to pay monthly at 9% of the annual rate, his payment would be
(a) $1443
(b) $1328
(c) $129.87
(d) $119.52

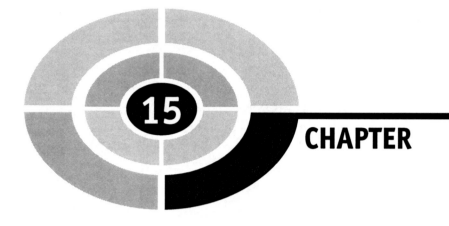

15

CHAPTER

Taxes

Introduction

In order to finance its operations, governments levy and collect **taxes**. These monies are used to pay the salaries and expenses of government employees and to enable governments to provide services such as police and fire protection and build schools, highways, and so on. Three of the most common taxes are sales tax, property tax, and income tax.

Sales Tax

Sales tax rates are determined by state governments and some local governments. Some states such as Alaska, Delaware, and Oregon have no state sales tax. The amount of the tax and the items that are taxable are also determined by the states; for example, there is no sales tax on food or prescription drugs in many states. Tax rates are subject to change and the rates used in this chapter are

current as of the writing of this book. The basic formula used to find the sales tax is

$$\text{Sales tax} = \text{Price} \times \text{Rate}$$

EXAMPLE: Find the sales tax and the total cost of a leather sofa priced at $499. The sales tax rate in Alabama is 4%.

SOLUTION:

$$\text{Sales tax} = \text{Price} \times \text{Rate}$$
$$= \$499 \times 0.04$$
$$= \$19.96$$

The total amount is $499 + $19.96 = $518.96.

The total cost of an item including tax can be found by the formula

$$\text{Total cost} = \text{Price} \times (1 + \text{Rate})$$

EXAMPLE: Find the total cost of a mirror costing $74.50 if the tax rate in Pennsylvania is 6%.

SOLUTION:

$$\text{Total cost} = \text{Price} \times (1 + \text{Rate})$$
$$= \$74.50 \times (1 + 0.06)$$
$$= \$74.50 \times 1.06$$
$$= \$78.97$$

Hence the total cost, tax included, is $78.97.

Note: One is added to the rate since the total cost is 100% + 6% or 106% of the cost.

Sometimes businesses list the price of an item that includes the sales tax. These situations usually occur when making change is inconvenient and time consuming. Some places include snack bars at swimming pools, amusement parks, and fairs. However, the vendors are required to pay the sales tax to the state or local municipalities so they must be able to compute the correct amount. The following formulas can be used:

$$\text{Price} = \frac{\text{Total cost}}{1 + \text{Rate}}$$

$$\text{Sales tax} = \text{Total cost} - \text{Price}$$

EXAMPLE: The total cost of a hamburger (tax included) is $2.75. Find the amount of sales tax if the rate is 5%.

SOLUTION:

$$\text{Price} = \frac{\text{Total cost}}{1 + \text{Rate}}$$

$$= \frac{\$2.75}{1 + 0.05}$$

$$= \frac{\$2.75}{1.05}$$

$$= \$2.62$$

$$\text{Sales tax} = \$2.75 - \$2.62 = \$0.13$$

Hence the actual cost of the hamburger is $2.62 and the sales tax is $0.13.

PRACTICE:

1. The sales tax rate in Oklahoma is 4.5%. Find the sales tax on a lamp costing $49.00.
2. A five-piece dining set costs $599. If the sales tax rate is 6.25%, find the sales tax and the total cost of the dining set.
3. If a set of wooden bookshelves costs $129 and the sales tax is 3.5%, find the total cost of the shelves.
4. Martha Irwin purchased an oval rug and said that the total cost of the rug including tax was $259.70. Find the price of the item and the sales tax if the tax rate was 6%.
5. Mark Johnston bought two chairs at a flea market for $125, tax included. If the sales tax rate is 5.5%, find the price of the item and the amount of the sales tax.

SOLUTIONS:

1. Sales tax $=$ Price $\times$ Rate
    $$= \$49 \times 0.045$$
    $$= \$2.21$$

2. Sales tax $=$ Price $\times$ Rate
    $$= \$599 \times 0.0625$$
    $$= \$37.44$$
    Total cost $= \$599 + \$37.44$
    $$= \$636.44$$

3. Total cost $=$ Price $\times (1 + \text{Rate})$
    $$= \$129 \times (1 + 0.035)$$
    $$= \$129 \times 1.035$$
    $$= \$133.52$$

4. $$\text{Price} = \frac{\text{Total cost}}{1 + \text{Rate}}$$
    $$= \frac{\$259.70}{1 + 0.06}$$
    $$= \frac{\$259.70}{1.06}$$
    $$= \$245$$
    Sales tax $= \$259.70 - \$245$
    $$= \$14.70$$

5. $$\text{Price} = \frac{\text{Total cost}}{1 + \text{Rate}}$$
    $$= \frac{\$125}{1 + 0.055}$$
    $$= \frac{\$125}{1.055}$$
    $$= \$118.48$$
    Sales tax $= \$125.00 - \$118.48$
    $$= \$6.52$$

Property Tax

Many municipalities and counties collect **property taxes**. These are taxes on land, houses, and buildings. These taxes are based on what is called the assessed value of the property. The **assessed value** is usually a percent of what is called the **market value**. The market value is an estimate of the worth of the property if it was sold today. Since the market value fluctuates from year to year, property is assessed periodically.

To find the assessed value of property, multiply the market value by the assessment rate.

EXAMPLE: Find the assessed value of a building that has an estimated market value of $150,000. The assessment rate is 30%.

SOLUTION:

$$\text{Assessed value} = \text{Market value} \times \text{Rate}$$

$$= \$150,000 \times 0.30$$

$$= \$45,000$$

Hence the assessed value of the building is $45,000.

The amount of the property tax is determined by different methods. A common method uses what is called a mill. A **mill** is one-thousandths of one dollar or $0.001. Municipalities who use this method levy taxes based on mills. For example, the property tax for Logan County is 85 mills. This means that the property owners must pay $85 in taxes for every $1000 of assessed value of their homes. If a home was assessed at $100,000, the property owner would pay $100 \times \$85 = \$8500$ in property taxes since $\$100,000 \div \$1000 = 100$.

In order to compute property taxes based on mills, use the following formula:

$$\text{Tax amount} = \frac{\text{Assessed value}}{\$1000} \times \text{Mills}$$

EXAMPLE: If a home is assessed for $130,000 and the property tax is 43 mills, find the amount of property tax the homeowner will pay.

SOLUTION:

$$\text{Tax amount} = \frac{\text{Assessed value}}{\$1000} \times \text{Mills}$$

$$= \frac{\$130,000}{\$1000} \times 43$$

$$= \$5590$$

Hence the property owner will pay a tax of $5590.

EXAMPLE: A home has a market value of $240,000. It is assessed at 25% of its market value and the tax rate is 56 mills. Find the amount of property tax.

SOLUTION:

$$\text{Assessed value} = \$240,000 \times 0.25$$

$$= \$60,000$$

$$\text{Property tax} = \frac{\text{Assessed value}}{\$1000} \times \text{Rate}$$

$$= \frac{\$60,000}{\$1000} \times 56$$

$$= \$3360$$

Sometimes property taxes are based on an amount per $1.00 of assessed value or on $100 of assessed value. In these cases, the following formulas are used:

(a)   Based on $1.00: Property tax $=$ Assessed value $\times$ Rate (amount)

(b)   Based on $100: Property tax $= \dfrac{\text{Assessed value}}{\$100} \times$ Rate (amount)

The rates are usually given in percents.

EXAMPLE: A home has an assessed value of $80,000. If the tax rate is $2 per $100, find the property tax.

SOLUTION:

$$\text{Property tax} = \frac{\text{Assessed value}}{\$100} \times \text{Rate (amount)}$$

$$= \frac{\$80,000}{\$100} \times \$2$$

$$= \$1600$$

Hence the property tax is $1600.

PRACTICE:

1.   Find the assessed value of an apartment building with a market value of $875,000 if the assessment rate is 35%.
2.   If an automobile service station is assessed at $155,000 and the tax rate is 73 mills, find the property tax.
3.   A hardware store has a market value of $1,250,000. If it is assessed at 50% of its market value and the millage is 75, find the property tax.

4. Find the property tax on a home that is assessed at $220,000 if the tax rate is $8.37 per $100.

5. Find the property tax on a vacant lot that is assessed at $20,000 if the tax rate is 1.5% per $1.00.

SOLUTIONS:

1. Assessed value $= $ Market value $\times$ Rate
$$= \$875,000 \times 0.35$$
$$= \$306,250$$

2. Property tax $= \dfrac{\text{Assessed value}}{\$1000} \times \text{Mills}$
$$= \dfrac{\$155,000}{\$1000} \times 73$$
$$= \$11,315$$

3. Assessed value $= $ Market value $\times$ Rate
$$= \$1,250,000 \times 0.50$$
$$= \$625,000$$
Property tax $= \dfrac{\text{Assessed value}}{\$1000} \times \text{Mills}$
$$= \dfrac{\$625,000}{\$1000} \times 75$$
$$= \$46,875$$

4. Property tax $= \dfrac{\text{Assessed value}}{\$100} \times \text{Amount}$
$$= \dfrac{\$220,000}{\$100} \times \$8.37$$
$$= \$18,414$$

5. Property value $= $ Assessed value $\times$ Rate
$$= \$20,000 \times 0.015$$
$$= \$300$$

Income Tax

The federal government and many state governments require wage earners to pay taxes on their wages. These taxes are called **income taxes**. The governments provide tax forms that are used to figure out how much tax to pay. Also, a booklet is provided by the governments that explains the procedures and the recent changes. Even though the tax laws change periodically, the basic procedure for calculating your income tax remains the same. *The explanation given here is only a brief introduction to income tax, and taxpayers should follow the instructions given in the government publications or consult a professional tax preparer when filing their income tax.*

Wage earners usually receive what is called a **W-2 form** from their employer. The W-2 form shows the employee's earned income, the federal income tax with-held, state income tax withheld, Social Security tax withheld, and the amount of Medicare tax withheld.

The total amount of income a person earns is called his or her **gross income**. Gross income includes salary, commissions, tips, bonuses, interest, royalties, etc. The **adjusted gross income** is computed by subtracting any allowable adjustments from the gross income. These adjustments are usually job expenses that are not reimbursed by the employer. Finally, the **taxable income** is computed by subtracting exemptions and deductions from the adjusted gross income.

Deductions include contributions to charities, interest paid on certain loans, taxes paid on property, medical insurance, etc. There are guidelines to follow when itemizing deductions. Consult the appropriate government publication.

There are four categories that a taxpayer selects, depending on his or her mari-tal status. A taxpayer is considered **single** if he or she has never married, is legally separated or divorced or widowed. If a husband and wife file a return together, they are considered to be **married filing jointly**. If a husband and wife file separately, they are considered **married filing separately**. Finally, the **head of household** category is for people who provide a home for certain other persons.

After determining your taxable income and your status, you can find how much you owe by consulting the tax table in the given publication. An abbrevi-ated version is shown in Table 15-1 on the next page. The table was obtained from the *IRS Booklet 2004 1040A*.

EXAMPLE: Find the amount of income tax a single taxpayer owes if her taxable income is $41,273.

SOLUTION:
Find the line in Table 15-1 showing $41,250–$41,300 since $41,273 falls be-tween these two numbers. Then look under the category "Single" to find the amount of tax owed. It is $7056. Hence the taxpayer owes the IRS $7056.

EXAMPLE: Find the amount of income tax a married couple filing jointly owes if their combined taxable income is $41,423.

SOLUTION:
Find the two values that $41,423 falls between the tax table. In this case, it is $41,400–$41,450. Then go to the column headed "Married filing jointly" and read the value. It is $5499. Hence the tax owed is $5499.

Table 15-1   IRS Tax Table

If Form 1040A, line 27, is—		And you are—			
At least	But less than	Single	Married filing jointly	Married filing separately	Head of a household
				Your tax is—	
41,000					
41,000	41,050	6,994	5,439	6,994	5,856
41,050	41,100	7,006	5,446	7,006	5,869
41,100	41,150	7,019	5,454	7,019	5,881
41,150	41,200	7,031	5,461	7,031	5,894
41,200	41,250	7,044	5,469	7,044	5,906
41,250	41,300	7,056	5,476	7,056	5,919
41,300	41,350	7,069	5,484	7,069	5,931
41,350	41,400	7,081	5,491	7,081	5,944
41,400	41,450	7,094	5,499	7,094	5,956
41,450	41,500	7,106	5,506	7,106	5,969
41,500	41,550	7,119	5,514	7,119	5,981
41,550	41,600	7,131	5,521	7,131	5,994
41,600	41,650	7,144	5,529	7,144	6,006
41,650	41,700	7,156	5,536	7,156	6,019
41,700	41,750	7,169	5,544	7,169	6,031
41,750	41,800	7,181	5,551	7,181	6,044
41,800	41,850	7,194	5,559	7,194	6,056
41,850	41,900	7,206	5,566	7,206	6,069
41,900	41,950	7,219	5,574	7,219	6,081
41,950	42,000	7,231	5,581	7,231	6,094

PRACTICE:

1. Find the amount of income tax paid by Helen Davis if she filed as a married person filing separately and her taxable income was $41,236.
2. Find the amount of income tax paid by Mr. and Mrs. Newman if they filed as a married filing jointly couple. Their taxable income was $41,560.
3. Harold Winter has a taxable income of $41,029 and filed as a head of household. What was his income tax?
4. Mark Weinstein's taxable income was $41,462. If he filed as a single person, find the amount of his income tax.
5. Betsy Lee filed her tax return as a single person. If her taxable income was $41,621, how much tax did she pay?

SOLUTIONS:

1. Since $41,236 falls between $41,200 and $41,250, find the value $7044 under the column head, "Married Filing Separately."
2. The value $41,560 falls between $41,550 and $41,600 and since the Newmans are filing jointly as a married couple, the amount of their income tax return is $5521.
3. Since $41,029 falls between $41,000 and $41,050 and Harold is filing as a "Head of household," his income tax is $5856.
4. Since Mark is filing as a single person and $41,462 falls between $41,450 and $41,500, his income tax is $7106.
5. Since Betsy is filing as a single person and her income of $40,621 falls between $41,600 and $41,650, her income tax is $7144.

Summary

This chapter explains sales tax, property, tax, and income tax.

Quiz

1. The sales tax of 6% on a lounge chair costing $25.95 is
   (a) $1.32
   (b) $1.87
   (c) $1.56
   (d) $1.49

2. If a radio costs $16.95 and the sales tax rate is 3.5%, then the total cost of the radio with tax is
   (a) $17.54
   (b) $0.59
   (c) $0.51
   (d) $17.51

3. If the market value of a house is $87,500 and it is assessed at 30% of market value, its assessed value is
   (a) $24,310
   (b) $27,450
   (c) $25,950
   (d) $26,250

4. If the property tax in Monroe County is 42 mills, the property tax on a house that is assessed at $143,750 is
   (a) $603.75
   (b) $7542.00

(c) $6037.50
(d) $754.20

5. The assessed value of a vacant lot is $20,000. If the property tax rate is 67 mills, then the property tax is
    (a) $13,400
    (b) $1200
    (c) $1340
    (d) $134.00

6. A small pizza shop has an estimated market value of $105,900. It is assessed at 25% of market value and the millage rate is 75 mills. The property tax is
    (a) $26,475.00
    (b) $19,856.25
    (c) $1985.63
    (d) $2647.50

7. The property tax rate is $8 per $100 in a certain city. The property tax on a home that is assessed at $22,500 is
    (a) $1625
    (b) $162.50
    (c) $180
    (d) $1800

8. When using a tax table to compute your income tax, you should find the tax based on your
    (a) gross income
    (b) adjusted gross income
    (c) taxable income
    (d) retail income

9. If Sam Higgins has a taxable income of $41,872 and he is filing as a single person, then according to Table 15-1, his income tax would be
    (a) $7194
    (b) $5559
    (c) $7206
    (d) $6056

10. If Martha Rotelli has a taxable income of $41,363 and is filing as a "Head of Household," her income tax based upon Table 15-1 is
    (a) $7081
    (b) $5491
    (c) $5931
    (d) $5944

16

Stocks and Bonds

Introduction

When a company incorporates, it is able to issue **stock**. If an investor purchases **shares** of stock, he or she becomes a part owner of the company; for example, if a company issues 1000 shares of stock and an investor purchases 250 shares, then the investor owns $\frac{1}{4}$ of the company. The investor is called a **shareholder**.

When the company makes money, it distributes part of the profit to its shareholders. This money is called a **dividend**. The stockholder receives a sum of money based on the number of shares of the stock that he or she owns. Sometimes if a company does not make a profit or its owners or managers decide to reinvest the money into the company, no dividends are paid.

Besides issuing stock, a company can also issue **bonds**. This is usually done to raise money for the company for startup costs or special projects. A person who purchases a bond is really lending money to the company. The company, in turn, repays the owner of the bond its **face value** plus interest.

Stocks can be bought and sold on a **stock exchange**. The price of stocks vary from day to day depending on conditions such as the profitability of the company, the economy, scandals, world conditions, etc. Investors need to buy and sell their stock through a **stockbroker**. The stockbroker charges a fee called a **commission** for his or her services. Bonds can also be bought and sold. This can be done by individual brokers and can even be traded online.

Investors usually own a combination of stocks and bonds. These stocks and bonds are listed in the investor's **portfolio**.

Sometimes investors hire a manager to handle their investments. The manager invests the money in stocks and bonds, follows the activity of the companies, and buys and sells in order to achieve the maximum possible profit for the group. This type of investment is called a **mutual fund**.

Stocks

In order to get information about a certain stock, you can refer to a stock table. These tables can be found in newspapers and online. The listings vary somewhat from newspaper to newspaper. In this case, a stock listing for Norfolk Southern will be used.

52 weeks								
HI	LO	STOCK	DIV	YLD%	PE	VOL (100S)	CLOSE	NET CHG
38.99	24.61	NSC	0.44	1.4	14	18091	32.45	−0.49

The first two columns give the highest and lowest selling prices for the stock during the past 52 weeks. In this case, they are $38.99 and $24.61 respectively. The column labeled STOCK contains the letters NSC. This is the symbol the company uses for trading. The column labeled DIV is the dividend per share that was paid to shareholders last year. In this case, it was $0.44 per share. The column labeled YLD% is the annual percentage yield. In this case, it is 1.4%. This percent can be compared to other investments such as savings accounts rates, CD rates, etc. The PE column is the price-to-earning ratio. It is the ratio of yesterday's closing price of the stock to its annual earning per share. In this case, the closing price of the stock, $32.45, is 14 times the annual earning per share. This concept will be explained in more detail after the next example.

The column labeled VOL (100S) means the number of shares in 100s that were traded yesterday. In this case, $18,091 \times 100 = 1,809,100$ shares were traded yesterday. The column labeled CLOSE was the price of the stock yesterday at closing time. The column labeled NET CHG is the change in the price of the stock between the day before yesterday and yesterday at closing time. In this case, the value of the stock decreased $0.49. In other words, the value of the stock the day before yesterday was $32.45 + $0.49 = $32.94. Since the net change was negative, a − appears in the column. When... appears in this column, it means that there was no change.

EXAMPLE: The following is a stock listing for the McGraw-Hill Company. Use the listing to answer the questions.

52 weeks								
HI	LO	STOCK	DIV	YLD%	PE	VOL (100S)	CLOSE	NET CHG
48	36.42	MHP	.66	1.5	22	16114	43.54	0.04

1.   What was the highest price that the stock sold for during the past 52 weeks?
2.   What was the lowest price that the stock sold for during the past 52 weeks?
3.   What was the amount of the dividend per share that McGraw-Hill paid last year?
4.   If a person owned 250 shares of stock, how much did the person make in dividends last year?
5.   How many shares were traded yesterday?
6.   What was the closing price per share yesterday?

SOLUTION:

1. $48.00
2. $36.42
3. $0.66
4.   250 × $0.66 = $165.00
5.   16114 × 100 = 1,611,400 shares
6. $43.54

As stated previously, the PE means the price-to-earnings ratio. It is found by using the following formula:

$$PE \text{ ratio} = \frac{\text{Yesterday's closing price}}{\text{Annual earnings per share}}$$

The annual earnings per share is found by dividing the company's total earnings by the number of shares that are owned by the stockholders for the last year. The annual earnings per share for a stock is found by subtracting expenses, taxes, losses, etc. from the gross revenues. These figures can be found in the companies' annual reports.

EXAMPLE: If the annual earnings per share for Norfolk Southern is $2.32, find the PE.

SOLUTION:

$$PE\ ratio = \frac{Yesterday's\ closing\ price}{Annual\ earnings\ per\ share}$$

$$= \frac{32.45}{2.32}$$

$$= 14\ (rounded)$$

This means that the price of a share of stock is 14 times the company's annual earnings per share. If you divide $1.00 by the PE ratio 14, you get 0.07, which means that for every dollar you invest in the company by purchasing its stock, the company makes 7¢. This, however, does not mean that the company pays a dividend of 7¢. The dividends paid are determined by the board of directors of the company, and they may want to use some of the profits for other purposes, such as expansion.

Another way of looking at the PE ratio is that you are paying the company $1.00 so that it can make 7¢. Now if the PE ratio for another company's stock is 20, then $1.00 ÷ 20 = 5¢. This means that you are paying the company $1.00 so that it can earn 5¢. Which is better? Obviously the investment in the first company is better. So in general, the lower the PE ratio is, the better the investment, but there are many other factors to consider when purchasing stock, and the company's PE ratio is only one factor to consider. Also remember that since the price of a company's stock is constantly changing, the PE ratio also changes.

Knowing the price per share of stock and the PE ratio, you can find the annual earnings per share for the last 12 months by using the following formula:

$$Annual\ earnings\ per\ share = \frac{Yesterday's\ closing\ price}{PE\ ratio}$$

EXAMPLE: If the closing price for Kellogg's stock is $45.55 and the PE ratio is 21, find the annual earnings per share for last year.

SOLUTION:

$$\text{Annual earnings per share} = \frac{\text{Yesterday's closing price}}{\text{PE ratio}}$$

$$= \frac{\$45.55}{21}$$

$$= \$2.17$$

Hence the annual earnings per share for Kellogg's is $2.17.

The current stock yield can be calculated by using the formula:

$$\text{Current stock yield} = \frac{\text{Annual dividend per share}}{\text{Closing price of stock}}$$

EXAMPLE: For the Norfolk Southern stock, the annual percent yield is 1.4%. Verify this by using the preceding formula.

SOLUTION:
The dividend per share is $0.44 and the closing price is $32.45; hence,

$$\text{Current stock yield} = \frac{\text{Annual dividend per share}}{\text{Closing price of stock}}$$

$$= \frac{\$0.44}{\$32.45}$$

$$= 0.0135$$

$$= 0.014 \text{ (rounded)}$$

$$= 1.4\%$$

After rounding, the figure agrees with the 1.4% shown in the listing.

To make money from the stock market, an investor must buy stock and collect dividends or buy stock when the price is low and sell it when the price goes up. In order to buy and sell stock, the investor must use a stockbroker. The broker instructs his representatives on the stock exchange to carry out the transactions. The broker charges the investor a commission. Commissions can vary among brokers. The amount the investor receives from the sale of a stock is called the **proceeds**. The proceeds are equal to the amount of the sale minus the broker's commission. Brokers can also make recommendations to investors concerning what stock to buy and sell. Consider the next several examples.

EXAMPLE: An investor purchased 600 shares of McKesson stock for $22.61 per share. If the broker's commission is 2%, find the amount of the commission and the amount the investor paid for the stocks including the commission fee.

SOLUTION:

Step1. Find the purchase price.

$$600 \text{ shares} \times \$22.61 = \$13,566.00$$

Step 2. Find the broker's commission.

$$\$13,566 \times 0.02 = \$271.32$$

Step 3. Find the sum of the purchase price and the commission.

$$\$13,566 + \$271.32 = \$13,837.32$$

Hence the investor paid $13,837.32 for the transaction.

EXAMPLE: A year later, the investor sold his 600 shares of McKesson stock for $43.44 each. If his broker charged 2% for the sale, find the commission and the amount the investor received (i.e., the proceeds).

SOLUTION:

Step 1. Find the total amount of the sale.

$$600 \text{ shares} \times \$43.44 = \$26,064.00$$

Step 2. Find the commission.

$$\$26,064.00 \times 0.02 = \$521.28$$

Step 3. Subtract the commission amount from the total amount of the sale to get the proceeds.

$$\$26,064.00 - \$521.28 = \$25,542.72$$

Hence the commission was $521.28 and the investor received $25,542.72.

With the previous information, you can figure how well your stock purchases did. This is called the **return on investment (ROI)**. In order to present a more accurate picture, you need to consider the dividends paid and the commissions of your stockbroker and use the following formula:

$$ROI = \frac{\text{Total gain}}{\text{Original cost of stock}} \times 100\%$$

where

$$\text{Total gain} = \text{Proceeds} + \text{Dividends} - \text{Original cost}$$

$$\text{Original cost} = \text{Cost of stock} + \text{Commission}$$

EXAMPLE: Use the information in the last two examples and find the rate of return on the sale of 600 shares of McKesson stock. Assume that the dividends paid were $0.66 per share.

SOLUTION:
The original cost of the stock including the commission was $13,837.32. The proceeds were $25,542.72 (see the previous examples). The total amount of the dividends is 600 shares × $0.66 = $396.
   The total gain is

$$\text{Total gain} = \text{Proceeds} + \text{Dividends} - \text{Original cost}$$
$$= \$25,542.72 + \$396.00 - \$13,837.32$$
$$= \$12,101.40$$

$$ROI = \frac{\text{Total gain}}{\text{Original cost of stock}} \times 100\%$$
$$= \frac{\$12,101.40}{\$13,837.32} \times 100\%$$
$$= 0.875 \text{ (rounded)} \times 100\%$$
$$= 87.5\%$$

Hence your return on your purchases is 87.5%.

Remember that a negative return means that you lost money. A positive return means that you made money. A return of 0% means that you broke even.

PRACTICE:

Use the following information for Exercises 1 to 10:

52 weeks								
HI	LO	STOCK	DIV	YLD%	PE	VOL (100s)	CLOSE	NET CHG
116.05	58.76	Sunoco	1.60	1.4	14	10948	116.81	0.76

1. What was the highest price that the Sunoco stock sold for during the last 52 weeks?
2. What was the lowest price that the Sunoco stock sold for during the last 52 weeks?
3. What was the amount of the dividend per share that the company paid last year?
4. If a person owned 150 shares, how much in dividends did the person make last year?
5. How many shares were traded yesterday?
6. What was the closing price of the stock yesterday?
7. Find the annual earnings per share of the stock.
8. If an investor purchased 150 shares of Sunoco stock at $83.43 and the broker's commission was 2.5%, find the amount of the commission and the total cost of the purchase.
9. If the investor sold 150 shares of the stock at $116.81 and the broker's fee was 2.5%, find the proceeds of the sale.
10. If the dividend per share the investor received was $1.60 per share, find the investor's return on investment.

SOLUTIONS:

1. $116.05
2. $58.76
3. $1.60
4. 150 shares × $1.60 = $240
5. 10,948 × 100 = 1,094,800
6. $116.81
7. Annual earnings $= \dfrac{\text{Closing price}}{\text{PE}}$

$$= \dfrac{\$116.81}{14}$$

$$= \$8.34$$

8.   150 shares $\times$ \$83.43 $=$ \$12,514.50

    Commission $=$ \$12,514.50 $\times$ 0.025
    $=$ \$312.86

    Total cost $=$ \$12,514.50 $+$ \$312.86 $=$ \$12,827.36

9.   150 shares $\times$ \$116.81 $=$ \$17,521.50

    Commission $=$ \$17,521.50 $\times$ 0.025 $=$ \$438.04

    Proceeds $=$ \$17,521.50 $-$ \$438.04 $=$ \$17,083.46

10.   Dividends $=$ 150 shares $\times$ \$1.60 $=$ \$240.00

$$\text{ROI} = \frac{\$17,083.46 + \$240.00 - \$12,827.36}{\$12,827.36} \times 100\%$$

$$= \frac{\$4496.10}{\$12,827.36} \times 100\%$$

$$= 0.35 \text{ (rounded)} \times 100\%$$

$$= 35\%$$

Bonds

When incorporated businesses and governments need to raise money, they can issue bonds. A bond is more or less a loan made by the purchaser to a corporation or government. The corporation or government then promises to pay interest to the owner of the bond. Corporate bonds are issued by corporations. Municipal bonds are issued by state and local governments, and treasury bonds are issued by the federal government.

Bonds have a face value that is usually $1000, a maturity date by which the money has to be repaid, and a fixed interest rate. Bonds can be bought and sold on the bonds market just like stocks. The prices of the bonds, just like stock prices, vary with market conditions.

Bonds pay a specific rate of interest and have a maturity date. They are listed in a way that is similar to stocks. The following is a listing for a Sprint bond:

| 52 weeks | | | | | WEEKLY | | | |
HIGH	LOW	NAME	CUR YLD	SALES ($1000s)	HIGH	LOW	LAST	NET CHG
114 1/2	95	Sprint 6 7/8 28	6.1	30	112	111	112	−2

The first two columns give the highest selling price and the lowest selling price over the past 52 weeks. These figures are $114\frac{1}{2}\%$ and 95% of the face value. The third column gives the name of the company issuing the bond, the annual interest, and the maturity year of the bond. In this case, the bond is being issued by Sprint. It pays $6\frac{7}{8}\%$ annual interest and it matures in 2028. The next column gives the current yield. This value is obtained by dividing the annual interest by the last selling price. In this case, it is 6.1%. The next column gives the volume in $1000s of the bonds traded yesterday. In this case, it is 30 × $1000 or $30,000. The next two columns give the weekly high and low. In this case, the high was 112% and the low was 111%. The next figure gives the closing price of the bond yesterday in a percent. In this case, it was 112%, and so at the close of the market yesterday, a $1000 bond sold for 112% × $10,000 or 1.12 × $1000 = $1120. The last column gives the net change in price as compared to last week. The net change is given as a percent of the face value. In this case, the price was 2% lower this week. In other words, last week it was 112% + 2% = 114%. So last week the bond sold for 114% × $1000 = $1140. Some bond listings are given in fractions; i.e., $98\frac{3}{8}$, or in decimals; i.e., 98.375.

EXAMPLE: Find the closing price of a $1000 bond if it is listed at 98.33%.

SOLUTION:
Multiply the face value of the bond by the closing percent. For a $1000 bond,

$$\$1000 \times 98.33\% = \$1000 \times 0.9833 = \$9833$$

The closing price is $9833.

There is a broker's fee or commission for selling bonds. It varies with the broker. This fee increases the cost of purchasing a bond and decreases the proceeds when the bond is sold.

EXAMPLE: Five bonds are purchased for $1000 and sold at the closing rate of 103.677%. If the broker charges a $6 fee for each bond bought or sold, find the amount the person made on the sale.

SOLUTION:

Step 1. Find the purchase price.

$$
\begin{aligned}
\text{Purchase price} &= \text{Cost of bonds} + \text{Commission} \\
&= 3 \times \$1000 + 3 \times \$6 \\
&= \$3000 + \$18 \\
&= \$3018
\end{aligned}
$$

Step 2. Find the amount of the sale.
Since the closing price of the bonds is 103.677%, the amount of the sale minus the commission is

$$3 \times 1.03667 \times \$1000 - 3 \times \$6 = \$3110.01 - \$18$$
$$= \$3092.01$$

Step 3. Find the amount the person made.

$$\$3092.01 - \$3018.00 = \$74.01$$

Hence the amount of money that the person made on the sale is $74.01.

If a bond sells for less than 100% of its face value, the owner will lose if he or she sells the bond.

When a bond is sold for less than its face value (usually $1000), the current yield is less than the coupon yield. When the bond is sold for more than its face value, the current yield is larger than its coupon yield. The formula used to determine the current yield is

$$\text{Current yield} = \frac{\text{Annual interest per bond}}{\text{Current price per bond}}$$

EXAMPLE: The Ford Motor Company bond has a coupon interest rate of 7.450%, and the closing price of the bond is 81.438. Find the current yield.

SOLUTION:

Step 1. Find the annual interest.

$$\text{Annual interest per bond} = 1000 \times 0.0745 = \$74.50$$

Step 2. Find the current price per bond.

$$\text{Current price per bond} = 1000 \times 0.81483 = \$814.83$$

Step 3. Substitute in the formula:

$$\text{Current yield} = \frac{\text{Annual interest per bond}}{\text{Current price per bond}}$$

$$= \frac{\$74.50}{\$814.83}$$
$$= 0.0914$$
$$= 9.14\%$$

The current yield is 9.14%.

PRACTICE:

1. A person purchased five $1000 bonds at a closing rate of 95.980%. If the broker's commission is $6 per bond, find the purchase price.
2. Brad James sold three $1000 bonds at the closing rate of 113.5%. If the broker's commission is $4 per bond, find the amount he made.
3. A $1000 bond is paying 8.125% interest. If it closes at 112.63%, find the current yield.
4. A $1000 bond is paying 2.75% interest. If it closes at 106.24%, find the current yield.
5. A $1000 bond was purchased when the rate was 98.125% and sold when the rate was 106.23%. If the broker's fee is $5 per transaction, find the amount made by the owner.

SOLUTIONS:

1. $5 \times \$1000 \times 0.95980 + 5 \times \$6 = \$4799 + \$30$
$$= \$4829$$

2. $3 \times \$1000 \times 1.135 - 3 \times \$4 = \$3405 - \$12$
$$= \$3393$$

3. Annual interest per bond $= \$1000 \times 0.08125 = \$81.25$
Current price per bond $= \$1000 \times 1.1263 = \$1126.30$

$$\text{Current yield} = \frac{\text{Annual interest per bond}}{\text{Current price per bond}} \times 100\%$$

$$= \frac{81.25}{\$1126.30} \times 100\%$$

$$= 7.21\%$$

4. Annual interest per bond $= \$1000 \times 0.0275 = \$27.50$
Current price per bond $= \$1000 \times 1.0624 = \$1062.40$

$$\text{Current yield} = \frac{\text{Annual interest per bond}}{\text{Current price per bond}} \times 100\%$$

$$= \frac{\$27.50}{\$1062.40} \times 100\%$$

$$= 2.59\%$$

5. $1000 \times 0.98125 + 5 = \$986.25$
    $1000 \times 1.0623 - \$5 = \$1057.30$
    $\text{Amount} = \$1057.30 - \$986.25 = \$71.05$

Summary

In order to raise money, corporations issue stock. A person can purchase shares of stock and become a part owner of a company. The board of directors can pay shareholders dividends on the stock that come from the profits of the company. Depending on various conditions of the company and the economy, the price of a company's stock can vary. Stocks are bought and sold on the stock market.

In addition to stocks, a company can issue bonds. There are different types of bonds. Local, state, and federal governments can issue bonds. Bonds pay interest and they can be bought and sold like stocks. A combination of stocks and bonds can be included in an investor's portfolio.

Quiz

Use the following information to answer Questions 1 to 10:

52 weeks HI	LOW	STOCK	DIV	YLD%	PE	VOL (100S)	CLOSE	NET CHG
42.27	33.71	Verizon	1.62	4.6	12	61231	35.14	.11

1. Last year Verizon paid a dividend of
    (a) $0.11
    (b) $4.60
    (c) $1.62
    (d) $12

2. The 52-week lowest price of Verizon stock was
    (a) $33.71
    (b) $16.20
    (c) $35.14
    (d) $42.27

3. The number of shares of Verizon stock that were sold yesterday was
    (a) 61,231
    (b) 12,000

(c) 46,000

(d) 6,123,100

4. The closing price of Verizon stock was
    (a) $33.71
    (b) $35.14
    (c) $35.25
    (d) $42.27

5. The price of Verizon stock the day before yesterday was
    (a) $35.25
    (b) $35.03
    (c) $33.71
    (d) $35.14

6. If a person owned 50 shares of Verizon, the amount in dividends he or she received was
    (a) $230
    (b) $81
    (c) $5.50
    (d) $230

7. The annual earnings per share of Verizon stock is
    (a) $2.93
    (b) $2.81
    (c) $3.52
    (d) $3.43

8. If an investor purchased 50 shares of Verizon stock at $34.00 and the broker's commission was 1.5%, the total cost of the purchase is
    (a) $1700
    (b) $1674.50
    (c) $25.50
    (d) $1725.50

9. If an investor sold 50 shares of Verizon stock for $35.14 and the broker's commission is 1.5%, the amount of the proceeds is
    (a) $1757.00
    (b) $26.36
    (c) $1783.36
    (d) $1730.64

10. An investor purchased 50 shares of Verizon stock at $34.00 and sold it for $35.14. The broker's commission is 1.5% and the dividend paid was $1.62. Find the return on investment.
    (a) 3%
    (b) 5%
    (c) 4%
    (d) 4.6%

11. If three $1000 bonds are purchased at a rate of 109.27% and the broker's commission is $4.50 per bond, the total cost of the transaction is
    (a) $3278.10
    (b) $1097.20
    (c) $1101.70
    (d) $3291.60

12. If a $1000 bond is paying 7.750% interest and is sold at a rate of 98.313%, the current yield is
    (a) 7.883%
    (b) 7.750%
    (c) 8.216%
    (d) 7.431%

13. Mary Carson sold five $1000 bonds at a closing cost rate of 94.562%. If her broker's commission is $3 per bond, her proceeds were
    (a) $4836.86
    (b) $4851.85
    (c) $4713.10
    (d) $4742.55

14. If a $1000 bond is paying 9.328% interest and it closes at 103.26%, the current yield is
    (a) 9.325%
    (b) 9.215%
    (c) 9.0335%
    (d) 9.435%

15. Four $1000 bonds were purchased at 97.125% and later sold at 102.5%. If the broker's commission is $5 per bond, the amount the person made was
    (a) $215
    (b) $175
    (c) $195
    (d) $255

17

Depreciation

Introduction

Businesses most often need to purchase equipment, furniture, buildings, and other necessary items in order to operate. These items are called **assets**. They are part of the cost of doing business. These costs can be deducted from the profits of the business for tax purposes. The federal government does not usually allow the business to deduct the total cost of the item purchased on 1 year's tax statement since the items can be used over a period of years. Instead, the businesses are permitted to deduct a portion of the cost of the item over a period of years called the **estimated lifetime** of the item. The worth of an item most often decreases over the years. This decrease in worth is due to what is called **depreciation**.

There are several methods that are used to figure depreciation. The most common ones are the straight-line method, the units-of-production method, the sum-of-the-years-digits method, the declining-balance method, and the modified accelerated cost-recovery system method (MACRS). Each method will be explained in this chapter.

The Straight-Line Method

The straight-line method is often used because it is the easiest one to compute. This method assumes that the items will depreciate by the same amount each year. It involves four factors:

1. The **original cost** of the item. This cost is the actual price that the business paid for the item plus any shipping costs and installation costs.
2. The **estimated lifetime** of the item. This could be stated by the number of years the item can be used or the number of hours of operation an item is used, such as machinery or in the number of miles a vehicle is driven over its lifetime as in the case of a delivery van.
3. The **scrap** or **resale value** of the item. When the item is no longer useful to the company, it may be sold to another company or even to a salvage dealer who can cut it up for its scrap value.
4. The **book value** of an item for a specific year, number of miles, hours, etc. of operation is the value of an item after depreciation is calculated.

In order to compute the yearly depreciation amount of an item, subtract the scrap value of the item from the original cost, and then divide the answer by the value of its estimated lifetime. The original cost minus the scrap value is called the **depreciable amount**.

EXAMPLE: A factory machine was purchased for $15,000 and has an estimated lifetime of 5 years. If the scrap value at the end of 5 years is estimated at $3000, find the amount of the depreciation for each year.

SOLUTION:
Find the depreciated amount.

$$\text{Depreciated amount} = \$15{,}000 - \$3000 = \$12{,}000$$

Divide the depreciation amount by the estimated lifetime.

$$\$12{,}000 \div 5 = \$2400 \text{ per year}$$

In other words, the value of the machine depreciates $2400 per year.

EXAMPLE: Find the book value at the end of 4 years of a digital video camera costing $24,000 with an expected lifetime of 6 years. The scrap value at the end of its lifetime is $3000.

SOLUTION:

Depreciable amount $= \$24,000 - \$3000 = \$21,000$

$$\$21,000 \div 6 = \$3500$$

The accumulated depreciation for 4 years is

$$\$3500 \times 4 = \$14,000$$

The book value of the camera at the end of 4 years is

$$\$24,000 - \$14,000 = \$10,000$$

No matter what depreciation method is used, a **depreciation schedule** can be made to keep track of an item's depreciation over its lifetime. The depreciation schedule should consist of four items. They are

1. the year
2. the depreciation during the year
3. the accumulated depreciation
4. the value of the item at the end of the year (sometimes called the book value)

Depreciation cannot be claimed when the book value is less than the scrap value of an item.

EXAMPLE: Make a straight-line depreciation schedule for a heating unit that costs \$900, has an estimated lifetime of 4 years, and a scrap value of \$100.

SOLUTION:

Step1. Find the depreciable amount.

$$\$900 - \$100 = \$800$$
$$\$800 \div 4 = \$200$$

Step 2. Find the book value of the unit at the end of the first year by subtracting the depreciation amount from the original cost.

$$\$900 - \$200 = \$700$$

Step 3. For the next year, subtract the depreciation amount from the book value of the unit for the previous year to get the book value for that year.

$$\$700 - \$200 = \$500$$

Step 4. Repeat Step 3 for the remaining years.

For year 3, $500 − $200 = $300

For year 4, $300 − $200 = $100

Step 5. Find the accumulated depreciation for each year by adding the depreciation for that year to the sum of the depreciation for the previous years.

For year 1, $200

For year 2, $200 + $200 = $400

For year 3, $400 + $200 = $600

For year 4, $600 + $200 = $800

Make a table as shown:

Year	Depreciation amount	Accumulated depreciation	Book value
1	$200	$200	$700
2	$200	$400	$500
3	$200	$600	$300
4	$200	$800	$100

PRACTICE:

1. Find the yearly depreciation, using the straight-line method, of 10 security uniforms costing $200 each and having a lifetime of 4 years. There is no scrap value.
2. A file cabinet costs $700. If it has an expected lifetime of 10 years, find the yearly depreciation using the straight-line method. The scrap value is $100.
3. Find the yearly depreciation of a lawn tractor costing $1800. It has an expected lifetime of 5 years and a scrap value of $200. Use the straight-line depreciation method.
4. Find the book value at the end of 60,000 miles of a bus costing $80,000 if it has an expected lifetime of 100,000 miles and a scrap value of $8000. Use the straight-line method.

5. Find the yearly depreciation of 15 table and chair sets for a restaurant costing a total of $60,000. The scrap value is $4000 and the expected lifetime is 8 years. Use the straight-line method. Make a depreciation schedule for the table and chair sets.

SOLUTIONS:

1. Depreciable value: $200 × 10 = $2000;
   Depreciation: $2000 ÷ 4 = $500
2. Depreciable value: $700 − $100 = $600;
   Depreciation: $600 ÷ 10 = $60
3. Depreciable value: $1800 − $200 = $1600;
   Depreciation: $1600 ÷ 5 = $320
4. Depreciable value: $80,000 − $8000 = $72,000;
   Book value: $72,000 × $\dfrac{60,000}{100,000}$ = $43,200
5. Depreciable value: $60,000 − $4000 = $56,000;
   Depreciation: $56,000 ÷ 8 = $7000

Year	Depreciation amount	Accumulated depreciation	Book value
1	$7000	$7000	$53,000
2	$7000	$14,000	$46,000
3	$7000	$21,000	$39,000
4	$7000	$28,000	$32,000
5	$7000	$35,000	$25,000
6	$7000	$42,000	$18,000
7	$7000	$48,000	$11,000
8	$7000	$56,000	$4000

Sum-of-the-Years-Digits Method

The straight-line method assumes that the item depreciated by the same amount each year. The **sum-of-the-years-digits** method assumes that the amount of the depreciation of an item is the largest in the first year and then gets smaller each year at a proportional rate. The reason for this method is that as an item is used, it begins to wear and becomes less efficient and requires more money to service it.

In order to compute the depreciation for each year, follow the steps shown in the next example:

EXAMPLE: A computer system costing $32,000 has an expected lifetime of 5 years. The scrap value is estimated to be $2000. Find the depreciation for each year using the sum-of-the-years-digits method.

SOLUTION:

Step 1. Find the depreciable amount.

$$\$32,000 - \$2000 = \$30,000$$

Step 2. Find the sum of the number of each year for the expected lifetime or the sum of the digits.

$$5 + 4 + 3 + 2 + 1 = 15$$

Step 3. Make a fraction using the year numbers in reverse order over the sum and multiply by the depreciation amount. Do this for each year as shown:

For year 1, $\frac{5}{15} \times \$30,000 = \$10,000$
For year 2, $\frac{4}{15} \times \$30,000 = \$8000$
For year 3, $\frac{3}{15} \times \$30,000 = \$6000$
For year 4, $\frac{2}{15} \times \$30,000 = \$4000$
For year 5, $\frac{1}{15} \times \$30,000 = \$2000$

In other words, the business can deduct $10,000 for depreciation the first year, $8000 the second year, etc. Note that the sum of the depreciation amounts is $30,000.

$$\$10,000 + \$8000 + \$6000 + \$4000 + \$2000 = \$30,000$$

EXAMPLE: A small truck costing $18,000 has an expected lifetime of 4 years and a scrap value of $2000. Find the amount of depreciation for each of the 4 years.

SOLUTION:

Step 1. Find the depreciable amount.

$$\$18{,}000 - \$2000 = \$16{,}000$$

Step 2. Find the sum of the digits.

$$4 + 3 + 2 + 1 = 10$$

Step 3. Find the depreciation for each year.

For year 1, $\frac{4}{10} \times \$16{,}000 = \$6400$

For year 2, $\frac{3}{10} \times \$16{,}000 = \$4800$

For year 3, $\frac{2}{10} \times \$16{,}000 = \$3200$

For year 4, $\frac{1}{10} \times \$16{,}000 = \$1600$

A depreciation schedule for this example can be made as shown:

Year	Depreciation amount	Accumulated depreciation	Book value
1	$6400	$6400	$11,600
2	$4800	$11,200	$6800
3	$3200	$14,400	$3600
4	$1600	$16,000	$2000

Recall from Chapter 12 that the sum of the numbers from 1 to n can be found using the formula $\frac{n(n+1)}{2}$. For example, the sum of the numbers from 1 to 10 can be found by substituting in the formula where $n = 10$.

$$\frac{10(10+1)}{2} = \frac{10(11)}{2} = \frac{110}{2} = 55$$

This can be verified by adding up the numbers $1 + 2 + 3 + 4 + 5 + 6 + 7 + 8 + 9 + 10 = 55$.

PRACTICE:

1. An automotive service center purchases an emission-testing machine for $44,000. Its expected lifetime is 7 years. The estimated scrap value is $2000. Find the yearly depreciation and the book value for the first 2 years using the sum-of-the-years- digits method.
2. A bank purchases 10 safety deposit boxes at a cost of $250 each. If the lifetime of the boxes is 20 years, find the depreciation for the first 3 years using the sum-of-the-years-digits method and the book value at the end of the third year. The estimated scrap value of each box is $10.
3. A library purchases some books for a total cost of $800. If the estimated lifetime value of the books is 4 years and the scrap value is $50, find the annual depreciation using the sum-of-the-years-digits method.
4. An x-ray machine used at an airport costs $75,000 when new. It has an estimated lifetime of 5 years. The scrap value is $5000. Find the annual depreciation using the sum-of-the-years-digits method.
5. A short-line railroad purchases a used switch engine for $48,000. It has an estimated lifetime of 6 years. The scrap value is $6000. Find the yearly depreciation using the sum-of-the-years-digits method. Make a depreciation schedule.

SOLUTIONS:

1. Depreciable amount: $44,000 − $2000 = $42,000
   Sum of digits: $7 + 6 + 5 + 4 + 3 + 2 + 1 = 28$
   For year 1, $\frac{7}{28} \times \$42,000 = \$10,500$
   Book value: $44,000 − $10,500 = $33,500
   For year 2, $\frac{6}{28} \times \$42,000 = \$9000$
   Book value: $33,500 − $9000 = $24,500
2. Original cost: $250 × 10 = $2500
   Depreciable value: $2500 − $10 × 10 = $2400
   Sum of digits: $\frac{20(21)}{2} = 210$
   For year 1, $\frac{20}{210} \times \$2400 = \$228.57$
   Book value: $2500 − $228.57 = $2271.43
   For year 2, $\frac{19}{210} \times \$2400 = \$217.14$

Book value: $2271.43 − $217.14 = $2054.29

For year 3, $\frac{18}{210}$ × $2400 = $205.71

Book value: $2054.29 − $205.71 = $1848.58

3. Depreciated value: $800 − $50 = $750

Sum of digits: $4 + 3 + 2 + 1 = 10$

For year 1, $\frac{4}{10}$ × $750 = $300

For year 2, $\frac{3}{10}$ × $750 = $225

For year 3, $\frac{2}{10}$ × $750 = $150

For year 4, $\frac{1}{10}$ × $\frac{\$750}{1}$ = $75

4. Depreciable value: $75,000 − $5000 = $70,000

Sum of digits: $5 + 4 + 3 + 2 + 1 = 15$

For year 1, $\frac{5}{15}$ × $70,000 = $23,333.33

For year 2, $\frac{4}{15}$ × $70,000 = $18,666.67

For year 3, $\frac{3}{15}$ × $70,000 = $14,000

For year 4, $\frac{2}{15}$ × $70,000 = $9333.33

For year 5, $\frac{1}{15}$ × $70,000 = $4666.67

5. Depreciable value: $48,000 − $6000 = $42,000

Sum of digits: $6 + 5 + 4 + 3 + 2 + 1 = 21$

For year 1, $\frac{6}{21}$ × $42,000 = $12,000

Book value: $48,000 − $12,000 = $36,000

For year 2, $\frac{5}{21}$ × $42,000 = $10,000

Book value: $36,000 − $10,000 = $26,000

For year 3, $\frac{4}{21}$ × $42,000 = $8000

Book value: $26,000 − $8000 = $18,000

For year 4, $\frac{3}{21}$ × $42,000 = $6000

Book value: $18,000 − $6000 = $12,000

For year 5, $\frac{2}{21}$ × $42,000 = $4000

Book value: $12,000 − $4000 = $8000

For year 6, $\frac{1}{21}$ × $42,000 = $2000

Book value: $8000 − $2000 = $6000

Year	Depreciation amount	Accumulated depreciation	Book value
1	$12,000	$12,000	$36,000
2	$10,000	$22,000	$26,000
3	$8000	$30,000	$18,000
4	$6000	$36,000	$12,000
5	$4000	$40,000	$8000
6	$2000	$42,000	$6000

Declining-Balance Method

The **declining-balance** method of computing depreciation is similar to sum-of-the-years-digits method and assumes that the largest amount of depreciation occurs during the first year then deceases for each succeeding year.

To compute the depreciation using the declining-balance method, it is first necessary to find a yearly depreciation rate. This is done by dividing 1 by the number of years of the expected lifetime of the item. This decimal then is used as a multiplier. If it is used as it is, then the depreciation is called a **straight-line declining balance**. It can also be doubled (i.e., multiplied by 2), and this type of depreciation is called the **double-declining balance**. After obtaining this factor, multiply the *original cost* by this factor to get the first year's depreciation, and then multiply the book values by this factor to get the depreciation for the rest of the years.

The multiplication continues for the estimated lifetime of the item or until the book value is equal to the scrap value of the time. Remember, you cannot depreciate the value of the item below its scrap value.

EXAMPLE: A cleaning company purchases 10 vacuum cleaners at a total of $4000. The expected lifetime of the vacuum cleaners is 4 years. The scrap value is $250. Using the double-declining balance method, find the yearly depreciation.

SOLUTION:

Step 1. Find the depreciation rate and double it.

$$\frac{1}{4} \times 2 = 0.50$$

Step 2. Find the depreciation for the first year.

$$\$4000 \times 0.5 = \$2000$$

Note: Always use the total cost, not the depreciation cost.

Step 3. Find the book value.

$$\$4000 - \$2000 = \$2000$$

Repeat the steps for the lifetime of the item. Use the book value in each case.

> For year 2, Depreciation: $\$2000 \times 0.05 = \$1000$
> Book value: $\$2000 - \$1000 = \$1000$
>
> For year 3, Depreciation: $\$1000 \times 0.05 = \$500$
> Book value: $\$1000 - \$500 = \$500$
>
> For year 4, Depreciation: $\$500 \times 0.5 = \$250$
> Book value: $\$500 - \$250 = \$250$

EXAMPLE: A delivery van costs $22,000 and has an estimated lifetime of 5 years. Its scrap value in 5 years is $2500. Find the depreciation using the double-declining balance.

SOLUTION:

> The depreciation rate is $\frac{1}{5} \times 2 = 0.4$.
> For year 1, Depreciation: $\$22,000 \times 0.4 = \$8800$
> Book value: $\$22,000 - \$8800 = \$13,200$
> For year 2, Depreciation: $\$13,200 \times 0.4 = \$5280$
> Book value: $\$13,200 - \$5280 = \$7920$
> For year 3, Deprecation: $\$7920 \times 0.40 = \$3168$
> Book value: $\$7920 - \$3168 = \$4752$
> For year 4, Depreciation: $\$4752 \times 0.40 = \$1900.80$
> Book value: $\$4752.00 - \$1900.08 = \$2851.20$

A depreciation table for this example is shown next:

Year	Depreciation amount	Accumulated depreciation	Book value
1	$8800.00	$8800.00	$13,200.00
2	$5280.00	$14,080.00	$7920.00
3	$3168.00	$17,248.00	$4752.00
4	$1900.80	$19,148.80	$2851.20

PRACTICE:

1. A soundboard for a theater's sound system costs $1500. Its estimated lifetime is 3 years. Its scrap value is $50. Find the annual depreciation using the double-declining method.
2. A photographer purchases a digital video camera for $24,000. Its estimated lifetime is 4 years. The scrap value is $1400. Find the annual depreciation using the double-declining balance method. Make a depreciation schedule for the item.
3. A large hotel chain purchases carpeting for its new building in Harrisburg. The cost and installation is $96,000. The estimated lifetime is 7 years. Its scrap value is $4000. Find the depreciation for the first 2 years using the double-declining balance method.
4. The same hotel chain purchases 80 beds with springs and mattresses for a total cost of $56,000. The estimated lifetime is 10 years. The scrap value is $600. Find the depreciation for the first 3 years using the double-declining method.
5. A bank purchases a security system costing $24,000 (including installation). The lifetime of the system is 12 years. Its scrap value is $1000. Find the depreciation for the first 2 years using the double-declining balance method.

SOLUTIONS:

1. The multiplier is $\frac{1}{3} \times 2 = \frac{2}{3}$.
    For year 1, Depreciation: $\frac{2}{3} \times \$1500 = \$1000$
    Book value: $\$1500 - \$1000 = \$500$
    For year 2, Depreciation: $\frac{2}{3} \times \$500 = \$333.33$

Book value: $500 − $333.33 = $166.67
For year 3, Depreciation: $\frac{2}{3}$ × $166.67 = $111.11
Book value: $166.67 − $111.11 = $55.56

2. The multiplier is $\frac{1}{4}$ × 2 = 0.50.
    For year 1, Depreciation: $24,000 × 0.50 = $12,000
    Book value: $24,000 − $12,000 = $12,000
    For year 2, Depreciation: $12,000 × 0.50 = $6000
    Book value: $12,000 − $6000 = $6000
    For year 3, Depreciation: $6000 × 0.50 = $3000
    Book value: $6000 − $3000 = $3000
    For year 4, Depreciation: $3000 × 0.50 = $1500
    Book value: $3000 − $1500 = $1500
    Depreciation schedule:

Year	Depreciation amount	Accumulated depreciation	Book value
1	$12,000	$12,000	$12,000
2	$6000	$18,000	$6000
3	$3000	$21,000	$3000
4	$1500	$22,500	$1500

3. The multiplier is $\frac{1}{7}$ × 2 = $\frac{2}{7}$ or 0.29 (rounded).
    For year 1, Depreciation: $96,000 × 0.29 = $27,840
    Book value: $96,000 − $27,840 = $68,160
    For year 2, Depreciation: $68,160.00 × 0.29 = $19,766.40
    Book value: $68,160.00 − $19,766.40 = $48,393.60

4. The multiplier is $\frac{1}{10}$ × 2 = 0.2
    For year 1, Depreciation: $56,000 × 0.2 = $11,200
    Book value: $56,000 − $11,200 = $44,800
    For year 2, Depreciation: $44,800 × 0.2 = $8960
    Book value: $44,800 − $8960 = $35,840
    For year 3, Depreciation: $35,840 × 0.2 = $7168
    Book value: $35840 − $7,168 = $28,672

5. The multiplier is $\frac{1}{12} \times 2 = \frac{2}{12}$ or $\frac{1}{6}$.

    For year 1, Depreciation: $24,000 \times \frac{1}{6} = \$4000$

    Book value: $24,000 - \$4000 = \$20,000$

    For year 2, Depreciation: $20,000 \times \frac{1}{6} = \$3333.33$

    Book value: $20,000 - \$3333.33 = \$16,666.67$

The Units-of-Production Method

When items (such as a snowplows) are used for periods of time (in the winter months) and then sit idle for another period of time (in the late spring, summer, and early fall months), the units-of-production method of depreciation is often used.

In order to use this method, you first find the depreciation per unit. This is found by dividing the depreciable value by the number of units that are produced during the expected lifetime of the product, and then multiply this number by the number of units produced.

EXAMPLE: A machine used to fill jars with vitamin pills costs $80,000. It is expected to fill 100,000 bottles during its lifetime. The scrap value of the machine is $10,000. Find the depreciation after the machine has filled 35,000 bottles.

SOLUTION:

$$\text{Unit depreciation} = \frac{\text{Depreciable value}}{\text{Units produced during its lifetime}}$$

$$= \frac{\$80,000 - \$10,000}{100,000}$$

$$= \$0.70$$

$$\text{Depreciation} = \text{Unit depreciation} \times \text{Number of units produced}$$

$$\$0.70 \times 35,000 = \$24,500$$

The depreciation is $24,500.

EXAMPLE: A taxicab company purchases a taxicab for $24,000. Its expected lifetime is 75,000 miles, and its scrap value is $6000. Find the depreciation after the cab has been driven 50,000 miles.

SOLUTION:

$$\text{Unit depreciation} = \frac{\$24,000 - \$6000}{75,000} = \$0.24$$

$$\text{Depreciation} = \$0.24 \times 50,000 = \$12,000$$

The depreciation is $12,000.

PRACTICE:

1. A small van is purchased for $32,000. Its expected lifetime is 50,000 miles. The scrap value is $2000. Find the depreciation after the van has been driven 18,000 miles.
2. A machine used to stamp serial numbers on labels for television sets costs $14,000. Its expected lifetime is to stamp 20,000 labels. Its scrap value is $500. Find the depreciation after 12,000 labels were made.
3. A bookbinding machine costs $32,000. It is expected to bind 20,000 books. Its scrap value is $4000. Find the depreciation after 10,000 books were bound.
4. A machine to peel potatoes costs an amusement park $18,000. It is expected to peel 8000 pounds of potatoes. Its scrap value is $2000. Find the depreciation after it has been used to peel 6000 pounds of potatoes.
5. A candle-making machine costs $20,000. It is expected to make 5000 candles. Its scrap value is $2000. Find the depreciation after making 4000 candles.

SOLUTIONS:

1. Depreciable value: $32,000 − $2000 = $30,000
   Unit depreciation: $\frac{30,000}{50,000} = \$0.60$
   Depreciation: $0.60 × 18,000 = $10,800
2. Depreciation value: $14,000 − $500 = $13,500
   Unit depreciation: $\frac{\$13,500}{20,000} = \$0.675$
   Depreciation: $0.675 × 12,000 = $8100
3. Depreciable value: $32,000 − $4000 = $28,000
   Unit depreciation: $\frac{\$28,000}{20,000} = \$1.40$
   Depreciation: $1.40 × 10,000 = $14,000

4. Depreciable value: $18,000 − $2000 = $16,000

   Unit depreciation: $\frac{\$16,000}{8000} = \$2.00$

   Depreciation: $2.00 × 6000 = $12,000

5. Depreciable value: $20,000 − $2000 = $18,000

   Unit depreciation: $\frac{\$18,000}{5000} = \$3.60$

   Depreciation: $3.60 × 4000 = $14,400

The MACRS Method

The Tax Reform Act of 1986 allows businesses to compute depreciation using *IRS Publication 534*. This form requires certain items to be depreciated over a period of 3 years, other items over a period of 5, 7, 10, 15, and 20 years. In addition, it gives a multiplier for each year so that the only thing that is necessary to do to compute depreciation is multiply the total cost of the item by the multiplier given in a table. For example, a piece of office furniture such as a desk costing $430 has a 7-year lifetime. To find the depreciation for the third year, multiply: $430 × 17.49% = $430 × 0.1749 = $75.21 The 17.49% comes from a table in the publication (see *IRS Publication 534* for more information).

Summary

Whenever an item is purchased and used by a business, its value decreases over time. The amount of the decrease is called depreciation. Several methods for computing depreciation were explained in this chapter. They were the straight-line method, the units-of-production method, the sum-of-the-years-digits method, and the declining-balance method. These methods are used for accounting purposes. For tax purposes, the MACRS method is used.

Quiz

1. The value of an item that declines over time is called
   (a) inventory
   (b) depreciation
   (c) declining value
   (d) assets

2. After an item's estimated lifetime, its worth is called the
   (a) depreciated value
   (b) straight-line value
   (c) scrap value
   (d) lifetime value

3. If the amount of depreciation remains the same for each year of an item's lifetime, the method used to calculate the depreciation was
   (a) straight-line method
   (b) sum-of-the-years-digits method
   (c) the declining-balance method
   (d) the MACRS method

4. The original cost of an item includes
   (a) the actual price of the item
   (b) the shipping cost of an item
   (c) the installation cost of an item
   (d) all of the above

5. The original cost of an item minus the scrap value of an item is called
   (a) depreciable value
   (b) estimated value
   (c) book value
   (d) straight-line value

6. The value of an item after the depreciation amount is subtracted is its
   (a) depreciable value
   (b) estimated value
   (c) book value
   (d) straight-line value

7. If the original cost of an item is $1250 and its scrap value is $175, then the depreciable value of the item is
   (a) $1425
   (b) $1150
   (c) $925
   (d) $1075

8. A hybrid (gas-electric) automobile was purchased as a company car. The original cost was $27,000. Its estimated lifetime is 5 years. The scrap value is $7000. Using the straight-line depreciation method, what is the depreciable value of the automobile?
   (a) $34,000
   (b) $20,000

(c) $5000
(d) $4000

9. Using the information in the previous problem, what is the annual depreciation amount if the straight-line method is used?
(a) $4000
(b) $5000
(c) $20,000
(d) $5400

10. A company purchased an air cleaner costing $450 for its laboratory. The estimated lifetime of the product is 4 years. Its scrap value is $30. What is the depreciation amount for the first year if the sum-of-the-years-digits method is used?
(a) $180
(b) $192
(c) $150
(d) $168

11. Using the information in the previous problem, what is the depreciation amount for the final year?
(a) $45
(b) $48
(c) $30
(d) $42

12. A food processing company purchased a machine that sterilizes jars used for baby food. The original cost of the machine was $28,000. The scrap value of the machine is $3000, and its estimated lifetime is 5 years. Using the double-declining balance method, what is the depreciation for the second year of its lifetime?
(a) $11,200
(b) $2000
(c) $6720
(d) $8000

13. A health club purchases an exercise bicycle at a cost of $1800. Its expected lifetime is 20,000 miles. Its scrap value is $200. Using the units-of-production method of depreciation, what is the unit depreciation factor?
(a) 0.09
(b) 0.9
(c) 0.08
(d) 0.8

14. Using the information in the previous problem, what is the depreciation after the bicycle has been in use for 12,000 miles?
    (a) $960
    (b) $1440
    (c) $1620
    (d) $1280

15. The depreciation method that is used on an IRS tax form is the
    (a) straight-line method
    (b) sum-of-the-years-digits method
    (c) declining-balance method
    (d) MACRS method

Inventory

Introduction

Successful businesses need to know how much merchandise they have on hand, the value of the merchandise, and how often they need to replace merchandise that has been sold. In order to determine these aspects, businesses use an inventory of the items. The merchandise and the value of the items a business has on hand to sell on a specific day are called its **inventory**. The inventory can be done weekly, monthly, quarterly, semiannually, or annually. Inventory is also used for financial statements and tax purposes.

When the author was in college, he worked in a large grocery store. Once a year, on a Sunday, all employees were asked to work out inventory. We had to count every single item on the shelves in the store. Today, with the advent of computers, the inventory process is much easier.

Cost of Goods Sold

Once the items in a store are counted, it is necessary to determine the **cost of goods sold**. The cost of goods sold is equal to the cost of goods available for sale minus the cost of the goods remaining. For example, if a store purchased 100 balloons at $0.25 each at the beginning of the month, then the cost of goods available for sale is $100 \times \$0.25 = \$25$. If there were five balloons left at the end of the month, then the cost of the remaining inventory would be $5 \times \$0.25 = \$1.25$. Hence the cost of the goods sold during the month is equal to $\$25.00 - \$1.25$ or $\$23.75$.

Unfortunately inventory is not always this simple since many items can be bought at different prices and also sold at different prices during the inventory period so there are several different ways that are used to determine the cost of goods sold. Some are explained here.

Consider the merchandise shown in Table 18-1. The table shows the inventory for a tote bag.

Table 18-1

Date of Purchase	Number of Units Purchased	Cost of Unit	Number of Units Remaining
March 1	18	$10	12
March 2	12	$8	7
April 16	13	$9	10
May 12	10	$10	

The first method used to calculate the cost of goods available is called the **specific identification inventory method**. Here all that is necessary to do is find the total cost of items purchased for the period and subtract the cost of the items remaining at the end of the period.

EXAMPLE: Use the inventory shown in Table 18-1 to find the cost of goods sold.

SOLUTION:

Step 1. Find the total cost of the items purchased (i.e., the cost of goods available for sale).

$$18 \times \$10 = \$180$$
$$12 \times \$8 = \$96$$
$$13 \times \$9 = \$117$$
$$10 \times \$10 = \$100$$
$$\text{Total} = \$180 + \$96 + \$117 + \$100 = \$493$$

Step 2. Find the cost of the items remaining.

$$12 \times \$10 = \$120$$
$$7 \times \$8 = \$56$$
$$10 \times \$9 = \$90$$
$$\text{Total} = \$120 + \$56 + \$90 = \$266$$

Step 3. Subtract $\$493 - \$266 = \$227$.
 Hence the cost of goods sold for that period is $227.

Another method used to determine the cost of goods sold is called the **weighted-average inventory method**. Here the cost of the number of items remaining is found by a weighted average that is subtracted from the cost of goods available for sale.

EXAMPLE: Find the cost of goods sold using the inventory shown in Table 18-1 by the weighted-average inventory method.

SOLUTION:

Step 1. Find the total cost of the items purchased.

$$18 \times \$10 = \$180$$
$$12 \times \$96 = \$96$$
$$13 \times \$9 = \$117$$
$$10 \times \$10 = \$100$$
$$\text{Total} = \$493$$

Step 2. Divide this value ($493) by the number of items available for sale. To find this value, add the number of items purchased given in the first column of Table 18-1.

$$\frac{\$493}{18 + 12 + 13 + 10} = \frac{\$493}{53} = \$9.30$$

Step 3. Multiply this value ($9.30) by the number of items in the ending inventory. This value is found by adding the numbers in the last column

of Table 18-1.

$$\$9.30 \times (12 + 7 + 10) = \$9.30 \times 29 = \$269.70$$

This value is the cost of the number of items remaining.
Step 4. Subtract this value from the cost of the merchandise purchased as found in Step 1.

$$\$493 - \$269.70 = \$223.30$$

Hence the cost of goods sold using the weighted-average method is $223.30.

This method is used often because it saves time by using an average. The average was found in Step 2. It is useful when a lot of purchases were made at different prices.

The third method used is called the **first-in, first-out method**. Hence it is assumed that the first items purchased were sold first and the items that remain to be sold first are from the last items purchased. The cost of the number of items remaining is determined by finding the cost of the items remaining to be sold based on the last and possibly next to the last purchase prices. This value is subtracted from the total cost of the merchandise purchased.

EXAMPLE: Use the inventory shown in Table 18-1 and find the cost of goods sold by the first-in, first-out method.

SOLUTION:

Step 1. Find the cost of goods available for sale. Use the method found in Step 1 of the previous two examples. The cost is $493.
Step 2. Find the cost per item based on the last items remaining based on the last items purchased. Add the numbers in the last column.

$$12 + 7 + 10 = 29$$

Hence there are 29 items remaining. Count backwards. On May 12, 10 items were purchased at $10 each; so $29 - 10 = 19$ items remain. On April 16, 13 items were purchased at a cost of $9 each: $19 - 13 = 6$. So 6 of the 12 items purchased on March 2 at a cost of $8 remain. Hence the cost of ending inventory is

$$10 \times \$10 = \$100$$

$$13 \times \$9 = \$117$$

$$6 \times \$8 = \$48$$

$$\text{Total} = \$100 + \$117 + \$48 = \$265$$

Step 3. Subtract this $265 from $493.

$$\$493 - \$265 = \$228$$

In this case, the cost of goods sold using the first-in, first-out method is $228.

A final way to determine cost of goods sold is the **last-in, first-out inventory method**. Here it is assumed that the last items purchased are the first items sold. In this case, it is assumed that the stock is not rotated; that is, the old stock is at the rear of the shelf and the new stock has been placed on the front of the shelf. (Not a good idea.) The items remaining to be sold are assumed to come from the first ones purchased. The cost of goods for sale is based on this premise and then the cost of goods remaining is subtracted from the cost of goods available for sale to get the cost of goods sold.

EXAMPLE: Use the inventory shown in Table 18-1 and find the cost of goods sold using the last-in, first-out inventory method.

SOLUTION:

Step 1. Find the total cost of goods available for sale. This amount was $493 (see Step 1 of the first two examples in this section).
Step 2. Find the cost of the items remaining assuming the number of items left came from the earliest items purchased. There are 29 items left (see Step 2 in the previous example). Eighteen items were purchased at $10, and $29 - 18 = 11$ were purchased at $8. Hence the cost of the number of items remaining is

$$18 \times \$10 = \$180$$

$$11 \times \$8 = \$88$$

$$\text{Total} = \$180 + \$88 = \$268$$

Step 3. Subtract this value ($268) from the cost of the goods available for sale.

$$\$493 - \$268 = \$225$$

Hence the cost of goods sold using the last-in, first-out method is $225.

The four methods give somewhat different answers (i.e., $227, $223.30, $228, and $225). Note that the answers are close. Each method has its advantages and disadvantages.

PRACTICE:

Use the following information on the cost of stepladders for Exercises 1 to 5.

Date of Purchase	Number of Units Purchased	Cost of Unit	Number of Units Remaining
July 1	24	$32	16
July 10	18	$38	9
July 18	20	$29	12
July 25	14	$30	

1. Find the cost of goods available for sale.
2. Find the cost of goods sold using the specific identification inventory method.
3. Find the cost of goods sold using the weighted-average inventory method.
4. Find the cost of goods sold using the first-in, first-out inventory method.
5. Find the cost of goods sold using the last-in, first-out inventory method.

Use the following information on the cost of soap dispensers for Exercises 6- to 10.

Date of Purchase	Number of Units Purchased	Cost of Unit	Number of Units Remaining
September 1	24	$18	5
September 6	18	$16	9
September 11	20	$20	4
September 19	32	$18	14
September 24	19	$20	7
September 30	10	$16	

6. Find the cost of goods available for sale.

7   Find the cost of goods sold using the specific identification inventory method.

8   Find the cost of goods sold using the weighted-average inventory method.

9   Find the cost of goods sold using the first-in, first-out inventory method.

10 Find the cost of goods sold using the last-in, first-out method.

SOLUTIONS:

1. Cost of goods available for sale is

$$24 \times \$32 = \$768$$
$$18 \times \$38 = \$684$$
$$20 \times \$29 = \$580$$
$$14 \times \$30 = \underline{\$420}$$
$$\text{Total} = \$2452$$

2. From Exercise 1, the cost of goods available for sale is $2452. The cost of goods remaining is

$$16 \times \$32 = \$512$$
$$9 \times \$38 = \$342$$
$$12 \times \$29 = \underline{\$348}$$
$$\text{Total} = \$1202$$

Hence the cost of goods sold using the specific identification inventory method is

$$\$2452 - \$1202 = \$1250$$

3. From Exercise 1, the cost of goods available for sale is $2452. The number of items available for sale is

$$24 + 18 + 20 + 14 = 76$$

The weighted average is $\frac{\$2452}{76} = \$32.26$.
The number of items remaining is $16 + 9 + 12 = 37$.
The cost of the goods remaining is $37 \times \$32.26 = \$1193.62$.

The cost of goods sold using the weighted-average method is

$$\$2452 - \$1193.62 = \$1258.38$$

4. From Exercise 1, the cost of goods available for sale is $2452. There are $16 + 9 + 12 = 37$ items remaining.
   Then 14 items were purchased at $30.
     20 items were purchased at $29.
     3 items were purchased at $38.
   The cost of the goods remaining is

$$
\begin{aligned}
14 \times \$30 &= \ \ \$420 \\
20 \times \$29 &= \ \ \$580 \\
3 \times \$38 &= \ \ \underline{\$114} \\
\text{Total} &= \$1114
\end{aligned}
$$

Hence the cost of goods sold using the first-in, first-out inventory method is

$$\$2452 - \$1114 = \$1338$$

5. From Exercise 1, the cost of goods available for sale is $2452. The number of items remaining for sale is 37 (see Exercise 3). Then the cost of the items remaining is

$$
\begin{aligned}
24 \times \$32 &= \ \ \$768 \\
13 \times \$38 &= \ \ \underline{\$494} \\
\text{Total} &= \$1262
\end{aligned}
$$

Hence the cost of goods sold using the last-in, first-out method is

$$\$2452 - \$1262 = \$1190$$

6. The cost of goods available for sale is

$$
\begin{aligned}
24 \times \$18 &= \ \ \$432 \\
18 \times \$16 &= \ \ \$288
\end{aligned}
$$

$$20 \times \$20 = \ \$400$$
$$32 \times \$18 = \ \$576$$
$$19 \times \$20 = \ \$380$$
$$10 \times \$16 = \ \underline{\$160}$$
$$\text{Total} = \$2236$$

7.   From Exercise 6, the cost of goods sold is \$2236. The cost of remaining goods is

$$5 \times \$18 = \$90$$
$$9 \times \$16 = \$144$$
$$4 \times \$20 = \$80$$
$$14 \times \$18 = \$252$$
$$7 \times \$20 = \underline{\$140}$$
$$\text{Total} = \$706$$

Hence the cost of goods sold using the specific identification inventory method is \$2236 - \$706 = \$1530

8.   From Exercise 6, the cost of goods sold is \$2236. The number of items available for sale is $24 + 18 + 20 + 32 + 19 + 10 = 123$.

The weighted average is $\dfrac{\$2236}{123} = \$18.18$.

The number of items remaining is

$$5 + 9 + 4 + 14 + 7 = 39$$

The cost of the remaining goods is

$$39 \times \$18.18 = \$709.02$$

The cost of goods sold using the weighted-average method is

$$\$2236.00 - \$709.02 = \$1526.98$$

9. From Exercise 6, the cost of goods sold is $2236, and the number of items remaining is $5 + 9 + 14 + 4 + 7 = 39$
Then the cost of remaining goods is

$$10 \times \$16 = \$160$$

$$19 \times \$20 = \$380$$

$$10 \times \$18 = \underline{\$180}$$

$$\text{Total} = \$720$$

Hence the cost of goods sold using the first-in, first-out method is

$$\$2236 - \$720 = \$1516$$

10. From Exercise 6, the cost of goods sold is $2236, and from Exercise 8, the number of items remaining is 39. Then the cost of remaining goods is

$$24 \times \$18 = \$432$$

$$15 \times \$16 = \underline{\$240}$$

$$\text{Total} = \$672$$

Hence the cost of goods sold using the last-in, first-out method is

$$\$2236 - \$672 = \$1564$$

The Retail Inventory Method

A common inventory method that is used often by department stores is called the **retail inventory method**. This method uses a ratio between the cost of goods available for sale and the retail value of the goods available for sale. The amount of the sales for the inventory period is multiplied by the ratio to get the cost of goods sold. The advantage of this method is that the information needed is easily obtained. The first example here uses the information in Table 18-1 for the cost value of the tote bags and has been included in Table 18-2 under "Cost Value." However, the additional information needed is the retail value of the tote bags and the amount of sales during the inventory period. This information is also shown in Table 18-2.

Table 18-2

Date of Purchase	Cost Value	Retail Value
March 1	$180	$270
March 2	$96	$180
April 16	$117	$195
May 12	$100	$150
Sales during the period		$375

EXAMPLE: Use the information shown in Tables 18-1 (on page 292) and 18-2 and the retail inventory method to find the cost of goods sold.

SOLUTION:

Step 1. Find the cost of goods available for sale. Add the cost values shown in Table 18-2.

$$\$180 + \$96 + \$117 + \$100 = \$493$$

2. Find the retail value of goods available for sale. Add the retail values shown in Table 18-2. (Do not include the amount of sales.)

$$\$270 + \$180 + \$195 + \$150 = \$795$$

3. Find the cost ratio.

$$\text{Ratio} = \frac{\text{Cost of goods available for sale}}{\text{Retail value of goods available for sale}}$$

$$= \frac{\$493}{\$795} = 0.62 \text{ (rounded)}$$

4. Multiply the amount of sales by the cost ratio to get the cost of goods sold.

$$\text{Cost of goods sold} = \$375 \times 0.62$$

$$= \$232.50$$

Hence the cost of goods sold is $232.50.

EXAMPLE: Use the retail inventory method to find the cost of goods sold given the following information:

Cost of goods available for sale:	$41,000
Retail value of goods available for sale:	$78,000
Sales for the inventory period:	$56,000

SOLUTION:

Step 1. Find the cost ratio.

$$\text{Cost ratio} = \frac{\$41,000}{\$78,000} = 0.53 \text{ (rounded)}$$

Step 2. Multiply the retail sales by the cost ratio to get the cost of goods sold. Cost of goods sold = Sales × Cost ratio

$$= \$56,000 \times 0.53$$

$$= \$29,680$$

PRACTICE:
Use the following information for Exercises 1 to 4:

Date	Cost Value	Retail Value
July 1	$2371	$3216
July 13	$1616	$2223
July 20	$897	$1031
July 25	$1055	$1431
Sales during the period		$4218

1. Find the cost of goods available for sale.
2. Find the retail value of the goods.
3. Find the cost ratio.
4. Find the cost of goods sold using the retail inventory method.

Use the following information for Exercise 5 to 8:

Date	Cost Value	Retail Value
September 1	$931	$1437
September 8	$265	$561
September 15	$416	$762
September 27	$221	$408
Total sales		$863

5.   Find the cost of goods available for sale.
6.   Find the retail value of goods available for sale.
7.   Find the cost ratio.
8.   Find the cost of goods sold using the retail inventory method.

SOLUTIONS:

1.   Cost of goods available for sale = $2371 + $1616 + $897 + $1055 = $5939
2.   Retail value of goods = $3216 + $2223 + $1031 + $1431 = $7901
3.   Cost ratio = $\dfrac{\$5939}{\$7901}$ = 0.752 (rounded)
4.   Cost of goods sold = 0.752 × $4218 = $3171.94
5.   Cost of goods available for sale = $931 + $265 + $416 + $221 = $1833
6.   Retail value of goods available for sale = $1437 + $561 + $762 + $408 = $3168
7.   Cost ratio = $\dfrac{\$1833}{\$3168}$ = 0.579 (rounded)
8.   Cost of goods sold = 0.579 × $863 = $499.68

Inventory Turnover Rate

The **inventory turnover rate** tells the business owner how often the merchandise needs to be replaced. For example, a turnover rate of 4 means that the merchandise has been sold and replaced four times over the period. A period could be a month, a year, or any designated time period. When the turnover rate is low, it generally means that the merchandise is not selling. There are many reasons for this. Perhaps the customers do not like the item. Perhaps the item is priced too high. Perhaps it is not being advertised properly.

On the other hand, when the inventory turnover rate is high, the merchandise may be priced much lower than the competitor's price, thus lowering profits. Perhaps the business is not purchasing enough items to keep the shelves stocked with the item.

There are no specific guidelines for a so-called good inventory turnover rate. When a business deals in perishable goods, a high turnover rate is desirable. For other non-perishable goods, the inventory turnover rates need to be compared with other similar businesses to see how well the sales are doing. Also rates can be compared to previous rates to see how things are selling. Generally speaking, for non-perishable goods, inventory rates of 3 or 4 for a 1-year period are considered good.

There are two methods used to calculate the inventory rate. One uses the cost prices and the other uses the retail prices of the merchandise.

To find the inventory turnover rate based on cost, first find the average cost inventory of the goods. This can be found by using the formula:

$$\text{Average inventory cost} = \frac{\text{Beginning inventory cost} + \text{Ending inventory cost}}{2}$$

Then use the next formula to find the inventory turnover rate based on cost.

$$\text{Rate based on cost} = \frac{\text{Cost of goods sold}}{\text{Average inventory cost}}$$

The rate can be calculated monthly, semiannually, or yearly.

EXAMPLE: For the month of July Pamela's Pots & Plants had net sales of $36,000. The cost of the inventory beginning July 1 was $20,000 and the cost of the inventory on July 31 was $12,000. Find the average inventory cost and inventory turnover rate based on cost.

SOLUTION:

$$\text{Average inventory cost} = \frac{\text{Beginning inventory cost} + \text{Ending inventory cost}}{2}$$

$$= \frac{\$20,000 + \$12,000}{2}$$

$$= \frac{\$32,000}{2}$$

$$= \$16,000$$

$$\text{Turnover rate} = \frac{\text{Cost of goods sold}}{\text{Average inventory cost}}$$

$$= \frac{\$36,000}{\$16,000}$$

$$= 2.25$$

The value is rounded to 2. Whole numbers are usually used. Hence the inventory's turnover rate based on cost is 2.

To find the inventory turnover rate based on retail, first find the average retail inventory using the following formula:

$$\text{Average inventory retail} = \frac{\text{Beginning inventory retail} + \text{Ending inventory retail}}{2}$$

Then use the next formula to find the inventory turnover rate based on retail.

$$\text{Rate based on retail} = \frac{\text{Net sales}}{\text{Average inventory retail}}$$

EXAMPLE: For the month of August Comfort Hot Tubs and Spas had net sales of $48,000. The beginning inventory retail was $24,000 and the ending inventory retail was $8000. Find the average inventory retail and the inventory turnover rate based on retail.

SOLUTION:

$$\text{Average inventory retail} = \frac{\text{Beginning inventory retail} + \text{Ending inventory retail}}{2}$$

$$= \frac{\$24,000 + \$8000}{2}$$

$$= \frac{\$32,000}{2}$$

$$= \$16,000$$

$$\text{Rate based on retail} = \frac{\text{Net sales}}{\text{Average inventory retail}}$$

$$= \frac{\$48,000}{\$16,000}$$

$$= 3$$

Hence the inventory turnover rate based on retail is 3.

EXAMPLE: For the month of April the Building Fitness Store had net sales of $60,000. The retail price of the inventory at the beginning of April was $50,000 and at the end of the month it was $10,000. Find the average inventory retail and the inventory rate at retail.

SOLUTION:

$$\text{Average inventory retail} = \frac{\text{Beginning inventory retail} + \text{Ending inventory retail}}{2}$$

$$= \frac{\$50,000 + \$10,000}{2}$$

$$= \frac{\$60,000}{2}$$

$$= \$30,000$$

$$\text{Inventory rate at retail} = \frac{\text{Net sales}}{\text{Average inventory retail}}$$

$$= \frac{\$60,000}{\$30,000}$$

$$= 2$$

Hence the inventory rate at retail is 2.

PRACTICE:

1. Betty's Beauty Supply has net sales of $18,000 at cost for the month of December. The cost of the inventory at the beginning of December was $10,000 and the cost of the inventory at the end of December was $8000. Find the average inventory cost and the turnover rate at cost for December.
2. Meyer's Hardware had sales of $11,000 at cost for the month of March. The cost of the inventory at the beginning of the month was $3,250 and the cost of the inventory at the end of the month was $2250. Find the average inventory cost and the turnover rate at cost for March.
3. Bull Dog's Fitness Equipment had retail sales of $42,500 for the month of May. The retail price of the inventory at the beginning of May was $11,015 and at the end of May was $10,235. Find the average inventory at retail and the turnover rate for May.
4. Comfort Hot Tubs and Spas had retail sales of $60,000 for the month of July. The retail price of the inventory at the beginning of July was $35,000 and at the end of July it was $25,000. Find the average inventory at retail and the inventory turnover rate for July.

5. Irwin Ornamental Iron Company had retail sales of $36,000 for October. The retail price of their inventory at the beginning of October was $8000 and at the end of October was $4000. Find the average inventory at retail and the inventory rate for October.

SOLUTIONS:

1. Average inventory cost $= \dfrac{\$10,000 + \$8000}{2}$

    $= \dfrac{\$18,000}{2}$

    $= \$9000$

    Turnover rate at cost $= \dfrac{\$18,000}{\$9000}$

    $= 2$

2. Average inventory cost $= \dfrac{\$3250 + \$2250}{2}$

    $= \dfrac{\$5500}{2}$

    $= \$2750$

    Turnover rate at cost $= \dfrac{\$11,000}{\$2750}$

    $= 4$

3. Average inventory at retail $= \dfrac{\$11,015 + \$10,235}{2}$

    $= \dfrac{\$21,250}{2}$

    $= \$10,625$

    Turnover rate at retail $= \dfrac{\$42,500}{\$10,625}$

    $= 4$

4. Average inventory at retail $= \dfrac{\$35,000 + \$25,000}{2}$

    $= \dfrac{\$60,000}{2}$

    $= \$30,000$

$$\text{Turnover rate at retail} = \frac{\$60,000}{\$30,000}$$

$$= 2$$

5. Average inventory retail $= \dfrac{\$8000 + \$4000}{2}$

$$= \frac{\$12,000}{2}$$

$$= \$6000$$

$$\text{Turnover rate at retail} = \frac{\$36,000}{\$6000}$$

$$= 6$$

Summary

Businesses need to keep track of the number of items they sell and the total cost of these items. They also need to know the retail value of the items. This information is used for financial statements, tax purposes, and future planning. In order to obtain these values, they inventory their stock. There are several methods that they can use. The ones explained in this chapter are the identification inventory method, the weighted-average inventory method, the first-in, first-out method, the last-in, first-out method, and the retail inventory method.

Businesses also use the inventory turnover rate to judge how often the merchandise is replaced during a specific inventory period.

Quiz

Use the following information on the cost of plastic portable water coolers to answer Questions 1 to 9:

Date of Purchase	Number of Items Purchased	Cost of Items	Number of Items Remaining
June 1	12	$28	3
June 15	22	$26	10
June 22	14	$25	8
June 30	6	$28	

1. The cost of goods available is
   (a) $107
   (b) $1243
   (c) $1426
   (d) $540

2. The cost of goods remaining using the specific identification method is
   (a) $632
   (b) $141
   (c) $544
   (d) $218

3. The cost of goods available for sale using the specific identification method is
   (a) $882
   (b) $764
   (c) $937
   (d) $1014

4. The average cost of the items available for sale is
   (a) $26.41
   (b) $32.18
   (c) $23.75
   (d) $45.26

5. The cost of goods sold using the weighted-average inventory method is
   (a) $914.56
   (b) $63.21
   (c) $731.58
   (d) $871.39

6. The cost of the items remaining using the first-in, first-out inventory method is
   (a) $625
   (b) $374
   (c) $544
   (d) $421

7. The cost of goods sold using the first-in, first-out inventory method is
   (a) $656
   (b) $882
   (c) $832
   (d) $715

8. The cost of the items remaining using the last-in, first-out inventory method is
   (a) $570
   (b) $931

(c) $673
(d) $411

9. The cost of goods sold using the last-in, first-out method is
    (a) $916
    (b) $538
    (c) $637
    (d) $856

Use the following information for Questions 10 to 13:

Date	Cost Value	Retail Value
April 1	$16	$25
April 11	$14	$29
April 22	$18	$30
April 29	$14	$28
Sales during the period		$42

10. The cost of goods available for sale is
    (a) $84
    (b) $21
    (c) $112
    (d) $62

11. The retail value of the goods available for sale is
    (a) $62
    (b) $84
    (c) $112
    (d) $42

12. The cost ratio is
    (a) 0.623
    (b) 0.554
    (c) 0.415
    (d) 0.712

13. The cost of goods sold using the retail inventory method is
    (a) $34.93
    (b) $21.60
    (c) $23.27
    (d) $41.67

14. The Diamond Jewelry Store had net sales of $26,500 for the month of January. The cost of the inventory at the beginning of January was $14,265 and the cost of the inventory at the end of January was $12,235. Based on this information, the turnover rate for January was

    (a) 2
    (b) 4
    (c) 3
    (d) 5

15. The No Leak Plumbing Supply Company had net sales of $6250 for June. The cost of inventory at the beginning of June was $2134.00 and the cost of inventory at the end of June was $2032.60. Based on this information, the inventory turnover rate for June was

    (a) 4
    (b) 2
    (c) 3
    (d) 5

Financial Statements

Introduction

The owner or owners of a business need to know the financial condition of their business in order to evaluate the status and the progress of the business and to make plans for the future. Investors and creditors also need to know the financial condition of a business before investing or lending money to the business. Stockholders are given yearly reports on the businesses they hold stock in. In order to report the financial condition of a business, financial statements are used. There are two basic types of financial statements: the *balance sheet* and the *income sheet*.

The Balance Sheet

A **balance sheet** explains the financial condition of a business at a specific point in time. It shows the *assets*, the *liabilities*, and the *net worth* or the *equity* of the business.

The **assets** of a business include any cash, equipment, buildings, and property the business owns. It also includes any money that is owed to the business by its customers. This money is called **accounts receivable**.

The **liabilities** of a business include any money owed by the business to other parties. For example, loans to banks, salaries and bonuses to employees, outstanding bills (called **accounts payable**), and mortgages are some of the liabilities of a business.

When the total amount of the liabilities is subtracted from the total amount of the assets, the amount left is called the **net worth** of the business. The net worth is also called the **owner's equity** or capital. For example, if the assets of a business are $500,000 and the liabilities are $350,000, then the net worth of the business is $500,000 − $350,000 = $150,000.

Many computer programs will enable you to prepare a balance sheet when the proper numbers are keyed in; however, for the purpose of this book, the principles of the balance sheet are explained without the aid of a computer.

In order to make a balance sheet, list the assets first and find the sum. Then draw a double line. Next list the liabilities and find the sum and draw a single line. Finally find the net worth or the owner's equity and find the total of the liabilities and owner's equity and draw a double line.

The basic equation is

$$\text{Assets} = \text{Liabilities} + \text{Owner's equity}$$

EXAMPLE: On December 31, the Miller Auto Parts store has the following assets: Cash—$6256; Accounts receivable—$8149; Merchandise—$42,871; Equipment—$24,331; Building—$80,000. The business has the following liabilities: Wages payable—$3210; Accounts payable—$3561; Mortgage—$62,327. Make a balance sheet for the business.

SOLUTION:

Assets	
Cash	$6256
Accounts receivable	8149
Merchandise	42,871
Equipment	24,331
Building	80,000
Total	$161,607
Liabilities and Owner's Equity	
Liabilities	
Wages payable	$3210
Accounts payable	3561
Mortgage	62,327
Total	$69,098
Owner's equity	
Net worth	$92,509
Total liabilities and owner's equity	$ 161,607

Note: The net worth is found by subtracting
$161,607 − $69,098 = $92,509.

The next step is to find the appropriate percents for the assets, the liabilities, and the equity using the formula:

$$\text{Percent} = \frac{\text{Amount}}{\text{Total}} \times 100\%$$

Assets

$$\text{Cash: } \frac{\$6256}{\$161,607} \times 100\% = 3.9\%$$

$$\text{Accounts receivable: } \frac{\$8149}{\$161,607} \times 100\% = 5.0\%$$

$$\text{Merchandise: } \frac{\$42,871}{\$161,607} \times 100\% = 26.5\%$$

$$\text{Equipment: } \frac{\$24,331}{\$161,607} \times 100\% = 15.1\%$$

$$\text{Building: } \frac{\$80,000}{\$161,607} \times 100\% = 49.5\%$$

Liabilities and equity

$$\text{Wages payable: } \frac{\$3210}{\$161,607} \times 100\% = 2.0\%$$

$$\text{Accounts payable: } \frac{\$3561}{\$161,607} \times 100\% = 2.2\%$$

$$\text{Mortgage: } \frac{\$62,327}{\$161,607} \times 100\% = 38.6\%$$

$$\text{Equity: } \frac{\$92,509}{\$161,607} \times 100\% = 57.2\%$$

Now the balance sheet can be completed by adding the percents as shown.

The total of the percents for the assets should add up to 100%. The total percents for the liabilities and owner's equity should add up to 100%.

(*Note*: In many cases, the sum of the percents will add up to a little less than 100% or a little greater than 100% due to rounding. In this case, it is permissible to adjust a percent when rounding so that the sum is 100%.)

Assets	Amount	Percents
Cash	$6256	3.9%
Accounts receivable	8149	5.0%
Merchandise	42,871	26.5%
Equipment	24,331	15.1%
Building	80,000	49.5%
Total	$161,607	100.0%
Liabilities and Owner's Equity		
Liabilities		
Wages payable	$3210	2.0%
Accounts payable	3561	2.2%
Mortgage	62,327	38.6%
Total	$69,098	42.8%
Owner's equity		
Net worth	$92,509	57.2%
Total liabilities	$161,607	100%

PRACTICE:

1. On December 31, the Ross Discount Electronic store has the following assets: Cash—$12,252; Accounts receivable—$9142; Merchandise—$18,360. They had the following liabilities: Wages payable—$4261; Accounts payable—$973; Operating expenses—$14,931. Prepare a balance sheet for the business.

2. On December 31, the Quality Printing Company had the following assets: Cash—$837; Accounts receivable—$275; Equipment—$8376; Office supplies—-$4160. They had the following liabilities: Accounts payable—$487; Wages payable—$321; Operating expenses—$5200. Prepare a balance sheet for the business.

3. On December 31, the Drip Free Plumbing Company had the following assets: Cash—$1641; Accounts receivable—$225; Merchandise—$3270; Office equipment—$3116. The business had the following liabilities: Accounts payable—$434; Wages payable—$165; Operating expenses—$2400. Prepare a balance sheet for the business.

4. On December 31, the Brick Oven Pizza Parlor had the following assets: Cash—$4261; Accounts receivable—$97; Equipment—$11,560; Building—$32,500. They had the following liabilities:

Accounts payable—$232; Wages payable—$316; Mortgage—$11,210.
Prepare a balance sheet for the company.

SOLUTION:

1.

Assets	Amount	Percent
Cash	$12,252	30.8%
Accounts receivable	9142	23.0%
Merchandise	18,360	46.2%
Total	$39,754	100%
Liabilities and Owner's Equity		
Liabilities		
Wages payable	$4261	10.7%
Accounts payable	973	2.4%
Merchandise	14,931	37.6%
Total	$20,165	50.7%
Owner's equity		
Net worth	$19,589	49.3%
Total liabilities	$39,754	100%

2.

Assets	Amount	Percent
Cash	$837	6.1%
Accounts receivable	275	2.0%
Equipment	8376	61.4%
Office supplies	4160	30.5%
Total	$13,648	100.0%
Liabilities and Owner's Equity		
Liabilities		
Accounts payable	$487	3.6%
Wages payable	321	2.4%
Overhead	$5200	38.0%
	$6008	44.0%
Owner's equity		
Net worth	$7640	56.0%
Total	$13,648	100.0%

3.

Assets	Amount	Percent
Cash	$1641	19.9%
Accounts receivable	225	2.7%
Merchandise	3270	39.6%
Office Equipment	3116	37.8%
Total	$8252	100%
Liabilities and Owner's Equity		
Liabilities		
Accounts payable	$434	5.2%
Wages payable	165	2.0%
Operating expenses	2400	29.0%
	$2999	36.2%
Owner's equity		
Net worth	$5253	63.8%
Total	$8252	100.0%

4.

Assets	Amount	Percent
Cash	$4261	8.8%
Accounts receivable	97	0.2%
Equipment	11,560	23.9%
Building	32,500	67.1%
Total	$48,418	100.0%
Liabilities and Owner's Equity		
Liabilities		
Accounts payable	$232	0.5%
Wages	316	0.7%
Mortgage	11,210	23.1%
Total	$11,758	24.3%
Owner's equity		
Net worth	$36,660	75.7%
Total	$48,418	100.0%

Income Statements

A balance sheet shows the financial condition of a business at a specific time whereas an **income statement** shows the net income of a business over a period of time.

The income statement shows items such as total sales, sales returns and allowances, cost of goods sold, gross profit, operating expenses, and net profit. The **net sales** is equal to the difference between the total sales and the amount of the returns and allowances. The cost of goods sold is equal to the difference between the cost of the beginning inventory and the cost of the ending inventory. The **gross profit** is the difference between the net sales and the cost of goods sold. **Operating expenses**, also called **overhead**, are any expenses incurred by doing business. These expenses include salaries, rent, maintenance, insurance, business permits, taxes, etc. The **net profit** is the difference between the gross profit and the operating expenses or overhead.

In order to prepare an income statement, list the values of the various items such as gross sales, net sales, cost of goods sold, operating expenses, and end with the net profit (see the next example).

EXAMPLE: The Pine Tree Nursery had the following records for a specific year:

> Gross sales: $62,587
> Returns and allowances: $1225
> Cost of beginning inventory: $18,387
> Cost of purchases: $22,631
> Cost of ending inventory: $6371
> Total of operating expenses: $15,433

Prepare an income statement for the business.

SOLUTION:

$$\text{Net sales} = \text{Gross sales} - \text{Returns and allowances}$$
$$= \$62,587 - \$1225 = \$61,362$$
$$\text{Cost of goods sold} = \text{Cost of beginning inventory} + \text{Cost of purchases}$$
$$- \text{Cost of ending inventory}$$
$$= \$18,387 + \$22,631 - \$6371 = \$34,647$$
$$\text{Gross profit} = \text{Net sales} - \text{Cost of goods sold}$$
$$= \$61,362 - \$34,647 = \$26,715$$
$$\text{Net profit} = \text{Gross profit} - \text{Operating expenses}$$

$$= \$26{,}715 - \$15{,}433$$
$$= \$11{,}282$$

The income statement will be

Gross sales	$62,587
Returns and allowances	−1225
Net sales	**$61,362**
Cost of beginning inventory	$18,387
Cost of purchases	22,631
Cost of ending inventory	−6371
Cost of goods sold	**$34,647**
Gross profit	$26,715
Total operating expenses	−15,433
Net profit	**$11,282**

PRACTICE:

1. The Tee Up Golf Shop has recorded the financial information for the month of May:

   Gross sales: $87,261
   Returns and allowances: $4582
   Cost of beginning inventory: $23,217
   Cost of the purchases: $18,571
   Cost of ending inventory: $9324
   Total operating expenses: $10,320

   Make an income statement for the business for May.

2. The Hot Fireplace Accessories Shop has recorded the following information for the month of February:

   Gross sales: $113,104
   Returns and allowances: $14,372
   Cost of beginning inventory: $63,412
   Cost of the purchases: $18,372
   Cost of ending inventory: $42,164
   Total operating expenses: $22,776

   Make an income statement for the business for the month of February.

3. The Green Grass Lawn Supply Company has recorded the following information for the month of August:

Gross sales: $57,961
Returns and allowances: $15,475
Cost of beginning inventory: $16,256
Cost of purchases: $18,368
Cost of ending inventory: $20,220
Salaries paid: $4315
Rent: $625
Utilities: $371
Insurance: $100
Maintenance: $464
Make an income statement for the business for the month of August.

SOLUTION:

1.

Gross sales	$87,261
Returns and allowances	−4582
Net sales	**$82,679**
Cost of beginning inventory	$23,217
Cost of purchases	18,571
Cost of ending inventory	−9324
Cost of goods sold	**$32,464**
Gross profit	$50,215
Total operating expenses	−10,320
Net profit	**$39,895**

2.

Gross sales	$113,104
Returns and allowances	−14,372
Net sales	**$98,732**
Cost of beginning inventory	$63,412
Cost of purchases	18,372
Cost of ending inventory	−42,164
Cost of goods sold	**$39,620**
Gross profit	$59,112
Total operating expenses	−22,776
Net Profit	**$36,336**

3. The total operating expenses are

Salaries paid	$4315
Rent	625
Utilities	371
Insurance	100
Maintenance	464
Total	$5875
Gross Sales	$57,961
Return and allowances	−15,475
Net sales	**$42,486**
Cost of beginning inventory	$16,256
Cost of purchases	18,368
Cost of ending inventory	−20,220
	$14,404
Gross profit	$28,082
Total operating expenses	−5875
Net profit	**$22,207**

Summary

Financial statements are used to show the financial condition of a business at any point in time or over a period of time such as a week, month, or year. There are two types of financial statements. They are the balance sheet and the income statement.

Businesses use balance sheets to show the financial condition of the business at any point in time. These statements contain monetary figures for the assets, liabilities, and the owner's equity or the net worth of the business.

Income statements show the financial condition of a business over a period of time. These statements show gross sales, the returns and allowances, the cost of goods sold, the operating expenses, and the net profit of a business.

Financial statements are used for securing loans, letting the investors know the condition of the business and for making plans for the future.

Quiz

1. The purpose of a balance sheet is to
   (a) show the financial condition of a business over a period of time
   (b) show the net income of a business over a period of time

(c) show the financial condition of a business at a single point in time

(d) show the net income of a business at any single point in time

2. Cash or properties owned by a business are called
   (a) assets
   (b) liabilities
   (c) the net worth of a business
   (d) the owner's equity

3. Moneys owed by the business to other parties are called
   (a) assets
   (b) liabilities
   (c) the net worth of a business
   (d) the owner's equity

4. The net worth of a business is found by
   (a) subtracting the accounts payable from the accounts receivable
   (b) subtracting the liabilities from the assets
   (c) subtracting the operating expenses from the gross profit
   (c) subtracting the amount of the returns and allowances from the gross sales

5. The cost of the beginning inventory of a business is $23,230, and the cost of the ending inventory is $16,273. If the cost of the purchases is $9260, then the cost of the goods sold is
   (a) $13,970
   (b) $30,243
   (c) $2303
   (d) $16,217

6. On a balance sheet, the sum of the assets should be equal to the
   (a) sum of the liabilities – the owner's equity
   (b) sum of liabilities
   (c) sum of the liabilities + the owner's equity
   (d) the owner's equity

7. The purpose of an income statement is to show
   (a) the financial condition of a business over a period of time
   (b) the net profit of a business over a period of time
   (c) the net income of a business at any specific point in time
   (d) the financial condition of a business at a specific point in time

8. Which is **not** considered an operating expense of a business?
   (a) Cash
   (b) Insurance

(c) Rent

(d) Taxes

9. The net profit of a business is found by subtracting
   (a) the net sales from the gross sales
   (b) the cost of ending inventory from the cost of the beginning inventory
   (c) the cost of goods sold from the net sales
   (d) the operating expenses from the gross profit

10. The total net sales of a business are $96,251 and the total operating expenses are $32,476. If the total of the cost of goods sold is $21,131, then the net profit of the business is
    (a) $107,596
    (b) $42,644
    (c) $84,906
    (d) $63,775

20

Statistics

Introduction

People in business can use statistics to interpret information and make knowledgeable decisions about their businesses.

Statistics uses what are called **data**. Data can be *categorical* or *numerical*. For example, the colors of the automobiles in a parking lot would be classified as categorical data since they would consist of white, blue, red, etc. The amounts of sales at a department store everyday for a month would be an example of numerical data since they would consist of numbers.

Statistics involves collecting, organizing, summarizing, and analyzing data. It also involves interpreting and drawing conclusions from the data.

Frequency Distributions

When data are collected, they are called **raw data**. Since it is difficult to make sense of raw data, statisticians organize the data by using a *frequency distribution*. A **frequency distribution** consists of a number of classes and the number of data values (called a frequency) contained in each class. The classes can be categorical or numerical. Numerical classes can be either a single number or a range of numbers.

EXAMPLE: The data show the way 30 employees get to work each day. Construct a categorical frequency distribution for the data:

$$A = \text{automobile}; B = \text{bus}; W = \text{walk}; T = \text{train}$$

A	A	B	A	W	T
B	A	A	A	B	A
T	A	B	B	A	W
A	T	W	B	A	A
W	A	B	W	T	A

SOLUTION:
Make a frequency distribution with four classes. Tally the data and then write the numerical frequency beside each class.

Class	Tally	Frequency
Automobile (A)	~~HHT~~ ~~HHT~~ ////	14
Bus (B)	~~HHT~~ //	7
Walk (W)	~~HHT~~	5
Train (T)	////	4
Total		30

In this case, almost half (14) of the employees get to work by automobile. The next largest category is people taking the bus (7).

EXAMPLE: The data show the number of hours of overtime 25 employees of a factory worked last week. Construct a frequency distribution for the data:

3	2	0	3	2
4	1	3	4	2
3	5	0	0	3
1	2	4	3	2
3	1	3	2	0

SOLUTION:
Since the range of the data values 0 to 5 is small, single class values can be used. The class values are 0, 1, 2, 3, 4, and 5. Tally the data as shown in the previous example and write the total beside each class.

Class	Tally	Frequency
0	////	4
1	///	3
2	~~////~~ /	6
3	~~////~~ ///	8
4	///	3
5	/	1
Total		25

In this case, we see that more than half of the employees worked 2 or 3 h overtime.

When the range of the data values is large, the data can be organized into classes that consist of more than one number; for example, 10 to 14, 15 to 19, 20 to 24, etc. In this situation, there are a few guidelines that can be used when setting up the classes. They are

1. Use from 5 to 15 classes.
2. Keep each class of the same width.
3. Do not leave out any class, even if the frequency of the classes is zero.
4. Make sure that there are enough classes for all the data.
5. Do not overlap the classes.

Note: There is no *single* best way to make a frequency distribution. As long as the guidelines are followed, the distribution you make can be different from the ones shown here.

EXAMPLE: The data represent the ages of 45 employees at the Cedar Glass Window Company. Make a frequency distribution for the data:

37	32	22	45	65
54	46	48	24	31
25	37	28	26	39
47	48	42	36	40
53	55	60	45	32
28	50	36	34	47
39	25	37	33	39
30	40	58	24	24
33	31	29	54	38

SOLUTION:

Step 1. Determine the number of classes.

In order to do this, subtract the smallest data value from the largest one:

$65 - 22 = 43$

Then divide the answer by the number of classes you want to have. The author likes to use 6, 7, or 8 classes, so I selected 6 classes. (You can select any number between 5 and 15. If you select a different number, you have a different distribution.)

$43 \div 6 = 7\frac{1}{6}$ (round this up to 8)

Hence, each class will be 8 units in width.

Step 2. Select a starting point. This will be a value equal to or less than your lowest data value. I selected 22. (If you select a different value, your distribution will be slightly different.)

Step 3. To get the lower class limits, add 8 starting at 22 and continue until you have 6 classes.

$22 + 8 = 30$
$30 + 8 = 38$
$38 + 8 = 46$
$46 + 8 = 54$
$54 + 8 = 62$
$62 + 8 = 70$

Step 4. Subtract 1 from each class value to get the upper class limit. The last value can be found by adding 8 to 61. The classes are

22 to 29
30 to 37
38 to 45
46 to 53
54 to 61
62 to 69

Step 5. Tally the data and write each frequency as shown:

Class	Tally	Frequency
22–29	⧸⧸⧸⧸ ⧸⧸⧸⧸	10
30–37	⧸⧸⧸⧸ ⧸⧸⧸⧸ ///	13
38–45	⧸⧸⧸⧸ ////	9
46–53	⧸⧸⧸⧸ //	7
54–61	⧸⧸⧸⧸	5
62–69	/	1
Total		45

After making the frequency distribution, a graph called a *histogram* can be drawn. The **histogram** uses vertical bars whose heights represent the frequency and whose widths represent the class values. Each bar should touch the adjacent one unless the class frequency is zero.

A histogram for the data given in the previous example is shown here. Make a scale on the vertical axis that can be used to show the frequencies. Show the class values below the horizontal axis. Make the heights of the bars correspond to the frequencies, as shown in Figure 20-1.

The histogram shows that the ages of the employees tend toward the left, which means that the majority of the employees are between the ages of 22 and 37 years.

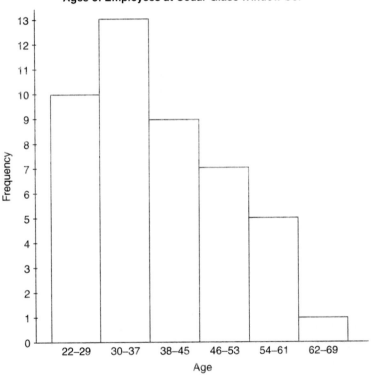

Fig. 20-1.

PRACTICE:
1. Newman's Health Food Store recorded the type of vitamins 30 customers purchased. Make a categorical frequency distribution for the data:

A = vitamin A; B = vitamin B complex; C = vitamin C; D = vitamin D; E = vitamin E

$$
\begin{array}{cccccc}
C & E & A & C & C & D \\
E & A & C & C & D & B \\
C & B & C & C & C & B \\
A & E & E & B & C & D \\
E & A & D & A & E & B \\
\end{array}
$$

2. The blood types of 25 patients at an emergency center were recorded. Make a categorical frequency distribution for the data:

$$
\begin{array}{ccccc}
A & B & O & AB & B \\
B & B & B & O & AB \\
AB & O & O & A & A \\
O & AB & A & B & O \\
B & O & O & B & B \\
\end{array}
$$

3. A survey of 50 families shows how many automobiles each family owns. Make a frequency distribution for the data:

$$
\begin{array}{ccccc}
2 & 1 & 0 & 1 & 2 \\
3 & 0 & 1 & 1 & 2 \\
1 & 2 & 1 & 2 & 1 \\
3 & 2 & 1 & 2 & 1 \\
5 & 3 & 2 & 2 & 1 \\
0 & 1 & 4 & 2 & 2 \\
2 & 1 & 2 & 1 & 3 \\
2 & 0 & 4 & 1 & 2 \\
3 & 2 & 2 & 2 & 1 \\
1 & 0 & 2 & 2 & 1 \\
\end{array}
$$

4. A researcher selected 36 pairs of men's athletic shoes from a catalog. The prices are shown. (The values have been rounded to the nearest dollar.) Make a frequency distribution for the data and draw a histogram:

$$
\begin{array}{cccccc}
42 & 50 & 54 & 62 & 80 & 79 \\
39 & 45 & 48 & 57 & 62 & 70 \\
29 & 32 & 55 & 62 & 68 & 49 \\
43 & 56 & 63 & 57 & 56 & 36 \\
44 & 53 & 29 & 45 & 48 & 59 \\
54 & 49 & 52 & 50 & 43 & 51 \\
\end{array}
$$

5. The data represent the number of homes sold last month in 40 munici-
    palities in a given state. Make a frequency distribution for the data and
    draw a histogram:

16	8	12	42	37
28	56	73	16	54
62	34	19	40	59
18	59	43	22	35
35	62	63	51	59
46	82	66	46	48
52	67	51	54	31
25	62	77	73	61

SOLUTIONS:

1.

Class	Tally	Frequency
A	ⵘ	5
B	ⵘ	5
C	ⵘ ⵘ	10
D	////	4
E	ⵘ /	6
Total		30

2.

Class	Tally	Frequency
A	////	4
B	ⵘ ////	9
AB	////	4
O	ⵘ ///	8
Total		25

3.

Class	Tally	Frequency
0	ⵘ	5
1	ⵘ ⵘ ⵘ //	17
2	ⵘ ⵘ ⵘ ⵘ	20
3	ⵘ	5
4	//	2
5	/	1
Total		50

4.

Class	Tally	Frequency
29–38	////	4
39–48	~~HHT~~ ////	9
49–58	~~HHT~~ ~~HHT~~ ////	14
59–68	~~HHT~~ /	6
69–78	/	1
79–88	//	2
Total		36

The histogram is shown in Figure 20-2.

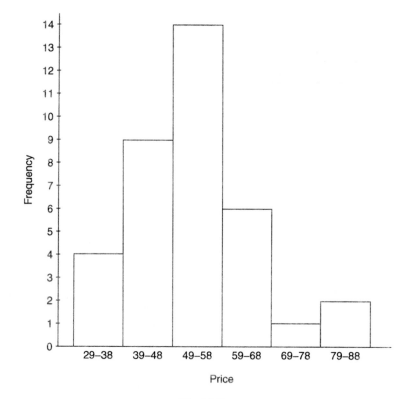

Fig. 20-2.

5.   Your answer may be different from the one shown:

Class	Tally	Frequency
0–14	//	2
15–29	~~HHT~~ //	7
30–44	~~HHT~~ ///	8
45–59	~~HHT~~ ~~HHT~~ //	12
60–74	~~HHT~~ ////	9
75–89	//	2
Total		40

The histogram is shown in Figure 20-3.

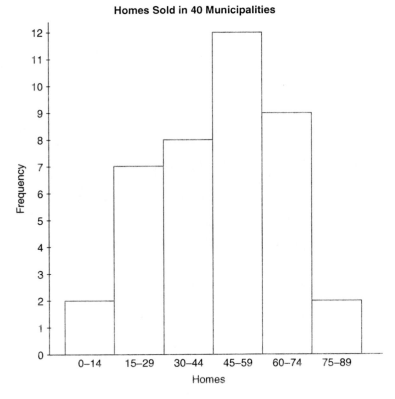

Fig. 20-3.

Measures of Average

In statistics, one way data are summarized is to use what are called measures of average. There are three common measures of average. They are the *mean, median,* and *mode.*

The **mean** is found by adding all the data values and dividing by the total number of data values. The symbol for the mean is $\overline{X}$ and the formula for the mean of n values is

$$\overline{X} = \frac{x_1 + x_2 + x_3 + \cdots + x_n}{n}$$

EXAMPLE: The manager of Henderson's Hardware Store recorded the number of power lawnmowers he sold each year for the last 5 years. The data are shown. Find the mean:

$$32 \quad 18 \quad 29 \quad 35 \quad 26$$

SOLUTION:

$$\overline{X} = \frac{32 + 18 + 29 + 35 + 26}{5} = \frac{140}{5} = 28$$

Hence the mean is 28 lawnmowers.

Sometimes it is necessary to find a *weighted mean.* In this case, some of the data values are worth more than other data values. The **weighted mean** is found by multiplying the data values by their corresponding weights, finding the sum of these products, and then dividing the total by the sum of the weights. The most common use of the weighted mean is finding a grade-point average as shown in the next example.

EXAMPLE: Harry Anderson's grades for the first semester are shown. Find his grade-point average.

Subject	Credits	Grade
Gen. Chemistry	5	C
College Algebra	4	B
English Comp 1	3	A
Philosophy	3	D
Total	15	

SOLUTION:
Let A = 4 points, B = 3 points, C = 2 points, D = 1 point, and F = 0 point.
Then find the sum of the weights (i.e., number of credits) and the numerical
values of the letter grades. Divide the sum by the total number of credits.

$$\overline{X} = \frac{5 \times 2 + 4 \times 3 + 3 \times 4 + 3 \times 1}{15}$$

$$= \frac{10 + 12 + 12 + 3}{15}$$

$$= \frac{37}{15} = 2.47 \text{ (rounded)}$$

Hence his grade-point average is 2.47.

The second measure of average is called the *median*. The **median** is at the
middle of the data when they are arranged in order. When there is an odd number
of data values, the median will be the middle data value. When there is an even
number of data values, the median will fall between the two middle values.

EXAMPLE: Find the median of 8, 6, 10, 12, 15, 16, and 14.

SOLUTION:
Arrange the data values in ascending order:

$$6, 8, 10, 12, 14, 15, 16$$

Since there are 7 values, find the middle value. It is 12.
Hence the median is 12.

EXAMPLE: Find the median of 24, 35, 18, 52, 45, and 33.

SOLUTION:
Arrange the data in ascending order:

$$18, 24, 33, 35, 45, 52$$

Since there is an even number of data values, namely 6, the median will fall
between the middle two values 33 and 35. Hence the median is $\frac{33+35}{2} = \frac{68}{2} = 34$.

The third commonly used measure of average is called the *mode*. The **mode**
is the data value that occurs most often.

EXAMPLE: Find the mode of 12, 18, 15, 16, 15, 14, and 6.

SOLUTION:
Since 15 occurs twice, which is more often than any other data value, the mode
is 15.

EXAMPLE: Find the mode of 8, 12, 17, 17, 22, 27, 32, 32, and 45.

SOLUTION:
In this case, the values 17 and 32 each occur twice. Hence the modes are 17 and 32. The data set is said to be **bimodal**.

EXAMPLE: Find the mode of 32, 14, 18, 16, 20, and 45.

SOLUTION:
In this case, each data value occurs once. Hence we say that there is no mode.
  Data sets can have no mode, one mode, or two or more modes.
  In statistics there are three measures that are called averages. For a data set they can be quite different, and so it is important to know which measure (mean, median, or mode) is being used.

PRACTICE:

1. The number of movies a video store rented during a 7-day period is shown. Find the mean, median, and mode for the data:

    156, 182, 147, 159, 165, 171, 159

2. The number of patrons at a swimming pool for a 10-day period is shown. Find the mean, median, and mode for the data:

    156, 268, 343, 249, 198, 118, 262, 227, 218, 173

3. The number of passengers on five runs of a local bus is shown. Find the mean, median, and mode for the data:

    76, 43, 57, 27, 38

4. The hourly wages in dollars of 8 employees working in a factory are shown. Find the mean, median, and mode for the data:

    $8.32, $5.98, $9.75, $10.29, $6.77, $9.75, $8.80, $5.98

5. The number of pizzas sold by Pizza Heaven over a 10-day period is shown. Find the mean, median, and mode for the data:

    87, 107, 96, 110, 101, 107, 82, 101, 97, 103

SOLUTIONS:

1. $\overline{X} = \dfrac{156 + 182 + 147 + 159 + 165 + 171 + 159}{7}$

    $= \dfrac{1139}{7} = 162.71$ (rounded)

Median $= 159$

Mode 159

2. $\overline{X} = \dfrac{156 + 268 + 343 + 249 + 198 + 118 + 262 + 227 + 218 + 173}{10}$

$= \dfrac{2212}{10} = 221.2$

Median $= 222.5$

No mode

3. $\overline{X} = \dfrac{76 + 43 + 57 + 27 + 38}{5} = \dfrac{241}{5} = 48.2$

Median $= 43$

No mode

4. $\overline{X} = \dfrac{8.32 + 5.98 + 9.75 + 10.29 + 6.77 + 9.75 + 8.80 + 5.98}{8}$

$= \dfrac{65.64}{8} = 8.205$

Median $= 8.56$

Mode $= \$5.98$ and $\$9.75$

5. $\overline{X} = \dfrac{87 + 107 + 96 + 110 + 101 + 107 + 82 + 101 + 97 + 103}{10}$

$= \dfrac{991}{10} = 99.1$

Median $= 101$

Mode $= 101$ and 107

Measures of Variability

Two data sets can have the same mean and still be quite different. Consider the two data sets:

Set A: 5, 10, 15, 20, 25

Set B: 13, 14, 15, 16, 17

Both sets have a mean of 15, but the variability of the data in each set is very different. Note that the data values in set A vary from 5 to 25 whereas the data values in set B vary from 13 to 17. For this reason, statisticians also use three common measures of variability to describe data. They are the *range,* the

variance, and the *standard deviation.* Measures of variability are also called measures of dispersion. The **range** is the difference between the smallest data value and the largest data value.

EXAMPLE: Find the range of data set A and data set B.

> Set A: 5, 10, 15, 20, 25
> Set B: 13, 14, 15, 16, 17

SOLUTION:
For data set A, the range is $25 - 5 = 20$.
For data set B, the range is $17 - 13 = 4$.
Hence the values in data set A are more variable than the values in data set B.

The range is a very rough indication of the variability of a data set since one extremely large data value or one extremely small data value can give an inaccurate picture of the variability of the data. For this reason, statisticians use the variance and the standard deviation to measure the variability of data.

The variance and standard deviation are related in that the square root of the variance is the standard deviation.

The procedure for calculating is somewhat complicated, and so the steps are shown in the next example.

EXAMPLE: Find the variance and standard deviation for the values in data set A.

$$\text{Set A} : 5, 10, 15, 20, 25$$

SOLUTION:

> Step 1. Find the mean.

$$\overline{X} = \frac{5 + 10 + 15 + 20 + 25}{5} = \frac{75}{5} = 15$$

Step 2. Subtract the mean from each data value.

$$5 - 15 = -10$$
$$10 - 15 = -5$$
$$15 - 15 = 0$$
$$20 - 15 = 5$$
$$25 - 15 = 10$$

Step 3. Square the answers and find the sum.

$$(-10)^2 + (-5)^2 + 0^2 + 5^2 + 10^2 = 100 + 25 + 0 + 25 + 100 = 250$$

Step 4. Divide this sum by the number of data values to get the variance.

$$\text{Variance} = \frac{250}{5} = 50$$

Step 5. Take the square root of the variance to get the standard deviation.

$$\text{Standard deviation} = \sqrt{50} = 7.07$$

Hence the variance is 50 and the standard deviation is 7.07.

Now you might say, "So what ?" The way you interpret the variance and the standard deviation are that for data sets, the larger the variance or standard deviation, the more variable the data are. For example, the standard deviation for data set B is 1.41, and so comparing 7.07 with 1.41, you can see that the data in data set A are much more variable than the data in data set B.

Another way to interpret the standard deviation is that for many data sets, most if not all of the data values fall within two standard deviations of the mean. For example, in data set A, the mean is 15 and the standard deviation is 7.07. $2 \times 7.07 = 14.14$. Now $15 - 14.14 = 0.86$, and $15 + 14.14 = 29.14$. So if you look at the data in data set A, the smallest value is 5 and the largest value is 15, and so all the values fall within two standard deviations of the mean.

Similar reasoning can be used for the data in data set B.

By using measures of average and measures of variability, statisticians can describe data and compare one data set with another one.

Note: The procedure for finding the variance and standard deviation uses n as a divisor. This formula gives the true variance and standard deviation for the specific data values. Most statistics books use $n - 1$ as a divisor. This gives what is called the "unbiased estimate" of the variance, which is useful when estimating the variance of a large number of data values called a population from a smaller number of data values obtained from the population. You will need to consult a statistics book for a more detailed explanation.

Calculator Tip

Many calculators have special keys to use to find the mean and standard deviation for data. The data values must be entered and then by pressing the key $\overline{X}$ the mean will be calculated. The key σ_x will compute the standard deviation and then the x^2 key will square it to get the variance. Since each calculator is different, it is recommended that you read the instructions to see how to use these keys.

PRACTICE:

1. The data show the number of miles per gallon five different four-wheel-drive sports utility vehicles get when off-roading. Find the range, variance, and standard deviation for the data:

    18, 14, 12, 16, 20

2. The data show the number of unhealthy air days last year for eight large cities. Find the range, variance, and standard deviation for the data:

    42, 35, 80, 68, 70, 50, 63, 64

3. The data show the ages of 10 customers who entered a computer store. Find the range, variance, and standard deviation for the data:

    36, 15, 21, 42, 30, 27, 19, 52, 41, 17

4. The data show the number of automobile accidents at a busy intersection for the past 6 years. Find the range, variance, and standard deviation for the data:

    15, 8, 3, 5, 6, 5

5. The data show the amount of state tax in cents on a pack of cigarettes for five states. Find the range, variance, and standard deviation for the data:

    20, 50, 18, 7, 5

SOLUTIONS:

1. Range $= 20 - 12 = 8$
    To find the variance and standard deviation
    (1) Find the mean.

$$\overline{X} = \frac{18 + 14 + 12 + 16 + 20}{5} = \frac{80}{5} = 16$$

(2) Subtract the mean from each value.
$18 - 16 = 2$
$14 - 16 = -2$
$12 - 16 = -4$
$16 - 16 = 0$
$20 - 16 = 4$

(3) Square the differences and find the sum.

$$2^2 + (-2)^2 + (-4)^2 + 0^2 + 4^2 = 4 + 4 + 16 + 0 + 16 = 40$$

(4) Divide by 5 to get the variance.

$$\frac{40}{5} = 8$$

(5) Find the square root of 8 to get the standard deviation.

$$\sqrt{8} = 2.83 \text{ (rounded)}$$

2.   Range $= 80 - 35 = 45$
Variance and standard deviation

$$\overline{X} = \frac{42 + 35 + 80 + 68 + 70 + 50 + 63 + 64}{8} = \frac{472}{8} = 59$$

$42 - 59 = -17$
$35 - 59 = -24$
$80 - 59 = 21$
$68 - 59 = 9$
$70 - 59 = 11$
$50 - 59 = -9$
$63 - 59 = 4$
$64 - 59 = 5$
$(-17)^2 + (-24)^2 + 21^2 + 9^2 + 11^2 + (-9)^2 + 4^2 + 5^2 = 1630$

$$\text{Variance} = \frac{1630}{8} = 203.75$$

Standard deviation $= \sqrt{203.75} = 14.27$ (rounded)

3.   Range $= 52 - 15 = 37$
Variance and standard deviation

$$\overline{X} = \frac{36 + 15 + 21 + 42 + 30 + 27 + 19 + 52 + 41 + 17}{10} = \frac{300}{10} = 30$$

$36 - 30 = 6$
$15 - 30 = -15$
$21 - 30 = -9$
$42 - 30 = 12$
$30 - 30 = 0$
$27 - 30 = -3$

$$19 - 30 = -11$$
$$52 - 30 = 22$$
$$41 - 30 = 11$$
$$17 - 30 = -13$$
$$6^2 + (-15)^2 + (-9)^2 + 12^2 + 0^2 + (-3)^2 + (-11)^2 + 22^2 + 11^2$$
$$+ (-13)^2 = 1390$$

$$\text{Variance} = \frac{1390}{10} = 139$$

$$\text{Standard deviation} = \sqrt{139} = 11.79 \text{ (rounded)}$$

4.   Range $= 15 - 3 = 12$
Variance and standard deviation

$$\overline{X} = \frac{15 + 8 + 3 + 5 + 6 + 5}{6} = \frac{42}{6} = 7$$

$$15 - 7 = 8$$
$$8 - 7 = 1$$
$$3 - 7 = -4$$
$$5 - 7 = -2$$
$$6 - 7 = -1$$
$$5 - 7 = -2$$
$$8^2 + 1^2 + (-4)^2 + (-2)^2 + (-1)^2 + (-2)^2 = 90$$

$$\text{Variance} = \frac{90}{6} = 15$$

$$\text{Standard deviation} = \sqrt{15} = 3.87 \text{ (rounded)}$$

5.   Range $= 50 - 5 = 45$
Variance and standard deviation

$$\overline{X} = \frac{20 + 50 + 18 + 7 + 5}{5} = \frac{100}{5} = 20$$

Variance and standard deviation
$$20 - 20 = 0$$
$$50 - 20 = 30$$
$$18 - 20 = -2$$
$$7 - 20 = -13$$
$$5 - 20 = -15$$

$$0^2 + 30^2 + (-2)^2 + (-13)^2 + (-15)^2 = 1298$$

$$\text{Variance} = \frac{1298}{5} = 259.6$$

$$\text{Standard deviation} = \sqrt{259.6} = 16.11 \text{ (rounded)}$$

Summary

Statistics involve collecting, organizing, summarizing, and drawing conclusions from data. To organize data, one can use a frequency distribution. There are two types of frequency distributions: categorical and numerical.

Data can be summarized by using measures of average and measures of variability. The three most commonly used measures of average are the mean, the median, and the mode. The mean is found by adding all the data values and dividing the sum by the total number of data values. The median is found by arranging the data values in order and then selecting the middle data value if there is an odd number of data values or selecting a value half way between the two middle values if there is an even number of data values. The mode is found by selecting the data value with the largest frequency.

There are three commonly used measures of variability. They are the range, the variance, and the standard deviation. The range is found by subtracting the smallest data value from the largest data value. The variance is found by summing the squares of the differences of the mean and each data value. The square root of the variance is the standard deviation.

There are many other statistical concepts, and this chapter provides only a brief introduction to some of them.

Quiz

1. Statistics involves
   (a) collecting, organizing, summarizing, and analyzing data
   (b) proving theories using data
   (c) predicting the future
   (d) manipulating data to get the conclusion you want

2. When data are first collected, they are called
   (a) unprocessed data
   (b) hypothesized data

   (c) raw data
   (d) undefined data

3. One way to organize data is to use a(n)
   (a) organizational chart
   (b) box system
   (c) process control organization
   (d) frequency distribution

4. A frequency distribution should have
   (a) 5 to 15 classes
   (b) 10 to 20 classes
   (c) 1 to 4 classes
   (d) 2 to 8 classes

5. Which is not a measure of average?
   (a) Median
   (b) Range
   (c) Mode
   (d) Mean

6. Which is not a measure of variability?
   (a) Variance
   (b) Range
   (c) Mode
   (d) Standard deviation

7. The mean of 8, 16, 12, 14, and 8 is
   (a) 8
   (b) 12
   (c) 11.6
   (d) 13

8. The median of 12, 27, 32, 16, 15, and 32 is
   (a) 15
   (b) 22.33 (rounded)
   (c) 20
   (d) 21.5

9. The median of 239, 162, 115, 118, and 280 is
   (a) 162
   (b) 182.8
   (c) 15
   (d) 138.5

10. The mode of 27, 43, 18, 27, 52, 16, 14, and 50 is
     (a) 27
     (b) 30.875
     (c) 38
     (d) 22.5

11. The mode of 9, 12, 6, 18, 24, and 10 is
     (a) 0
     (b) 13.17 (rounded)
     (c) 11
     (d) none

12. The mode of 3, 8, 6, 2, 8, 4, 5, and 6 is
     (a) 3
     (b) 5.25
     (c) 8
     (d) 6 and 8

13. The range of 5, 12, 32, 17, and 19 is
     (a) 14
     (b) 27
     (c) 17
     (d) 8.92 (rounded)

14. The variance of 6, 24, 32, 17, 15, and 14 is
     (a) 8.19 (rounded)
     (b) 26
     (c) 7
     (d) 67

15. The standard deviation of 3, 10, 7, 5, 14, 17, and 7 is
     (a) 14
     (b) 4.63 (rounded)
     (c) 21.44 (rounded)
     (d) 5

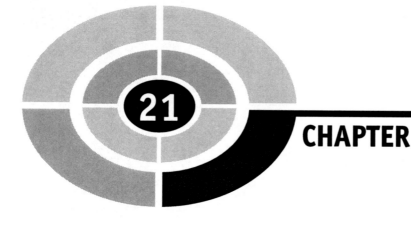

CHAPTER

Charts and Graphs

Introduction

There are many applications of statistical charts and graphs in business. Well-made statistical graphs make it easier (as opposed to tables of numbers) for people to understand and interpret numerical information. These graphs can be used in written reports, verbal presentations, and advertisements explaining budgets, environmental issues, growths of companies, and many other topics.

Charts and graphs can be drawn using computer programs; however, it is still necessary to know the mechanics of a chart or graph in order to make a simple, easy-to-read, and most important, accurate representation of the data.

The most common types of graphs are the bar graph, the Pareto graph, the pie graph, the time series graph, the scatter plot, and the stem and leaf plot. These are the ones that will be explained in this chapter. (All data in this chapter are hypothetical unless otherwise noted.)

The Bar Graph and Pareto Graph

There are three kinds of bar graphs: the horizontal bar graph, the vertical bar graph, and the Pareto graph. When drawing a bar graph, make sure all the bars are of the same width.

EXAMPLE: The average life of US monitory notes is shown. Draw a horizontal bar graph, vertical bar graph, and a Pareto graph for the data:

$1	1 month
$5	2 years
$10	3 years
$20	4 years
$50	9 years
$100	9 years

Source: Federal Reserve

SOLUTION:

For a horizontal bar graph, make vertical and horizontal axes. Use a scale of 0 to 9 units on the horizontal axis. Draw the bars horizontally to represent the data values. Make sure that all bars are of the same width, and that there are spaces between them. See Fig. 21-1.

For a vertical bar graph, draw the axes and place the scale of 0 to 9 units on the vertical axis. Draw the bars vertically to represent the data. Make sure that all the bars are of the same width, and that there are spaces between the bars. See Fig. 21-2.

For the Pareto graph, draw the axes and the scale in the same way as is done for the vertical bar graph. The bars should start with the largest data value and descend to the smallest data value. Also, the bars should touch each other. See Fig. 21-3.

PRACTICE:

1. The following data show the number of crimes committed in a city during a 3-month period. Draw a horizontal and vertical bar graph for the data:

Type	Number
Homicides	8
Robberies	22
Assaults	14
Auto thefts	12

Lifetimes of Monitory Notes

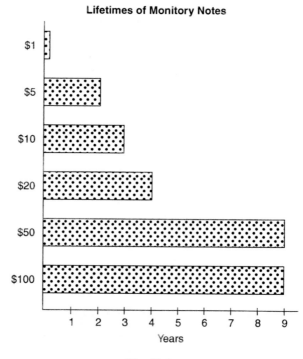

Fig. 21-1.

Lifetimes of Monitory Notes

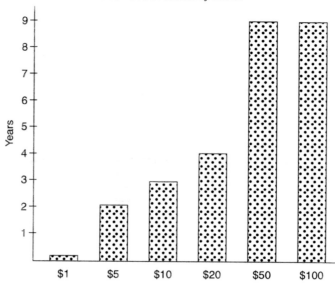

Fig. 21-2.

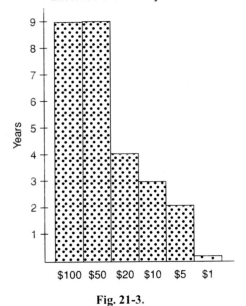

Fig. 21-3.

2. The following data show the number of registered motorcycles in certain municipalities for a specific year. Draw a Pareto chart for the data:

Municipality	Number
West Irwin	54
Cedar Creek	32
Keystone	41
Mount Newton	36
South Penn	18

3. The following data show the number of tons of trash recycled in a certain city for a given week. Draw a Pareto chart for the data:

Type	Amount
Paper	635
Aluminum	423
Glass	187
Plastic	98

SOLUTIONS:

1.

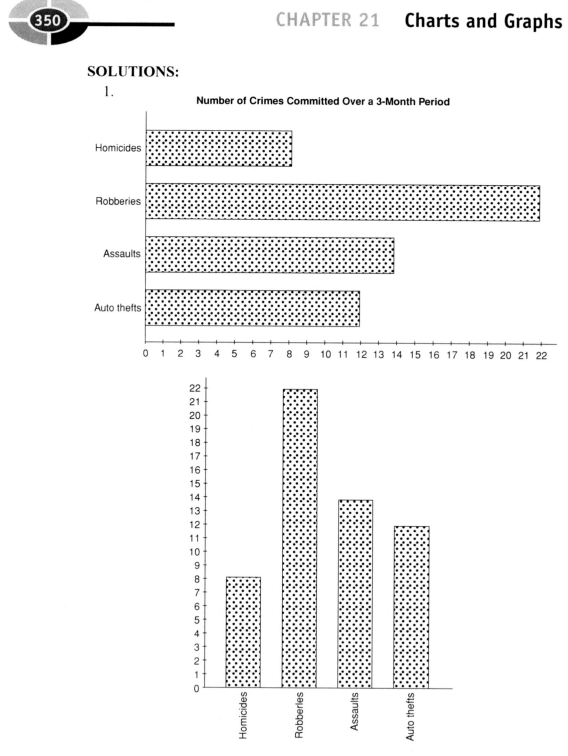

Fig. 21-4.

2.

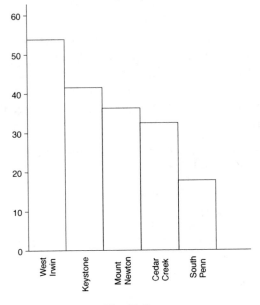

Number of Registered Motorcycles

Fig. 21-5.

3.

Tons of Trash

Fig. 21-6.

The Pie Graph

The pie graph uses a circle, and it is divided into sections that are proportional to the data. These sections usually represent parts of a whole.

In order to construct a pie graph, find the percent for each category and then multiply each percent by 360° since there are 360° in a circle. Draw the graph using a protractor to measure the angles. If you do not know how to use a protractor, consult a geometry book.

EXAMPLE: The costs of operating expenses for Miller's Flower Shop for May are shown. Draw a pie graph for the data:

Category	Amount
Salaries	$1200
Rent	700
Utilities	350
Materials	900
Other	200
Total	$3350

SOLUTION:

Find the percents for each class. Use the formula percent $= \frac{\text{Amount}}{\text{Total}} \times 100\%$.

For salaries: $\frac{\$1200}{\$3350} \times 100\% = 36\%$ (rounded)

For rent: $\frac{\$700}{\$3350} \times 100\% = 21\%$ (rounded)

For utilities: $\frac{\$350}{\$3350} \times 100\% = 10\%$ (rounded)

For materials: $\frac{\$900}{\$3350} \times 100\% = 27\%$ (rounded)

For other: $\frac{\$200}{\$3350} \times 100\% = 6\%$ (rounded)

Next, find the number of degrees for each category. Use the formula: degrees = percent $\times$ 360°.

Note: Make sure to change the percent to a decimal before multiplying.

For salaries: $0.36 \times 360° = 129.6°$
For rent: $0.21 \times 360° = 75.6°$
For utilities: $0.10 \times 360° = 36.0°$
For materials: $0.27 \times 360° = 97.2°$
For other: $0.06 \times 360° = 21.6°$

Using a protractor, draw the graph as shown in Figure 21-7:

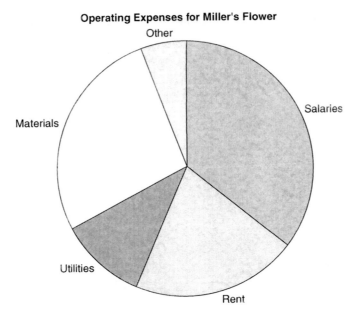

Fig. 21-7.

PRACTICE:

1. The following information shows the housing arrangement for 30 students in a business mathematics class. Draw a pie graph for the data:

Dormitory	16
Apartment	7
House	4
Mobile home	1
Condominium	2

2. The following data show the number of students in five elementary school students in East Harrison School District. Construct a pie graph for the data.

School	Number of students
Eastside	240
Forest	322
Fawcett	165
Bennet	263
Summit	110

3. In a small company, the educational achievements of its employees are shown. Construct a pie graph for the data:

Achievement	Number
High school diploma	87
Associate's degree	54
Bachelor's degree	39
Graduate degree	20

SOLUTIONS:

1.

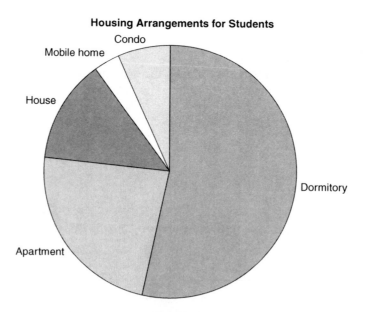

Fig. 21-8.

2.

Number of Students Enrolled in Each School

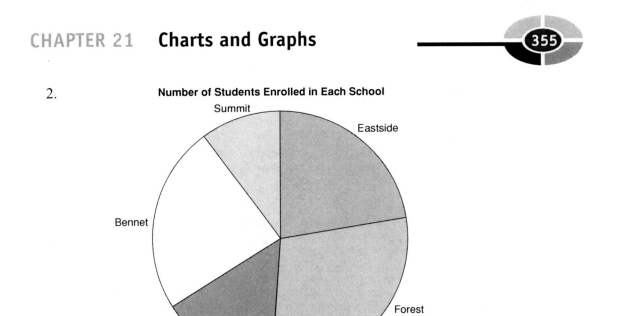

Fig. 21-9.

3.

Achievement of Employees

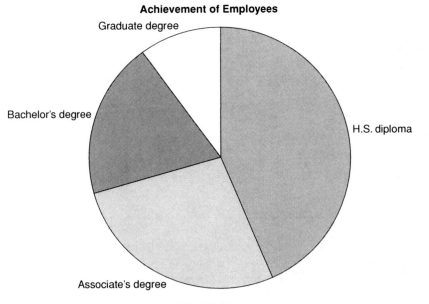

Fig. 21-10.

The Time Series Graph

When data are collected over a period of time (i.e., hours, days, weeks, years, etc.), they can be analyzed using a **time series graph**. The scale along the x-axis represents the time and the scale on the y-axis represents the data values. The data values are connected with broken line segments.

When analyzing the graph, look for trends or patterns. In other words, are the values increasing or decreasing over time? Also look at the segments to see if they rise or decline steeply over the time periods indicating a rapid increase or decrease over the time period.

EXAMPLE: Records for a large school district show the approximate number of students over the last 15 years. Draw a time series graph and explain the trend if one exists.

Year	1985	1990	1995	2000	2005
Students	50	20	10.5	5	4

SOLUTION:
Draw the x- and y-axes. Place the years on the x-axis and numbers of students on the y-axis. Plot the points and connect them with line segments as shown (see Figure 21-11):

The graph shows that there are fewer students per computer as time goes on. One possible reason is that school districts have probably purchased more computers.

PRACTICE:

1. The data show the number of automobiles in millions registered in the United States. Draw a time series graph and analyze the graph.

Year	1925	1950	1970	2000
Number	16	41	106	140

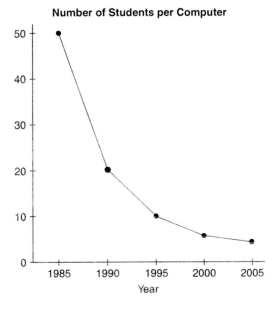

Number of Students per Computer

Fig. 21-11.

2. The data show the number of sports-talk radio stations in the United States over the last several years. Draw a time series graph and suggest any trends that might appear.

Year	1995	1997	1999	2001	2003
Number	146	224	258	342	427

3. The data show the number of snow blowers that McClain's Hardware Store sold over the last several seasons. Draw a time series graph and explain any trends.

Year	2000	2001	2002	2003	2004	2005
Number	37	45	50	27	29	20

SOLUTIONS:

1.

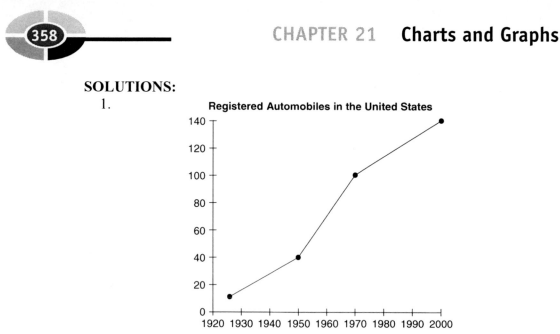

Fig. 21-12.

There is an increasing trend from 1925 to 2000.

2.

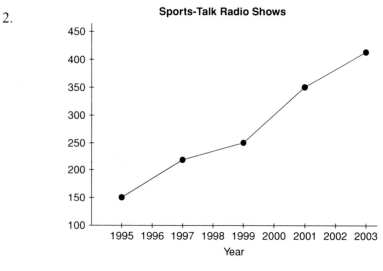

Fig. 21-13.

The graph shows that the number of sports-talk radio stations is increasing over the years.

3.

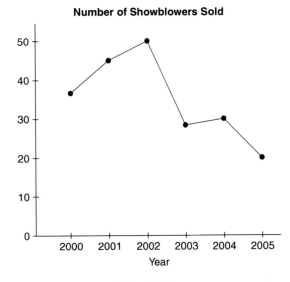

Number of Showblowers Sold

Fig. 21-14.

The graph shows an increase in snow-blower sales up to 2002; hence, there is a decline in sales.

The Scatter Diagrams

Many times statisticians wish to see if there is a relationship between the corresponding measures of two variables. In this case, they use what is called a *scatter diagram*. A **scatter diagram** is a graph of paired data. One variable is designated as the x variable and the other variable is designated as the y variable. For example, automobile manufacturers might want to see if the number of miles per gallon an automobile gets is related to the weight of the automobile. In this case, a sample of automobiles is selected and the weight and the number of miles per gallon of each automobile are recorded. The weights can be the x variable and the miles per gallon can be the y variable. Then the pair (x, y) is plotted on a graph. The plot is analyzed to see if there is a pattern.

The basic patterns are shown in Figure 21-15.

The patterns in part A shows a positive, somewhat linear relationship which means as the values of the x variable increase, the values of the y variable increase. The pattern shown in part B shows a negative, somewhat linear relationship. This means that as the values of the x variable increase, the values of the y variable decrease. The patterns in part C and D show examples of nonlinear relationships. If there is no discernable pattern, as shown in part E, it can be concluded that there is no relationship between the variables.

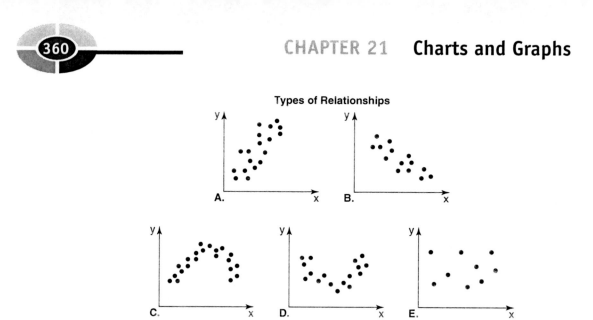

Fig. 21-15.

EXAMPLE: The data shown represent the heights in feet of 10 tall buildings in Columbus, Ohio. Draw a scatter diagram and determine the type of relationship, if one exists, between the variables.

Heights, x	624	555	530	512	503	485	464	456	438	408
Stories, y	47	33	37	33	40	27	31	34	27	30

SOLUTION:

Step 1. Draw the x- and y-axes. Make two scales as shown in Figure 21-16.
Step 2. Plot the points on the graph as shown.

The relationship is positive and somewhat linear which means that the variables of heights and number of stories of buildings both increase at the same time.

PRACTICE:

1. The data show the tuition in hundreds of dollars and the number of full-time faculty for eight selected colleges in the United States. Draw a scatter diagram and determine the typical relationship if one exists.

Tuition	$12	23	16	8	22	19	14	22
No. of Faculty	14	188	177	85	141	92	58	206

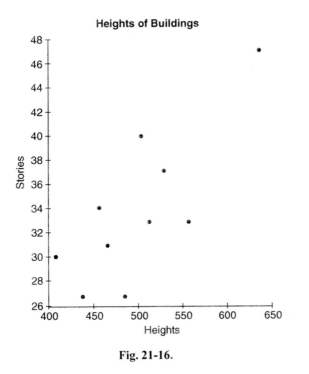

Fig. 21-16.

2. The data show the number of gold and silver medals won by various countries in the Olympic games for a specific year. Draw and analyze a scatter plot for the data:

Gold, x	12	10	11	6	2	6	4	4
Silver, y	16	13	7	3	4	6	4	5

3. The data show some of the numbers of concert shows of musical groups and the gross incomes in millions of dollars the groups earned from these tours. Construct and analyze a scatter plot for the data:

Numbers, x	63	54	88	125	96	72
Gross income, y	$134	83	76	118	108	106

SOLUTIONS:

1.

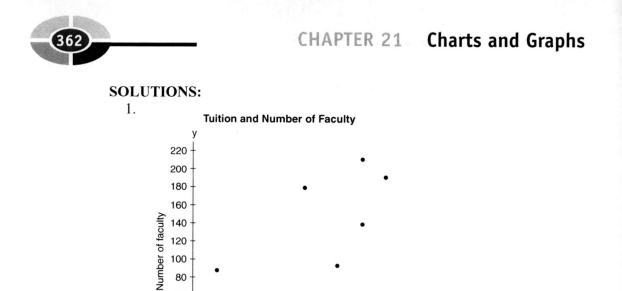

There is a positive relationship between the tuition and the number of faculty in the selected colleges.

Fig. 21-17.

2.

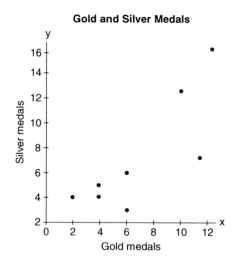

There is a slight positive relationship between the number of gold and silver medals a team won.

Fig. 21-18.

3.

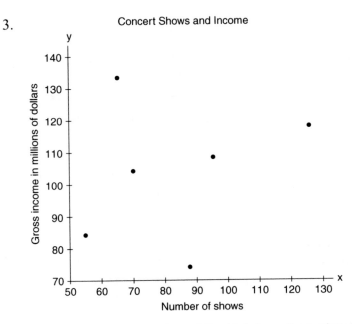

Concert Shows and Income

There does not appear to be a relationship between the number of concert shows and the gross income of the shows.

Fig. 21-19.

The Stem and Leaf Plot

As shown previously, one way to organize data and show the nature of the data is to use a frequency distribution and a histogram. Another way to organize data is to use a *stem and leaf plot*. This plot is a combination of a frequency distribution and a histogram. The **stem and leaf plot** uses part of the data values to form classes. The next example shows how to construct a stem and leaf plot.

EXAMPLE: At an outpatient-testing center, the number of blood tests given each day for 20 days is shown. Construct a stem and leaf plot for the data:

$$
\begin{array}{ccccc}
26 & 33 & 19 & 33 & 12 \\
13 & 45 & 9 & 52 & 22 \\
38 & 30 & 34 & 31 & 47 \\
37 & 51 & 48 & 54 & 45 \\
\end{array}
$$

SOLUTION:

Step 1. Arrange the data in order. (This step is not absolutely necessary, but it helps in drawing the plot.)

9, 12, 13, 19, 22, 26, 30, 31, 33, 33, 34, 37, 38, 45, 45, 47, 48, 51, 52, 54

Step 2. Separate the data according to the first digit as shown:

9,   12,   13,   19,   22,   26
30,   31,   33,   33,   34,   37,   38
45,   45,   47,   48,   51,   52,   54

Step 3. Make a display using the leading digit as the stem, and the trailing digit as the leaf. For example, for the data value 36, the 3 is the stem digit and the 6 is the leaf digit. The plot can be constructed as shown:

```
0 | 9
1 | 2  3  9
2 | 2  6
3 | 0  1  3  3  4  7  8
4 | 5  5  7  8
5 | 1  2  4
```

The plot shows that the class with the most values (7) is 30 to 39.

PRACTICE:

1.   The number of automobile thefts is shown for a 30-day period in a large city. Construct a stem and leaf plot for the data:

22   38   14   62   53   41
32   43   44   27   49   51
27   16   37   25   32   30
29   41   32   46   25   43
38   20   48   26   41   38

2. The ages of 30 CEO's of large companies are shown. Construct a stem and leaf plot for the data:

62	70	64	56	48	63
59	61	63	55	52	47
65	73	75	60	59	61
48	57	56	63	74	63
61	69	67	56	65	78

3. The number of passengers on buses over a 24-hour period is shown. Construct a stem and leaf plot for the data:

37	42	45	18	16	10
36	22	27	14	22	25
35	31	19	20	40	37
24	28	16	39	27	25

SOLUTIONS:

1. | 1 | 4 | 6 | | | | | |
    |---|---|---|---|---|---|---|---|
    | 2 | 0 | 2 | 5 | 5 | 6 | 7 | 7 | 9 |
    | 3 | 0 | 2 | 2 | 2 | 7 | 8 | 8 | 8 |
    | 4 | 1 | 1 | 1 | 3 | 3 | 4 | 6 | 8 | 9 |
    | 5 | 1 | 3 |
    | 6 | 2 |

    The majority of days the number of auto thefts increased was between 20 and 49 inclusive.

2. | 4 | 7 | 8 | 8 | | | | | |
    |---|---|---|---|---|---|---|---|---|
    | 5 | 2 | 5 | 6 | 6 | 6 | 7 | 9 | 9 |
    | 6 | 0 | 1 | 1 | 1 | 2 | 3 | 3 | 3 | 3 | 4 | 5 | 5 | 7 | 9 |
    | 7 | 0 | 3 | 4 | 5 | 8 |

    The age group with the largest frequency was between 60 and 69 inclusive.

3. | 1 | 0 | 4 | 6 | 6 | 8 | 9 |
|---|---|---|---|---|---|---|
| 2 | 0 | 2 | 2 | 4 | 5 | 5 | 7 | 7 | 8 |
| 3 | 1 | 5 | 6 | 7 | 7 | 9 |
| 4 | 0 | 2 | 5 |

The largest group of passengers was between 20 and 29 inclusive.

Summary

In statistics, graphs are used to give a visual representation of data. For most people, graphs are easier to understand than a group of numbers. The most common kinds of graphs that are used are the bar graph, the pie graph, the time series graph, the scatter plot, and the stem and leaf plot.

Each graph has a special use. For example, when the data are collected over a period of time, the time series graph is used. When one is interested in showing the relationships between the parts to the whole, the pie graph is used, etc.

Graphs should be easy to read, accurate, and have a source.

Quiz

1. A graph which is a combination of a frequency distribution and histogram is called a
   (a) scatter plot
   (b) pie graph
   (c) Pareto chart
   (d) stem and leaf plot

2. A graph that uses vertical bars that touch each other is called a
   (a) scatter plot
   (b) Pareto graph
   (c) pie graph
   (d) time series graph

3. When drawing a time series graph, the units of time should be placed along
   (a) the x-axis
   (b) the y-axis
   (c) either axis
   (d) both axes

4. The sum of percents of each section in a pie graph should be
    (a) 100%
    (b) 50%
    (c) 25%
    (d) 10%

5. When the data are collected over several years and the researcher is looking for a trend, the most appropriate graph to use would be a
    (a) pie graph
    (b) stem and leaf plot
    (c) time series graph
    (d) trend graph

6. When statisticians wish to see if there is a relationship between two variables, the most appropriate type of graph to use would be a
    (a) scatter plot
    (b) horizontal bar graph
    (c) stem and leaf plot
    (d) pie graph

7. Which is not a characteristic of a well-drawn graph?
    (a) It should have a source of information
    (b) It should be complex in nature
    (c) It should be easy to read
    (d) It should be accurate

8. Which graph does not have x- and y-axes?
    (a) Vertical bar graph
    (b) Pie graph
    (c) Scatter plot
    (d) Pareto graph

9. In a scatter plot, a positive relationship exists if, generally,
    (a) as the x values increase, the y values increase
    (b) as the x values decrease, the y values increase
    (c) as the x values increase, the y values decrease
    (d) as the x values increase, the y values increase and decrease

10. When drawing a vertical bar graph, the bars should always
    (a) be of the same height
    (b) be of the same width
    (c) vary in width
    (d) be horizontal

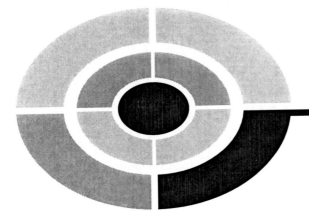

Final Exam

1. $2\frac{1}{2} + 3\frac{1}{8} - 1\frac{3}{4} =$

   (a) $7\frac{3}{8}$

   (b) $3\frac{7}{8}$

   (c) $6\frac{1}{8}$

   (d) $5\frac{5}{8}$

2. Round 8.3271 to the nearest hundredth.
   (a) 8.32
   (b) 8.372
   (c) 8.3
   (d) 8.33

3. Change 0.45 to a reduced fraction.
   (a) $\dfrac{9}{20}$
   (b) $\dfrac{1}{8}$
   (c) $\dfrac{4}{9}$
   (d) $\dfrac{45}{99}$

4. $18.756 \div 3.6 =$
   (a) 52.1
   (b) 5.21
   (c) 0.521
   (d) 521

5. Write 64% as a reduced fraction.
   (a) $\dfrac{3}{5}$
   (b) $\dfrac{1}{64}$
   (c) $\dfrac{16}{25}$
   (d) $\dfrac{2}{3}$

6. 16% of what number is 90.88?
   (a) 5.68
   (b) 14.5408
   (c) 1454.08
   (d) 568

7. Simplify $9 \times \{38 - 6[3(4 + 1)]\}$.
   (a) 4320
   (b) -252
   (c) 515
   (d) -468

8. Simplify $\dfrac{27 - 12}{8 - 3}$.
   (a) 22.5
   (b) 3
   (c) 1.5
   (d) 5

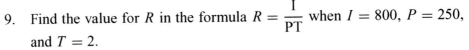
9. Find the value for R in the formula $R = \dfrac{I}{PT}$ when $I = 800$, $P = 250$, and $T = 2$.
   - (a) 1.6
   - (b) 6.4
   - (c) 5.2
   - (d) 3.2

10. Find the value for P in the formula $P = R(1 + N)^x$ when $R = 20$, $N = 10$, and $x = 2$.
    - (a) 2020
    - (b) 220
    - (c) 2420
    - (d) 202

11. In a person's account register, the previous balance is $62.50. If the person wrote two checks for $18.52 and $24.76 and deposited $75.00, the balance would be
    - (a) $19.22
    - (b) $94.22
    - (c) $31.72
    - (d) $30.78

12. If the bank statement balance is $525.60 and the total of outstanding credit and debit are $129.32 and $231.60, then the adjusted balance is
    - (a) $886.52
    - (b) $164.68
    - (c) $423.38
    - (d) $396.28

13. If a person earns $20,514 a year and is paid biweekly, the person's gross pay will be
    - (a) $789
    - (b) $854.75
    - (c) $1709.50
    - (d) $394.50

14. An employee earns $9.70 per hour and gets $1\frac{1}{2}$ times his salary for all hours he works over 40 h per week. If the person works 49 h this week, his gross pay will be
    - (a) $388.00
    - (b) $712.95
    - (c) $475.30
    - (d) $518.95

15. A factory worker earns $0.75 for each ashtray up to 50 that he paints per day. He gets $1.00 for each ashtray over 50 he paints per day. Yesterday he painted 68 ashtrays. His gross pay is
    (a) $51.00
    (b) $69.00
    (c) $55.50
    (d) $68.00

16. If a salesperson sold $18,250 worth of furniture and received a commission of $1368.75, his commission rate is
    (a) 7.5%
    (b) 6%
    (c) 6.6%
    (d) 7%

17. Find a person's net pay if he earned $3260 last week and his federal income tax deduction was $684.60. Social Security and Medicare were also deducted.
    (a) $2326.01
    (b) $2575.40
    (c) $984.52
    (d) $2960.80

18. If a wristwatch costs $24 and is marked up 80% on cost, the selling price is
    (a) $19.20
    (b) $28.80
    (c) $32.50
    (d) $43.20

19. If a textbook sells for $60 and the markup is $20, then the markup rate on the cost is
    (a) 25%
    (b) 50%
    (c) 33.3%
    (d) 66.7%

20. If a pearl necklace costs $85 and sells for $136, the markup rate on the selling price is
    (a) 60%
    (b) 37.5%
    (c) 62.5%
    (d) 54.6%

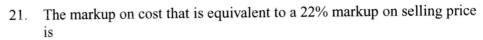

21. The markup on cost that is equivalent to a 22% markup on selling price is
    (a) 28.2%
    (b) 18%
    (c) 31%
    (d) 25%

22. A grandfather clock is marked down 30%. If the selling price was $400, the reduced price is
    (a) $120
    (b) $280
    (c) $240
    (d) $160

23. A pharmacist purchases 60 bottles of vitamin C tablets that sell for $2.00 a bottle. He estimates that 5% of the bottles will have to be thrown out because of the expiration date. In order to account for this fact, he should sell them for
    (a) $2.15
    (b) $2.18
    (c) $2.11
    (d) $2.07

24. A men's topcoat had a list price of $160. If a trade discount series of 15/10/5 was offered, how much should the buyer pay?
    (a) $104
    (b) $136
    (c) $116.28
    (d) $122.40

25. An invoice dated January 25 for $325 was received with the following terms: $\frac{3}{10}, \frac{2}{15}, \frac{n}{30}$. If the bill was paid on February 6, how much did the buyer pay?
    (a) $318.50
    (b) $315.25
    (c) $325
    (d) $308.75

26. If an invoice was dated April 29 and had the terms $\frac{2}{10}$EOM, the last day for the buyer to pay the invoice and get a 2% discount would be
    (a) May 9
    (b) June 10

(c) June 9

(d) May 10

27. An ear pin had a list price of $150. A trade discount series of 10/5 was offered. The invoice had the terms $\frac{3}{10}$, $\frac{n}{30}$. If the bill is paid within 10 days, the buyer paid

(a) $128.25

(b) $123

(c) $123.68

(d) $124.40

28. The Melody Music Company borrowed $5000 at 6% interest for 3 years. The simple interest was

(a) $300

(b) $150

(c) $900

(d) $600

29. If the simple interest paid on a $1500 loan for 2 years was $240, the rate is

(a) 6%

(b) 5%

(c) $7\frac{1}{2}$%

(d) 8%

30. The exact number of days between April 5 and October 24 is

(a) 202

(b) 196

(c) 182

(d) 163

31. The due date for a 60-day loan made on September 7 using ordinary time is

(a) November 6

(b) November 8

(c) November 7

(d) November 5

32. The interest rate on a $950 loan for 27 days was 4%. Find the interest using the banker's rule.

(a) $2.81

(b) $2.62

(c) $2.75

(d) $2.85

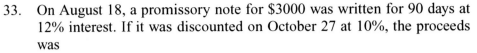

33. On August 18, a promissory note for $3000 was written for 90 days at 12% interest. If it was discounted on October 27 at 10%, the proceeds was
    (a) $90
    (b) $3072.83
    (c) $3090
    (d) $17.17

34. The future value of $2150 invested at 6% compounded quarterly for 4 years is
    (a) $2666
    (b) $2814.52
    (c) $2547.16
    (d) $2728.32

35. The effective rate equivalent to 10% compounded quarterly is
    (a) 10.38%
    (b) 10.25%
    (c) 10.12%
    (d) 10.06%

36. The present value of $3600 compounded semiannually at 5% for 8 years is
    (a) $2627.32
    (b) $2425.05
    (c) $2513.98
    (d) $2562.18

37. The semiannual payment for an ordinary annuity is $960. If the interest rate is 4% and the term is 6 years, the future value of the annuity will be
    (a) $12,875.61
    (b) $13,133.12
    (c) $12,467.72
    (d) $13,014.72

38. An annuity due is paying 10%. If quarterly payments of $500 are made for 3 years, the future value of the annuity will be
    (a) $6897.78
    (b) $7204.63
    (c) $6538.79
    (d) $7070.22

39. Mary Ishler wants to remodel her home office in 5 years. She estimates the cost to be $12,000. If she purchases an ordinary annuity paying 8% annually, her payment will be
    (a) $2316.27
    (b) $2045.48
    (c) $1998.62
    (d) $2135.63

40. Mike purchased a microwave oven for $30 down payment and 12 payments of $15 each. The total price of the oven is
    (a) $180
    (b) $210
    (c) $150
    (d) $375

41. If Shirley borrowed $6000 for 3 years with 5% simple interest, her monthly payment would be
    (a) $191.67
    (b) $166.67
    (c) $170.00
    (d) $186.33

42. Ken borrowed $3350 for 2 years at 5% simple interest and he paid off the loan in 18 months. Using the rule of 78s, find the amount of interest he saved.
    (a) $83.75
    (b) $52.61
    (c) $48.96
    (d) $23.45

43. Michael borrowed $6200 for 15 months at 12% interest. The annual percentage rate if the loan is paid back in equal monthly payments is
    (a) 15.8%
    (b) 22.5%
    (c) 18.2%
    (d) 19.1%

44. A home is sold for $98,000. If the buyer made a 30% down payment, he would need to obtain a mortgage for
    (a) $29,400
    (b) $27,000
    (c) $63,000
    (d) $68,600

45. If a home was purchased with a mortgage of $121,500 and the buyer had to pay 3 points, the value of the 3 points would be
    (a) $117,855
    (b) $36,450
    (c) $85,050
    (d) $3645

46. If a person obtained a $62,000 mortgage for 20 years and his payment was $480.50, then the total interest he would pay is
    (a) $115,200
    (b) $53,320
    (c) $86,230
    (d) $47,430

47. The owner of an auto repair building worth $130,000 insured it for $100,000. How much would the insurance company pay if a fire caused $56,000 in damage?
    (a) $56,000
    (b) $53,846.15
    (c) $52,000.06
    (d) $48,276.31

48. The annual premium on a fire insurance policy dated March 5 was $860. If the policy was cancelled on December 31, the policyholder refund would be
    (a) $709.21
    (b) $125.88
    (c) $150.79
    (d) $562.18

49. The terms of an automobile insurance policy are 50/100/75. The total amount the insurance company will pay for property damage is
    (a) $50,000
    (b) $100,000
    (c) $75,000
    (d) $225,000

50. A person purchased a $40,000 life insurance policy. If the premium rate is $6.47 per $1000, the yearly premium would be
    (a) $258.80
    (b) $618.24
    (c) $327.16
    (d) $491.77

51. If a CD collection costs $59.95 and the sales tax rate is 7%, the sales tax will be
    (a) $64.15
    (b) $3.60
    (c) $3.00
    (d) $4.20

52. A house is assessed at $85,000. If the property tax rate is 56 mills, then the property tax will be
    (a) $5525
    (b) $4760
    (c) $552.50
    (d) $476

53. Using Table 15-1 on page 254, find the income tax paid by a person filing as "Single" and having a taxable income of $41,866.
    (a) $7206
    (b) $7194
    (c) $7219
    (d) $7181

54. A person purchased 200 shares of stock for $83.26. He sold the stock for $95.03 a share. If his broker charged a 2% commission on both transactions, the return on the investment is
    (a) 12%
    (b) 13%
    (c) 14%
    (d) 15%

55. A $1000 bond was purchased when the rate was 97.25% and sold when the rate was 103.51%. If the broker's fee is $3 per transaction, then the amount made by the owner on the sale is
    (a) $62.60
    (b) $56.60
    (c) $59.60
    (d) $58.60

56. A $1000 bond is paying 5.51% interest. If it closes at 103.28%, the current yield is
    (a) 5.34%
    (b) 6.27%
    (c) 4.83%
    (d) 7.16%

57. Find the book value at the end of 3 years of a treadmill costing $800 if it has a lifetime of 4 years and a scrap value of $80. Use the straight-line method of depreciation.
   (a) $540
   (b) $260
   (c) $200
   (d) $600

58. An electronic security system costing $24,000 is purchased for a building. It has an estimated lifetime of 8 years. It has no scrap value. The amount of depreciation for year 5 using the sum-of-the-years-digits method is
   (a) $2666.67
   (b) $15,000
   (c) $3333.33
   (d) $9000

59. A high school band purchases new uniforms at a cost of $12,000. The lifetime of the uniforms is 5 years. Using the double-declining method, the amount of depreciation for year 2 is
   (a) $4800
   (b) $2880
   (c) $7200
   (d) $2400

60. A mold used to make ceramic logs costs $8000. It is estimated that it can make 1000 castings. It has no scrap value. Using the units-of-production method, find the amount of depreciation after it has been used to make 600 sets of ceramic logs.
   (a) $5400
   (b) $3200
   (c) $4200
   (d) $4800

61. A storeowner purchased five packages of headphones at $19, three packages at $15, and four packages at $20. The cost of goods available for sale is
   (a) $220
   (b) $212
   (c) $176
   (d) $198

62. Using the information in Problem 61, the average cost of an item is
    (a) $17.67
    (b) $18.33
    (c) $14.67
    (d) $16.50

63. For the month of November, the cost of goods available for sale was $23,000 and the retail value of the goods was $42,000. If the total sales for the month were $35,000, then the cost of goods sold using the retail inventory method is
    (a) $63,913.04
    (b) $33,810.02
    (c) $26,227.16
    (d) $19,166.67

64. The net sales for Tomorrow's Video Store last year was $63,000. If the cost of inventory at the beginning of the year was $43,000 and the cost of the inventory at the end of the year was $20,000, then the turnover rate is
    (a) 3
    (b) 2
    (c) 4
    (d) 5

65. For a business, the beginning inventory is $82,362 and the cost of the ending inventory is $43,213. If the cost of the purchases is $21,162, then the cost of goods sold is
    (a) $104,413
    (b) $17,987
    (c) $60,311
    (d) $146,737

66. For a business, the gross profit was $86,211 and the operating expenses were $48,377. The net profit is
    (a) $134,588
    (b) $37,834
    (c) $21,433
    (d) $15,643

67. Find the mean of 18, 32, 14, 16, and 25.
    (a) 21
    (b) 18
    (c) 23
    (d) 14

68. Find the median of 12, 23, 14, 22, 16, and 10.
    (a) 16.17
    (b) 18
    (c) 22
    (d) 15

69. Find the mode of 8, 6, 3, 5, 10, 12, and 14.
    (a) 4
    (b) No mode
    (c) 7
    (d) 8

70. Find the mode of 3, 5, 12, 4, 6, 3, 5, 10, and 15.
    (a) 7
    (b) 3 and 5
    (c) 6
    (d) 4

71. Find the range of 41, 6, 18, 22, 36, and 50.
    (a) 9
    (b) 44
    (c) 29
    (d) 35

72. Find the variance of 14, 19, 22, 12, 18, and 20.
    (a) 17.5
    (b) 3.45
    (c) 11.92
    (d) 8

73. Find the standard deviation of 9, 27, 12, 18, and 6.
    (a) 7.45
    (b) 21
    (c) 55.44
    (d) 14.4

74. A graph that shows the relationship between the parts and the whole is called a
    (a) Pareto graph
    (b) stem and leaf plot
    (c) pie graph
    (d) histogram

75. A graph that is sort of a combination of a frequency distribution and histogram is called
    (a) pie graph
    (b) Pareto graph
    (c) scatter plot
    (d) stem and leaf plot

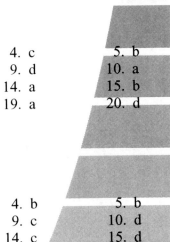

Answers to Quizzes and Final Exam

CHAPTER 1

1. c	2. d	3. a	4. c	5. b
6. a	7. d	8. a	9. d	10. a
11. b	12. b	13. d	14. a	15. b
16. c	17. d	18. b	19. a	20. d

CHAPTER 2

1. b	2. d	3. c	4. b	5. b
6. d	7. a	8. b	9. c	10. d
11. b	12. c	13. a	14. c	15. d

Answers

CHAPTER 3

1. c	2. c	3. b	4. a	5. d
6. a	7. d	8. b	9. d	10. a
11. b	12. c	13. a	14. d	15. b
16. a	17. a	18. b	19. c	20. d

CHAPTER 4

1. d	2. a	3. b	4. d	5. c
6. d	7. a	8. a	9. b	10. d
11. c	12. d	13. a	14. c	15. d

CHAPTER 5

1. c	2. a	3. d	4. d	5. b
6. d	7. b	8. c	9. a	10. b

CHAPTER 6

1. c	2. d	3. a	4. c	5. a
6. b	7. b	8. c	9. d	10. b
11. a	12. b	13. c	14. d	15. d

CHAPTER 7

1. a	2. d	3. b	4. d	5. b
6. c	7. c	8. b	9. a	10. c

CHAPTER 8

1. d   2. a   3. c   4. c   5. c
6. a   7. d   8. c   9. b   10. a

CHAPTER 9

1. a   2. c   3. d   4. b   5. a
6. b   7. b   8. b   9. a   10. b
11. c   12. a   13. a   14. c

CHAPTER 10

1. a   2. d   3. c   4. a   5. c
6. b   7. d   8. d   9. b   10. c

CHAPTER 11

1. d   2. b   3. a   4. c   5. c
6. c   7. b   8. a   9. b   10. d

CHAPTER 12

1. d   2. b   3. c   4. d   5. a
6. c   7. c   8. b   9. d   10. b
11. b

CHAPTER 13

1. c   2. b   3. a   4. d   5. a
6. c   7. b   8. b   9. d   10. c

Answers

CHAPTER 14

| 1. d | 2. b | 3. d | 4. d | 5. c |
| 6. a | 7. c | 8. d | 9. b | 10. c |

CHAPTER 15

| 1. c | 2. a | 3. d | 4. c | 5. c |
| 6. c | 7. d | 8. c | 9. c | 10. d |

CHAPTER 16

1. c	2. a	3. d	4. b	5. b
6. b	7. a	8. d	9. d	10. b
11. d	12. a	13. c	14. c	15. b

CHAPTER 17

1. b	2. c	3. a	4. d	5. a
6. c	7. d	8. b	9. a	10. d
11. d	12. c	13. c	14. a	15. d

CHAPTER 18

1. c	2. c	3. a	4. a	5. d
6. c	7. b	8. a	9. d	10. d
11. c	12. b	13. c	14. a	15. c

CHAPTER 19

1. c	2. a	3. b	4. b	5. d
6. c	7. b	8. a	9. d	10. b

CHAPTER 20

1. a	2. c	3. d	4. a	5. b
6. c	7. c	8. d	9. a	10. a
11. d	12. d	13. b	14. d	15. b

CHAPTER 21

1. d	2. b	3. a	4. a	5. c
6. a	7. b	8. b	9. a	10. b

FINAL EXAM

1. b	2. d	3. a	4. b	5. c
6. d	7. d	8. b	9. a	10. c
11. b	12. c	13. a	14. d	15. c
16. a	17. a	18. d	19. b	20. b
21. a	22. b	23. c	24. c	25. a
26. b	27. d	28. c	29. d	30. a
31. c	32. d	33. b	34. d	35. a
36. b	37. a	38. d	39. b	40. b
41. a	42. d	43. b	44. d	45. d
46. b	47. b	48. c	49. c	50. a
51. d	52. b	53. a	54. c	55. b
56. a	57. b	58. a	59. b	60. d
61. a	62. b	63. d	64. b	65. c
66. b	67. a	68. d	69. b	70. b
71. b	72. c	73. a	74. c	75. d

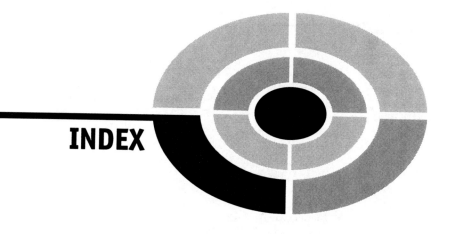

INDEX

Index

Index

Index

Index

ABOUT THE AUTHOR

Allan G. Bluman has taught mathematics and statistics in high school, college, and graduate school for 39 years. He received his Ed.D. from the University of Pittsburgh and has written three mathematics textbooks published by McGraw-Hill, as well as the hugely popular *Pre-Algebra Demystified, Probability Demystified,* and *Math Word Problems Demystified.* Dr. Bluman is the recipient of an "Apple for the Teacher" award for bringing excellence to the learning environment and the "Most Successful Revision of a Textbook" award from McGraw-Hill. His biographical record appears in *Who's Who in American Education,* 5th edition.

CPSIA information can be obtained
at www.ICGtesting.com
Printed in the USA
FFOW01n0452140618
47139742-49711FF